GLOBAL DESIGN
ELSEWHERE ENVISIONED

PEDER ANKER, LOUISE HARPMAN, MITCHELL JOACHIM

PRESTEL
MUNICH · LONDON · NEW YORK

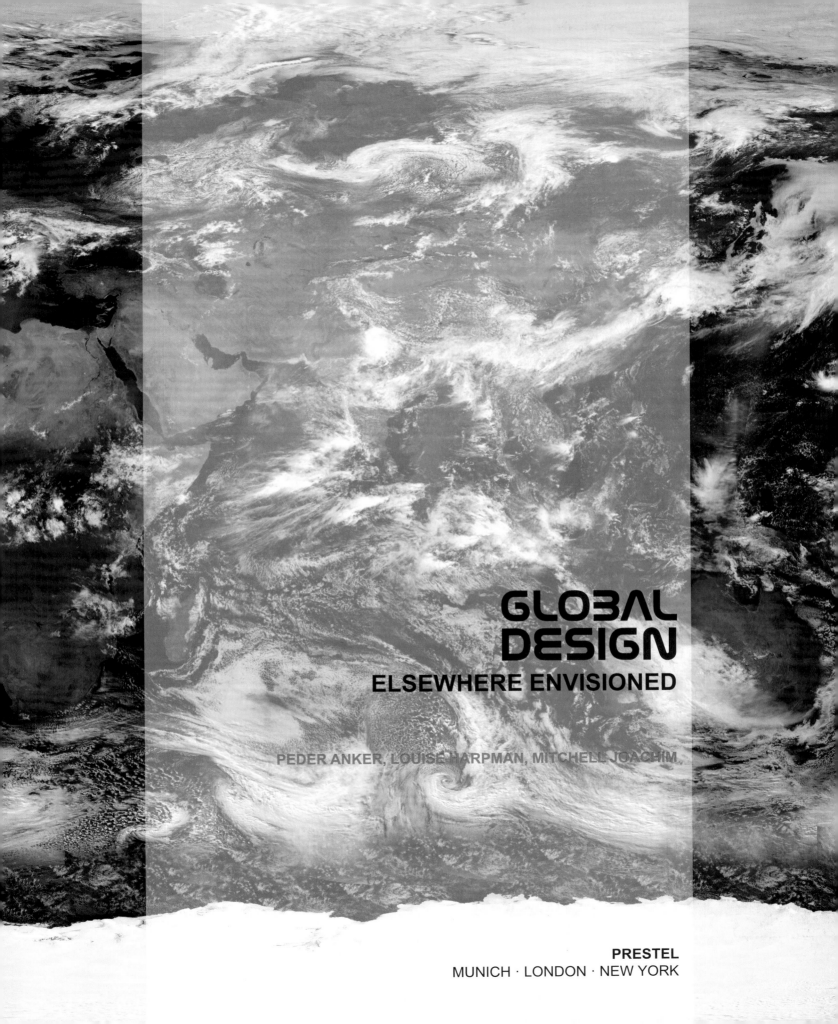

GLOBAL DESIGN
ELSEWHERE ENVISIONED

PEDER ANKER, LOUISE HARPMAN, MITCHELL JOACHIM

PRESTEL
MUNICH · LONDON · NEW YORK

CONTENTS

INTRODUCTION: ELSEWHERE ENVISIONED

The effects of global warming pose drastic challenges to the architecture, landscape architecture, and urban design communities. The immediate response has been a turn toward a host of energy-saving technologies or behavior modifications. What has rarely been addressed, however, is the problem of scale. How can the designer ensure that global solutions do not come at the expense of local traditions, cultures, and environments? By placing human rational, emotional, technological, and social needs at the center of our environmental concerns, we propose a new Global Design initiative.

For the last twenty years, the most celebrated architectural designs have been decadent buildings. Projects of all types have exploited untold resources to craft magnificent displays of power and culture. Regardless of location, these technologically-driven constructions represent the last bastions of form-driven modernism and operate within a stylized international routine to produce beautiful "Bilbao-ifications" that proliferate across many borders and regimes. Wherever these artifacts are located, the point is the same: to be recognized as "signature" buildings, as "iconic," and above all, as globally significant. While some might applaud the beauty or the formal gymnastics of these structures, we challenge the mindless destruction of nature that supports their existence.

At the same time we have witnessed an Albert Speer syndrome among a generation of architects disillusioned with the ideologies of the Cold War. A turn toward cynicism has allowed them to design a propaganda television tower for the Chinese government, to take pride in being architects for Saudi dictators, to shore up the reputations of Russian oligarchs, and to ignore slave labor conditions on building sites in Qatar. They have shown a disregard for basic human rights and for the environment. They are simply doing what their clients pay them to do. Appalled by their arrogance, a new generation of designers has taken seriously both social and environmental concerns, while advancing a modern design aesthetic. All architects must acknowledge that they are active citizens, not passive consumers. This book belongs within that emerging dialogue.

That architects should care about people and the land they engage with is, of course, not new. Indeed, it was once at the heart of the modernist program. Here is what Walter Gropius once told his students at Harvard: "[T]he greatest responsibility of the planner and architect, I believe, is the protection and development of our habitat. Man has evolved a mutual relationship with nature on earth, but his power to change its surface has grown so tremendously that this may become a curse instead of a blessing. . . . *Until we love and respect the land almost religiously, its fatal deterioration will go on.*"[1]

In resurrecting this lost modernist Global Design program, we do not regard the periphery as our antagonist. The periphery is defined by boundaries—disciplinal and spatial, as well as intellectual. What we propose is to collapse the global and the local, since environmental problems are not limited to a particular location. This brings us to architecture, the related design disciplines, and to the many actors and agents who imagine their practices scaling to address different issues and locations. Despite the necessity of envisioning the global in order to achieve effective design solutions, the notion that an individual can have the ability to perceive the global in its entirety requires a great deal of hubris—it is simply too difficult

to imagine every part of the globe as connected all together, all the time. The term "global" is therefore elusive and problematic, because we can only grasp the local. We instead embrace the desire for propinquity and topophilia.[2] It's vital to uphold a sense of nearness to places, identity, and culture, irrespective of actual distance.

We come to know our own locale in fragments. It is hard to have a complete understanding of the city beyond your neighborhood and beyond the things that are connected viscerally to your daily life. Thus, the vision of the global—the vision of saving the Earth—always seems to collapse into local issues. It is hard to create something global, since the local pulls you back. That is a good thing—something we embrace. If you follow the social networks, the money, and the materials, they will always point back to the local setting—the person or community group who needs *that* building for *that* location, the materials that can resist *that* type of weather, the bulk and uses that are appropriate for *those* zoning regulations. Local knowledge is deep and abiding, but it can't be used to dull our response to larger issues.

We are already seeing the bridging and breaking of disciplinary boundaries, where design problems demand greater fluidity and design research is one way to blur those boundaries. With Global Design, we are foregrounding a number of practices who see their work as informed by both local and global concerns and whose projects expand traditional definitions of practice. To address the increasing complexity of building in this interconnected world, architects and designers can rarely avoid engaging big business, politics, and the finance industry. Architects are trained to understand and operate within an "open set" of conditions. As the design disciplines expand to embrace other areas of knowledge, it is our hope that the design process—which promotes research, innovation, and experimentation—will bring its methodology and rigor to these "other" determinants of built form.

Global movements in architecture are nothing new. The difference is that today they move at a hyperbolic pace. From concepts and ideas, architectural expression is found within a milieu of radically diverse cultural inputs simultaneously configured. A blog post with a rendering of a new Japanese office tower influences designers in Egypt before people in New York are even awake. Design and critical reactions soar across political and geographical boundaries every moment, in a near-continual feedback loop. Forms morph with instantaneity in direct response to published online images of speculative structures any place on earth. Architectural manifestos, movements, and isms rise and fall within the space of a few days or weeks. In the early part of the twentieth century, it took Le Corbusier and the CIAM founding architects decades to establish themselves and disseminate their views. Today, architecture exists in the concomitant and ever-shifting present and needs to reconcile itself against a global platform. To work in isolation is nearly impossible and almost certainly the demise of any firm. Design is relevant everywhere all at once. All buildings matter, especially in their resource inputs and waste streams. What then can we say of globalized architecture in the context of our planet's declining ecological health and global warming? Is there an elsewhere to envision?

We need to remember the inevitability of constant interactions between the global and the local with regard to worldwide challenges. The invasive process of fracking for shale gas, for example, is deeply problematic on a local or regional level, but it is not actually *the* problem. The problem is the insatiable global demand for cheap hydrocarbons. Many fields need to act in unison to solve issues of this magnitude. Thus, we look at the global picture and attempt to operate on it through a local lens. It becomes very difficult to address the dynamic set of interrelated problems, because so much of current global thinking claims to represent all people, all places, and all times. But designers are not astronauts, looking at the Earth from outer space. Instead, we need to understand our human condition as integrated within and bounded by the environment.

The Google-Earth view that zooms in on nature is a dominant trend in current understandings of design—a trend we try to avoid in this book. That view privileges an elevated, empowered, and distinctly human perspective that reduces nature to an abstract visual database. Because it is photographic, it is literally a surface treatment of the planet. Though the view of the Earth as a whole from outer space may look beautiful and innocent at first sight, it enables a type of planning and design which is not only insensitive to local environmental conditions and cultures, but also alienates humans from themselves. This view mobilizes narrow managerial rationalities at the expense of a more widely defined human condition. Yet, to empower ourselves at our opponent's expense, we purposely have appropriated NASA typography and images to develop a visual language that begins to create proximity between individual responsibility and the global environmental crisis. Already the disasters at Chernobyl and Fukushima have demonstrated long-reaching influences on worldwide environmental health, migration, and, ultimately, global financial markets. Effects of scale are transferred constantly between the minute and the colossal, where small changes ramify into massive effects and vice versa. Global Design posits that we must try to operate at several scales simultaneously without privileging one format, as thinking and working inside strict categories of scale is both outdated and counterintuitive.

Charles and Ray Eames provided an important case study forty years ago, which is still relevant today. Illustrated in their film *Powers of Ten*, scale is conveniently defined in neat square-shaped frames. Their animation bridges different perceptions of scale along a continuum, as they seek to empower viewers to see the environment from multiple, but nested points of view. Unfortunately, some viewers also interpret this to mean designers ought to bracket places and things in specific scales—this is a common misconception of the *Powers of Ten* message. Nothing happens in only one frame of space and time. Framing can help to study a phenomenon at a particular moment, but nothing is static. Moreover, artificially binding a place to a numerical scale is to some extent arbitrary. Design cannot and should not be compiled into tidy categories defined by scale and size.

Our overarching aim is to develop a language of design that can create productive relationships between local problems, individual accountability, and the urgent environmental challenges posed by global warming. We see environmental problems as a crisis of human alienation from the natural world, and our Global Design initiative explores ways in which design can reformat the unfortunate separation. In our plea for proximity between the individual and the global, we explore, in the words of Maurice Merleau-Ponty, design that is "as close to the beyond as to things near" when we evoke "our power to imagine ourselves elsewhere."[3]

---

1. Walter Gropius, *Scope of Total Architecture* (New York: Harper & Brothers, [1943] 1955), 184. Gropius's emphasis.
2. Yi-Fu Tuan, *Topophilia: A Study of Environmental Perception, Attitudes, and Values* (New York: Columbia University Press, 1990).
3. Maurice Merleau-Ponty, *L'Oeil et l'Esprit* (Paris: Gallimard, 1964), 83. Our translation.

GLOBAL DESIGN

JONATHAN BELL, ELLIE STATHAKI

Global Design New York University (GDNYU) was established to highlight innovative design with an emphasis on contextual practice, a sense of place, and an eco-sensitive approach. Spanning architecture, urbanism, and design, this initiative has been created to explore what it means to be experimental today, how architects utilitize research and conceptual design, and, above all, how these approaches shape our response to the landscape that surrounds us.

Most of the practices involved in GDNYU have a base in Europe and the United States, but their work and concerns speak to an international audience. The work is wide-ranging, offering a variety of different approaches to the relationship between research and reality. A few years ago, much of the architecture showcased in this book would have been the preserve of fantasy, such as the eye-catching streamlined and stylized forms of Berlin-based practice J. Mayer H., and the provocatively distinctive forms by young studios like Bloom and ATMOS.

While major advances in design and construction technology have transformed the architect's palette, there is also a new rigor and simplicity emerging in young practice. The pragmatic, clean, and functional creations of London-based David Kohn Architects, Basel's HHF, and New York's Architecture Research Office all incorporate craft, pattern, technology, and digital processes, producing work that is sober and utilitarian, yet still connected to the many possibilities of the digital world.

The widespread use of digital tools might initially have suggested the slow disappearance of regional variations in architectural design. Yet as this book demonstrates, the opposite has happened, as the intersection between research and practice has seen the emergence of several local trends.

At first glance these diverse selections of offices seem to have no obvious common denominator. However, their connections are under the skin, links that show how architecture culture has learned to accommodate the digital diaspora in order to produce designs that are not only fit for purpose and truly appropriate for the twenty-first century, but which are born out of a tailor-made, experimental outlook. At the heart of this emerging work is the tendency of architects to draw inspiration from each project's physical and social locale, be it through direct research or the sharing of ideas and approaches.

These practices share an architectural sensitivity and research-based approach that is irrespective of office size or place of origin. At GDNYU, young and dynamic practices such as Studio Weave, Aberrant Architecture, Interboro Partners, and Lateral Office sit side by side with larger international studios such as Bjarke Ingels Group (BIG). The work they showcase is as rooted in its socio-geographical context and local tradition as it is inspired by modern technology and innovation. It takes the global architectural debate about sustainability and creativity to the next level while simultaneously having a strong sense of the local conditions that shape plan, form, and program.

GDNYU Directors Louise Harpman and Mitchell Joachim are each principals of research-focused practices in New York, while Peder Anker is an historian of science who writes about technology and the environment. This initiative is aiming high, looking to build an informal network of like-minded architects to promote relevant discourse. Their own participation is key to their approach. Accordingly, Specht Harpman's (the firm Harpman co-directs with partner Scott Specht) updated version of the zerohouse concept is a versatile prefabricated solar-powered dwelling with a net-zero energy profile, while Mitchell Joachim's Terreform One studio offers team projects such as Urbaneering Brooklyn 2110, one of several futuristic visions of the city developed by the practice, all of which address site-specific urban issues such as waste, mobility, and shelter.

Never before has there been such a strong sense of a global architecture community. Whereas the connections and cross-pollinations that shaped the common threads in International Modernism over half a century ago were driven by the physical movement of architects around the world, today's debate is instant and universal. The digital realm has brought architecture to a wider audience, and it has brought a hitherto unprecedented amount of data and feedback into the architectural process. GDNYU harnesses the energy of this process and methodology, translating the virtual into the real. Issues are shared, as are responses, and the potential for collaboration and conversation is vastly increased.

GDNYU presents architecture with a strong human focus, examining how contemporary methods of research and practice distill global concerns into a local context. Bringing together academics, architects, urbanists, and historians, this collection includes work of all scales—from small installations to larger building work, landscape, and urban design —and explores different applications of environmentally-friendly design within them.

Organized by New York University and the Gallatin School of Individualized Study, GDNYU will continue to be involved in planning annual design conferences, exhibitions, and books following the successes of the first New York and London events, with upcoming events in the Far East, the Middle East, and South America. Casting the net far and wide across the globe, GDNYU is committed to raising the bar for an ongoing, stimulating interdisciplinary discussion about cities, ecology, and design.

ARCHITECTURE OF THE WORLD: OEKOUMENOS REDUX [1]

HASHIM SARKIS

THE LIMITS OF THE INHABITED WORLD

Can architecture express the global? Can it leap out of its specificity and contingency—out of its material boundaries—to address such an esoteric, yet ubiquitous, entity (or is it a concept)? If the answer is to be yes, as the title of this book confirms, then architecture's formulation must rely on a definition of the global that is most nurturing of this possibility. Geography, I propose, may provide such a definition.

In his canonical treatise *The Biological Foundations of Human Geography* (1943), French geographer Maximilien Sorre (1880–1962) develops the theoretical and spatial construct of the *oekoumene*.[2] The oekoumene, he proposes, is the space of adaptation between humans and their environment.[3] Drawing from the Greco-Roman etymology for "inhabited world" and from the German and French schools of geography, particularly from his mentor and the founder of human geography in France, Paul Vidal de la Blache, Sorre brings to geography an emphasis on the human in a social sense. The mobility of humans also distinguishes them from other creatures that tend to be more localized in their inhabitation of the Earth and therefore less adaptable to different climatic conditions. The mobility and adaptability of humans led them to reach the limits of the inhabited world a long time ago. The process of inhabiting the Earth over the course of history did not rely as much on spreading the footprint of humankind as on densifying settlements and changing migration patterns. While there may still be unoccupied voids in the oekoumene, these do not interfere in its conception as a totality of possible inhabitation. Geography becomes the science of the oekoumene. However, the oekoumene is not static. It is animated by the mobility and growth of the human population and by the development of different methods of adaptation that transform the countenance, or physiognomy, of this world.

Sorre's book deepens the study of how this adaptation takes place. Even though his foundations are biological, the links between the natural and the cultural are understood not to be causal, but based on possibility. The environment guides certain forms of adaptation. It does not cause them. Borrowing from Blache, Sorre refers to these forms of adaptation as "forms of life."

Genre de vie (translated to English as "form of life," "way of life," or even "lifestyle"), according to Vidal, Sorre, and a long tradition of human geography after them, is "the set of habitual behaviors, cultural forms, and social interactions that characterize a given cultural group in/of a particular landscape."[4] These forms of life include individual and group actions on the environment and qualities of the environment itself. They change from one place to the other, bestowing each place with unique qualities, and they can be applied to explain the environments of cities as well as rural areas. These forms of life are dynamic, but they nevertheless register longer-term patterns that characterize each culture socially and spatially. Sorre studies different habitats and identifies recurring patterns of settlement, of housing, and of land use. By inhabiting the world, humans produce varieties of its inhabitation that are as much expressions of the locus as they are expressions of the oekoumenical in its expanse.

Sorre was not the first link between the concept of oekoumene and architecture. Before him, Jean Brunhes, another major disciple of Vidal de la Blache, appealed to the young Le Corbusier and influenced his urban theories, particularly his formulation of *The Three Human Establishments.*[5] American historian Lewis Mumford had also used this concept in his *Technics and Civilization* (1934). Following World War II, the concept was readily adopted by a range of theorists and scholars such as Constantinos Doxiadis, who used it as "ecumenopolis" to describe a future world made of one connected city. More recently the concept has been used by French geographer Augustin Berque, who develops an ontological reading of landscape through the concept of the écoumene.[6] German philosopher Peter Sloterdijk has also leaned on this term to help historicize the phenomenon of globalization and to distinguish between early ecumenes—be it the Roman Empire or the age of navigation, where a unifying idea of humanity brought different peoples together—and the Second Ecumene of globalization, where humans across the globe find themselves living in similar situations in which they are all bound by a sense of shared risks and displacement in the world.[7]

The strong influence of Sorre's oekoumenos, particularly on architecture, came by way of Aldo Rossi's interpretation of the universal as city and of *genres de vie* as architectural typologies. In his canonical *The Architecture of the City*, Rossi translates the recurring patterns of environmental adaptation into architectural typologies, and the universal setting of these different patterns into the city.[8] In its structuralist interpretations, typology gives architecture deeper, longer-term patterns through which it can mark and express its relationship with society and place. Yet what is most perplexing about Rossi and his followers is the unquestioned equation between the oekoumene and the city, especially considering that Vidal de la Blache and Sorre wanted to transcend the city and include the rural environments as *genres de vie* worth examining and including in the oekoumene.

Additionally, the relationship between the *genres de vie* and the oekoumene has been, for the most part, reduced to a tension—a contrast between the regional and the universal, the local and the global. What has therefore been lost in translation between geography and architecture is the recognition of the oekoumene as the limit and expression of the world and not the city. What has also been lost is the idea that architecture could be seen, in its specificity and locality, as the expression of the world created out of the yearning for unison among forms emanating from different places. Instead of "the architecture of the city," can we then speak of "the architecture of the inhabited world"?

LEAVING COSMOPOLIS

Much of today's literature about urban development presents the city as the ultimate expression of globalization's impact on human settlements and on the general patterns of land use. The spatial outcome of globalization is produced out of migration patterns, ecological and other collective risks, and unfathomable "flows" of capital. These are generating new forms of social, economic, and political organization that specialists are still trying to delineate and understand. They are all unprecedented, we are told, and if they could only be carefully modeled and well analyzed, and if some of their undesirable impact could be circumvented, they could lead to more effective individual emancipation and better forms of collective life. When it comes to spatial modeling, however, we are generally noticing the recurrence of centralized metropolitan patterns of urbanization: concentrations of capital and communication in a few highly connected spots on the surface of the Earth produce a radical redistribution of resources, and new hierarchies emerge. Diffusions occur as well, but when carefully analyzed, they either are themselves diffused or they reproduce patterns of organization similar to the metropolitan.[9]

Granted, if we can agree to this diagnosis, urbanization and urban settlements are rising at an unprecedented scale and pace. They are invading new settings: the third world, rural areas, and deserts. We have also undoubtedly benefited enormously from two decades of rigorous documentation and analysis of new settlement conditions across the world. This literature, however, persists in describing the new phenomena through established gradients of density and centrality such as urban-suburban-rural, with conventional land-use categories and within the confines of nation-states. Many radically different morphologies and typologies are being recorded, but their collective impact remains the city, as big or fast-paced as it may have become.

To be sure—whether coming from within the disciplines of urbanism, landscape, geography, or ecology—we are witnessing an increasing number of new positions that respond to the complexity of the problem by proposing more complex interdisciplinary approaches. These positions, however, as analytically rigorous as they may be, are ultimately so preoccupied with the nature of their interdisciplinarity that they tend to forget the object of their inquiry. No matter how novel the combination of tools, these interdisciplinary propositions do not seem to offer better insight into the way that global economic and social changes have transformed the built environment, and how architects can better address and express this new condition.

If this murky category of urban is everywhere, shouldn't its omnipresence weaken it as a specific category of living? If beyond density, the concept implies multiplicity, should we not begin to search for multiplicity within its pervasiveness? If, on the other hand, one of the ambitions of architecture is to make visible emerging social conditions, why are we not seeing the world as a possible scale of operation? If financial and demographic flows are challenging national boundaries, why is our imagination about space still bound to the city and city-region-state order? Can we find an equivalent to the scope of globalization in the space of the world, as one spatial entity?

THE CITY-WORLD: A BRIEF HISTORY

An age, Gilles Deleuze repeats after Michel Foucault, does not precede the visibilities that fill it. The image of a city-world predates the advent of globalization, but it has yet to come into consciousness as a representative visibility. The representation may be too literal, but the world conceived as one spatial entity corresponds with the scope of globalization, where national and natural borders do not set limits to the physical environment and to its perception.

Early science-fiction writers such as H. G. Wells foretold of the whole world at war with itself, followed by a period of peace in which the unified conception acquired during wartime is maintained. Led by technocrats, the world operates as one entity—as a city-world. Science fiction has continued to reimagine the world as a single entity, whether in Asimov's Trantor or in more popular renditions such as Star Wars' Coruscant and Death Star. Admittedly, these worlds differ considerably in their governance, social and spatial organization, density, and degree of urbanization, but they do anticipate and rehearse the yearning for a spatial totality at the global scale.

Discerning this type of yearning from a totalizing project such as that of empire or colonialism is as necessary as it is difficult. In the context of imagining the world as one entity, we cannot overlook the grounds that such political aspirations cleared. As emphasized by the likes of Fredric Jameson and Bruno Latour, the necessity of the separation between the pursuit of totalities and of totalizing projects is important if we are to persist in developing clearer mappings or representations of the world. Jameson's reference to Kevin Lynch's cognitive mapping parallels Latour's reference to the phenomenon of the nineteenth century panorama.[10]

In architecture, the classical project and, in related ways, that of the early Modernist universalism culminating in the International Style have aspired to a certain sameness (read equality, universality, unity) across national boundaries. This aspiration was driven more by a temporal understanding of the world than a spatial one—the world it imagined wanted to move in sync. Not that a spatial conception was lacking, but it was lagging. The aspiration for sameness of high Modernism emulated and expressed the aspiration for equality among human beings and states. The criticisms of this project are all too familiar and they have helped us discern the indelible ties between formal and political projects. The very geography that produced the oekumene also produced essentialized differences among nation-states, as well as colonization. Here again, however, we should not miss out on the outlooks of connectedness and continuity that Modern architecture effected across the world. As visibilities, they should be able to live past their political associations.

From the 1930s onward, the qualities of connectedness, continuity, and sameness transform from wish images into projected outcomes of development. Jean Gottman's premonition featured a Megalopolis where cities grow and connect to create regional bands of urbanization enabled by expanding communication and transport. This premonition was magnified to the scale of the world and turned into an inevitability by Constantinos Doxiadis

ARCHITECTURE OF THE WORLD GDNVYU ELSEWHERE ENVISONED

in his proposition for an Ecumenopolis, a city-world formed out of settlements around major routes of transportation. Slowly, all development is drawn to this infrastructural grid while clearing the rest of the planet for agriculture and conservation of natural resources. Speed of movement and proximity of people to each other guided Doxiadis's anticipatory and remedial approach to urban planning. His contemporaries and fellow world-warriors, such as Yona Friedman, Superstudio, Constant Nieuwenhuys, and Buckminster Fuller, all aspired to a worldly conception of their domain of operation that transcended locality and city.

Friedman scaffolded a parallel, open, and floating world on top of the ground-bound and sequestered one we inhabit—accelerating spatial mobility, diffusing boundaries, and multiplying uses and connections. For Superstudio, the connectivity of the world's citizens to each other depended on the establishment of a fictive, smooth infrastructure that provided continuity and connectivity against the Earth's geographic hurdles—minimizing the architectural superstructure to almost nothing. Fuller's obsession with mapping the world in ways that could make its finitude and fragility visible led him to invent such representational devices as his famous maps, as well as the geoscope. The world was a scopic and geometric projection from space that readily replaced the physical earth as lightly as he wished to tread on it. Even though the scope of Unitary Urbanism continued to be the metropolis, the degree of diffusion of activities and land uses proposed by Nieuwenhuys clearly transgressed the centrist models of development toward more fluid continuities that heralded the global space of New Babylon.

Not of all of these attempts at representing and imagining the world stemmed from a need to shape the larger totality, but they all stemmed from dissatisfaction with the urban models of high Modernism. The overwhelming revocation of these models by postmodernist urban theories has, in many ways, consolidated the Modernist centralized understanding of the city. This revocation has also ratified the city as the largest scope of the inhabited environment while detracting from the radical attributes of these late Modernist experiments in which the world as one entity was articulated in architectural terms.

The renewed interest in this cast of renegade characters and their imagination has primarily stressed a systemic versus object-oriented approach to urbanism.[11] The environmental and democratic motivations of this approach no doubt make it more attractive and current, but even in the present reiteration of these visions, the rendering of the world as one entity has not been stressed. The global city has somehow eclipsed the city-world. The difference between the two models is enormous, but the city-world should not be seen as the opposite of the world-city (or of the global city or cosmopolis, or whatever name will be applied to it in the coming years). The city-world is the scope, spatial parameters, geometries, land-uses, and infrastructures that connect the world and make us actively take part in its description, its construction, and its perception as a totality—world-cities included. The identification of this entity relies heavily on new modes of perception and tools of representation—on a worldly subject and a mediated (seen through the media) world.

"WORLDLINESS"

Difficulties abound in conceptualizing the world as one architectural entity, but these difficulties are being slowly, if inadvertently, superseded. This is caused by the fact that the world as a concept is constantly producing new *genres de vie* that are searching for architectural articulation. The seeming immodesty of such a proposition disguising itself as inevitability, combined with its imperial scope, should be countered with the scale and scope of risks that contemporary society confronts—be they generated by environmental, nuclear, or public health concerns. This call for collective atonement may turn out to be just another rhetorical device, but the scope of action in response to these risks is generating a worldwide response, including the coordination of the world's spatial resources, putting into question the global city model. The capacity to understand and map the lived environment beyond the scope of the city, corresponding to new patterns of global mobility and demographic shifts, is now greatly enhanced by new technologies, as well as by modes of representation and communication that make us constantly aware of the world as one entity. The lack of corresponding governing authority to coordinate shaping the world remains a major impediment to conceptualizing the world. This lack of corresponding governing authority, however, may weaken the totalizing dimension of architecture and urban planning, and mobilize architects to think of ways in which the qualities of the forms they produce—their sameness, repetitiveness, connectedness to larger geographic attributes like the horizon or trans-regional phenomena—can mobilize the physical and aesthetic dimensions of form in more effective ways than a servile association with a political project.

Most importantly, while the emancipatory dimensions of such a scope of imagination and operations—which predate the global city to as far back as Heraclites—have been all-too-easily bundled with the larger package of globalization, several social theorists and philosophers, such as Jean Luc-Nancy, Kostas Axelos, and Michel Serres, have recovered the project of being in the world from the asphyxiating weight of globalization discourse.[12] Furthermore, and despite valid criticisms that have accompanied its resurgence, the discourse on cosmopolitanism has helped imagine the subject of the world as a positively nomadic stranger whose constant yearning for being here and there simultaneously produces ways of describing and representing the world as the scope of individual imagination. The writings of Edward Said on worldliness and those of Anthony Appiah on strangeness are particularly poignant on this issue.[13] Could this desire for displacement not be expressed in architectural terms?

World history—as an established field of inquiry into the history of the world as a set of collective phenomena—has also helped generate historiographic and spatial models for this investigation. In this respect, recent work on the history and historiography of the Mediterranean is compelling. The Mediterranean that is most relevant to the idea of the world is that of historian David Abulafia, who speaks of distant shores with a frequency of communication between them. Abulafia has argued that what most characterizes the Mediterranean is a geography of opposed but accessible shores with a frequency of exchange. In this conception, the edges of the Mediterranean consist of cities and towns that are loosely connected with their hinterland but are mostly connected via trading communities and businesses. The opposing shorelines could and should be read as different and nested scales.[14]

Most pertinent in Abulafia's proposal is the idea that the Mediterranean is a model that can be applied to the world. The increasing sameness within cities and between each city and the rest of the world points to the dissolution of place and to the acceleration of development. This acceleration of development brings us to the point where we can anticipate a world moving in a real-estate development sync, especially following the most recent recession and the global risks it generated, and perhaps even because of the recession and its associated risks. These global risks include security and economic vulnerability that tie every city's patterns to those of the world, sometimes bringing individual cities to the point of brinkmanship and collapse, perhaps, as some argue, to speak to the world.[15]

We ought to think again about whether sameness in the world is a sign of poverty of form or of an untapped richness—a new source of inspiration for urbanism and architecture. This sameness is not dull. It points to the fact that we are all worldly, that we work to link to the world from where we are—to achieve a sense of the totality and to anticipate a city-world before and beyond globalization—a city-world that flows with Heraclitus's river, where identities could be constantly constructed, and constructed in part by design.

THE WORLD AS AN ARCHITECTURAL QUESTION

But how do architects respond when the world is placed on their table as an architectural question? Increasingly, architects are being compelled to address and transform larger contexts and to give these contexts more legible and expressive form. Architects are being called upon to design infrastructural and urban systems, and to imagine solutions to regional and rural questions. The Grand Paris competition in Paris was a case in point. Problems that had been confined to the domains of engineering, ecology, or regional planning are now looking for articulation by design. If architectural historians like Lewis Mumford and Carl Condit and their generation were fascinated by the geonomic role that architecture could play around large-scale development projects such as the Tennessee Valley Authority, we are now noting a proliferation of such projects to the point that urban architecture has become "geo-architecture."[16] This situation has opened up a range of technical and formal possibilities that had previously been out of reach for designers. The need to address these "geographic" aspects has also encouraged designers to reexamine their tools and develop means to link attributes that had once been understood to be either separate or external to their disciplines. The importance of questions regarding sustainability and risk are beginning to put measurable standards in front of architects—forcing them to think about the world as a physical scope of impact, if not of operation.

Engaging the geographic, however, does not only mean a shift in scale. This has also come to affect the formal repertoire of architecture, even at a smaller scale, with more architects becoming interested in forms that reflect the geographic connectedness of architecture. Engaging the geographic enables architecture to bridge the very large and the very small (networks and frameworks), or to provide forms that embody geographic references (such as continuous surfaces or environmentally integrated buildings).

Curiously, while most of the research around these various attributes has tended to be quite intense, the parallel tracks of inquiry have remained disconnected. For example, the discussion about continuous surfaces in architecture ignores the importance of continuity of ground in landscape ecology. Even if there is not a common cause driving these different geographic tendencies, a synthesis is possible, and perhaps even necessary, to expand on the formal possibilities of architecture and its social role. This makes the need to articulate the geographic paradigm all the more urgent, because the role of synthesis that geography aspired to play between the physical, the economic, and the social is now being increasingly delegated to design.

The term geographic is used here primarily in a metaphorical way to designate a connection to the physical context. The paradigm does overlap, however, with the discipline of geography. Some clarification is necessary in this respect to benefit from the overlap while avoiding confusion. The history of geography is strongly linked to the history of discovery and colonization. The instruments for the discovery of territory were extended into its documentation and then, in turn, into its appropriation and transformation. And yet the discipline has evolved to become more diverse and broad—to become institutionalized around geographic societies; to split into human and physical geography producing very different approaches and even subject matters; then to disintegrate (as in the case of Harvard) and migrate into other disciplines (sociology, public health, information systems); and finally to be revived around central contemporary issues such as globalization. The paradigmatic role of geography in our thinking about design in this proposition could be taken in the narrower sense of geographic as an attempt to study the relationship between the social and the physical at a larger territorial scale, but also to forge a synthesis along the lines of "high" geography by design. It may not be an exaggeration to propose that something like a geographic attitude—in both method and content—is guiding different strands of design thinking today toward convergence. Or, that a geographic aesthetic dominates formal pursuits in the same way that the machine aesthetic inspired functionalism at the turn of the century, and for that, it would be important to study the extent and potentials of such a tendency.[17] As an example, and as a way of pushing these formal possibilities, the question of human settlements could be cast at the scale of the world. Within this scale, the marks of the urban centralities would be diffused and we can identify new spatial patterns that transcend the limitations of cosmopolis and help us imagine a better city-world where residences of peripheries or suburbs find themselves to be at the centers of other conglomerations. This would be a city-world where, when we compare tract developments across the globe, we find similarities that can link north and south in unexpected ways.

"WORLDMAKING"

According to Nelson Goodman, "the way the world is" is not predetermined.[18] Moreover, it is not useful to draw an exact distinction between what is given (out there) and what is represented (mental or cognitive). To speak of the world means to speak of one of its representations or constructions. If two equally rigorous representations seem incompatible, this implies two incompatible but nevertheless possible worlds. Truth or "rightness of rendering" can only be determined instrumentally, within a construction and around the purpose for which it is constructed. Goodman has always called on philosophers to examine the way artists construct worlds through their media and techniques. Art anticipates and elucidates the idea of world-making.

Goodman's proposition bridges between the logical and semiological approaches to the question of representation, but its emphasis on the world as the space in which a scope of operation is internally consistent (and therefore real) could be linked to the proposal of thinking of the world as an entity. As per Latour's conceptualization of the totality in his *Reassembling the Social*, we ought to take these panoramic representations seriously, because they provide the "only occasion to see the 'whole story' *as a whole*." He goes on:

> Their totalizing views should not be despised as an act of professional megalomania, but they should be adding, like everything else, to the multiplicity of sites we want to deploy. Far from being the place where everything happens, as in their director's

dreams, they are local sites to be added to as so many new places dotting the flattened landscape we try to map. But even after such a downsizing, their role may become central since they allow spectators, listeners, and readers to be equipped with a desire for wholeness and centrality. It is from those powerful stories that we get our metaphors for what "binds us together," the passions we are supposed to share, the general outline of society's architecture, the master narratives with which we are disciplined. It is inside their narrow boundaries that we get our commonsensical idea that interactions occur in a "wider" context; that there is an "up" and a "down"; that there is a "local" nested inside a "global"; and that there might be a Zeitgeist the spirit of which has yet to be devised.[19]

Along these lines, we should think of the ability of architects to construct new worlds and to encourage new forms of inhabitation, or habits, in these worlds. This *constructionist* position in architecture could be expanded to provide a more strategic tension between the internal world that the architectural object represents and the world outside it—more strategic, that is, and perhaps even more expressive, than the parallel pursuit of autonomy through this mechanism may have allowed.

The functional dimension of architecture should remain important in this process, but it should be addressed as forms of life—as inhabitation. In that sense, these habits of living should be interrogated and revised to allow for the formation and expression of new habits. This is the core of world-making à la Goodman, but it could also be expanded here to express how ways of inhabitation in their contingency relate to an idealized world.

From this constructionist approach, we can also infer that these smaller worlds through which art rehearses a larger world are predicated on the fact that we inhabit these new contexts with new eyes—that the new habits of living encourage new habits of representation and seeing, which in turn help to achieve another level of significance to architecture. This significance is one that maintains a higher openness to the experiences of its inhabitants. They are acquired rather than imposed. At one level then, the idea that the attributes of sameness, repetition, placelessness, scalelessness, and homogeneity that have so far been scaring us and compelling us to obsessively articulate and differentiate by architecture could be turned into a treasure trove of qualities waiting to be reexplored. Could the incessant sameness between a building in Shanghai, a building in provincial Ukraine, and one in São Paulo allude to a desire to connect the world together by this repetition at a time when the "small differences" between those places are being "narcissistically" exaggerated?[20] Marc Augé sees the phenomenon of star architects giving localities their signature and place markers on the face of the Earth as being an acknowledgment of this placelessness.[21] Perhaps it could also be seen as a place-holder until other ways of expressing placelessness can be found.

Conversely, and along with Jacques Rancière, we can also conceive of this global architecture as one that imagines new "forms of art" which do not fully relate to the forms of life that globalization has produced, but which displace them in order to make us more aware of their artifice.[22] This idea suggests that architecture, by virtue of its ability to balance between internal worlds and external ones, should maintain a certain level of operative autonomy and behave more like an object that sits in the flows, rather than a plug into the networks of systemic thinkers (blinded by the utilitarian exigencies of ecology or technology). But then, isn't this strategic withdrawal one of the more eloquent expressions of the global condition?

1. An earlier version of this paper was first delivered as a lecture titled "The World According to Architecture" at New York University's "Global Design" conference on May 26, 2011. A paper of the same title appeared in *New Geographies 4: Scales of the Earth*, ed. El Hadi Jazairy (Cambridge, MA: Harvard Graduate School of Design, 2011), 104–8. My gratitude goes to Peder Anker, Louise Harpman, and to Mitchell Joaquim for their kind invitation to be part of both the conference and the book. I am deeply indebted to the students in the New Geographies seminar that I teach at the GSD who studied the world-making architects with me and took a stab at designing their own worlds. I am also grateful to Amin Alsaden for his comments on the draft.

2. The term will appear in different spellings depending how the respective users spell the Greek original.

3. Maximilien Sorre, *Les fondements biologiques de la géographie humaine* (Paris: A. Colin, 1943–1952).

4. John Horton and Peter Kraftl, *Cultural Geographies: An Introduction* (London: Routledge, 2013), 11.

5. See Hashim Sarkis, "Geo-Architecture: A Prehistory for an Emerging Aesthetic," *Harvard Design Magazine 37* (spring 2014).

6. See Constantinos Doxiadis, *Ecumenopolis: The Settlement of the Future* (Athens: Athens Center of Ekistics, 1967). See also Augustin Berque, "Beyond Modern Landscape," *AA Files 25* (summer 1993) and Augustin Berque, *Ecoumène: Introduction à l'étude des milieu humains* (Paris: Belin, 2000).

7. Peter Sloterdijk, *In the World Interior of Capital* (Cambridge, UK, and Malden, MA: Polity Press, 2013), 143–49.

8. Aldo Rossi, *The Architecture of the City* (Cambridge, MA: MIT Press, 1977).

9. See for example Milton Santos, *La Nature de l'Espace, technique et temps, raison et émotion* (Paris: l'Harmattan, 1997).

10. See for example Fredric Jameson, *Postmodernism, or the Cultural Logic of Late Capitalism* (Durham: Duke University Press, 1991) 52–53. See also Bruno Latour, *Reassembling the Social: An Introduction to Actor-Network-Theory* (Oxford and New York: Oxford University Press, 2005).

11. See Marc Augé, "Architecture as Illusion and Allusion," in *The City of Flows, Territories, Agencies, and Institutions*, ed. Mauro Magatti and Laura Gherardi (Milano-Torino: Bruno Mondarodi, 2010).

12. See Stuart Elden, "The Space of the World," in *New Geographies 4*, 26–31.

13. See Edward Said, *Reflections of Exile and Other Essays* (Cambridge, MA: Harvard University Press, 2000). See also Kwame Anthony Appiah, *Cosmopolitanism: Ethics in a World of Strangers*, (New York: W. W. Norton & Co., 2006).

14. David Abulafia, *The Great Sea: A Human History of the Mediterranean* (London and New York: Allen Lane, 2011).

15. Ulrich Beck, *The Cosmopolitan Vision* (Cambridge, UK, and Malden, MA: Polity Press, 2006).

16. This term appears early on in the work of historian Carl Condit in relation to the TVA projects, but also in the writings of Le Corbusier on "the three human establishments." See Hashim Sarkis, "Geo-Architecture."

17. See David Gissen, "Architecture's Geographic Turns," in *Log 12* (2008).

18. Nelson Goodman, *Ways of Worldmaking* (Indianapolis: Hackett Pub. Co., 1978).

19. Bruno Latour, *Reassembling the Social*, 189.

20. In reference, of course, to Sigmund Freud's much borrowed, but equally helpful, concept of "narcissism of small differences."

21. Marc Augé, "Architecture as Illusion and Allusion," in *The City of Flows, Territories, Agencies, and Institutions*, ed. Mauro Magatti and Laura Gherardi (Milano-Torino: Bruno Mondarodi, 2010).

22. Jacques Rancière, *Aesthetics and Its Discontents* (London: Polity Press, 2004), 1–44.

SCAPE

KATE ORFF

ZEREGA AVENUE EMS STATION | Bronx, New York

Located on the site of a community garden in the Bronx, the new Zerega Avenue EMS Station project simultaneously meets the functional needs of the New York City Fire Department and enriches the surrounding community. SCAPE's proposal takes a large-scale sustainable systems approach to the site, which benefits the relocated garden, now on an adjacent property. The landscape is designed to incorporate storm-water management practices in the form of perimeter and interior parking swales that collect and channel water runoff, cisterns that collect excess rainwater to reuse on-site and supply to the relocated community garden next door, and a green roof that will optimize rainwater absorption and act as a fifth façade to the neighboring Castle Hill Housing Towers.

BLUE WALL ENVIRONMENTAL CENTER | Greenville, South Carolina

Situated in the uniform forest of the Blue Ridge Mountains, the Blue Wall Environmental Center provides a visitor experience that exposes the historical, cultural, ecological, and hydrological layers of its surroundings. A series of rooms act as unique destinations to support diverse programming and educational experiences. Each room is a "microclimate" dedicated to a specific theme, experience, or particular type of flora and fauna, acting as an aberration to the uniform nature of the surrounding forest. Each room is built within the former campsite, taking advantage of the existing site conditions while fully reconstructing the ecology and identity of the landscape. This approach provides unique and compelling experiences in every season. Designed to attract visitors year-round, the Blue Wall Environmental Center is part nature sanctuary, part art-park, part eco-retreat, and part rural event space.

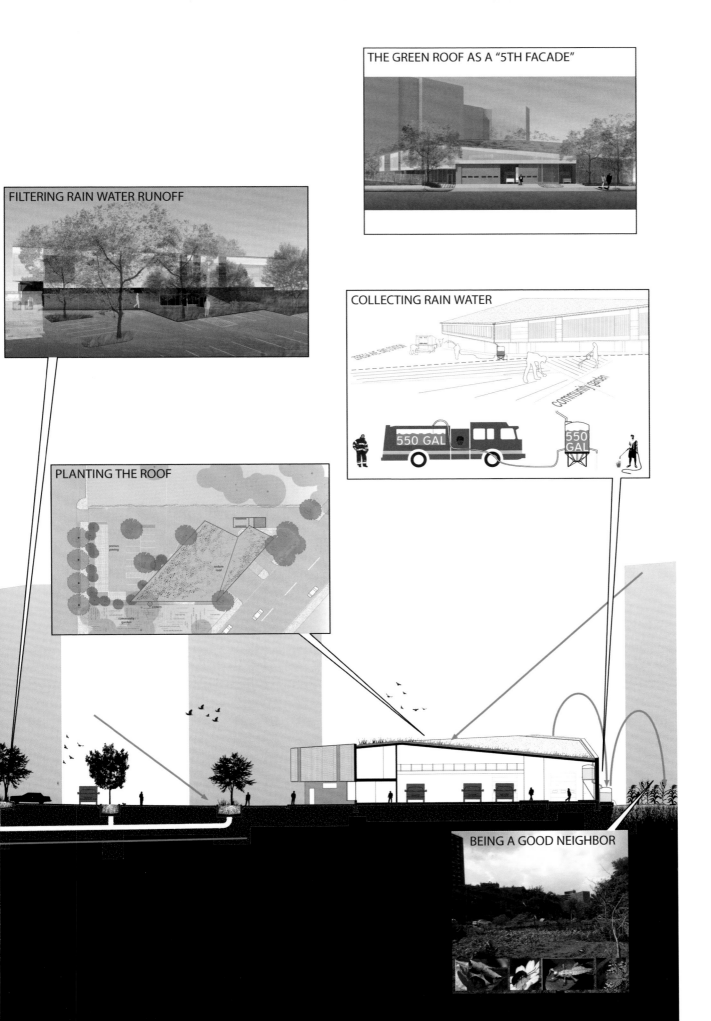

THE GREEN ROOF AS A "5TH FACADE"

FILTERING RAIN WATER RUNOFF

COLLECTING RAIN WATER

550 GAL

550 GAL

PLANTING THE ROOF

BEING A GOOD NEIGHBOR

SCAPE GDNYU ELSEWHERE ENVISONED

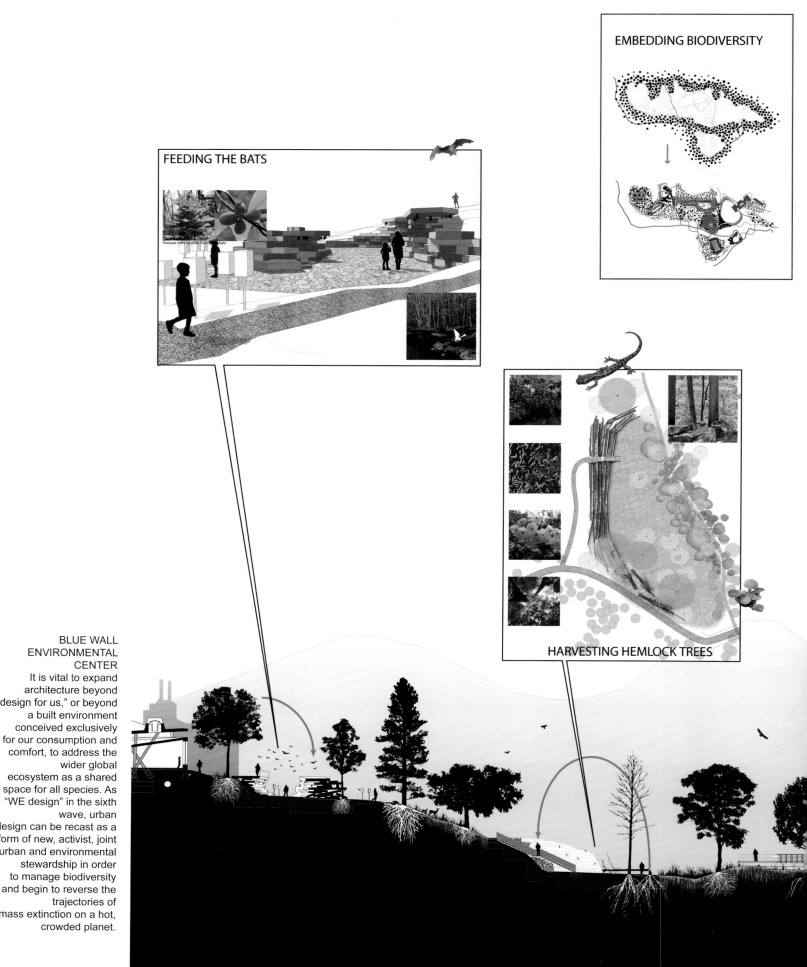

EMBEDDING BIODIVERSITY

FEEDING THE BATS

Pawpaw trees provide fruit for the bats

HARVESTING HEMLOCK TREES

BLUE WALL ENVIRONMENTAL CENTER

It is vital to expand architecture beyond "design for us," or beyond a built environment conceived exclusively for our consumption and comfort, to address the wider global ecosystem as a shared space for all species. As "WE design" in the sixth wave, urban design can be recast as a form of new, activist, joint urban and environmental stewardship in order to manage biodiversity and begin to reverse the trajectories of mass extinction on a hot, crowded planet.

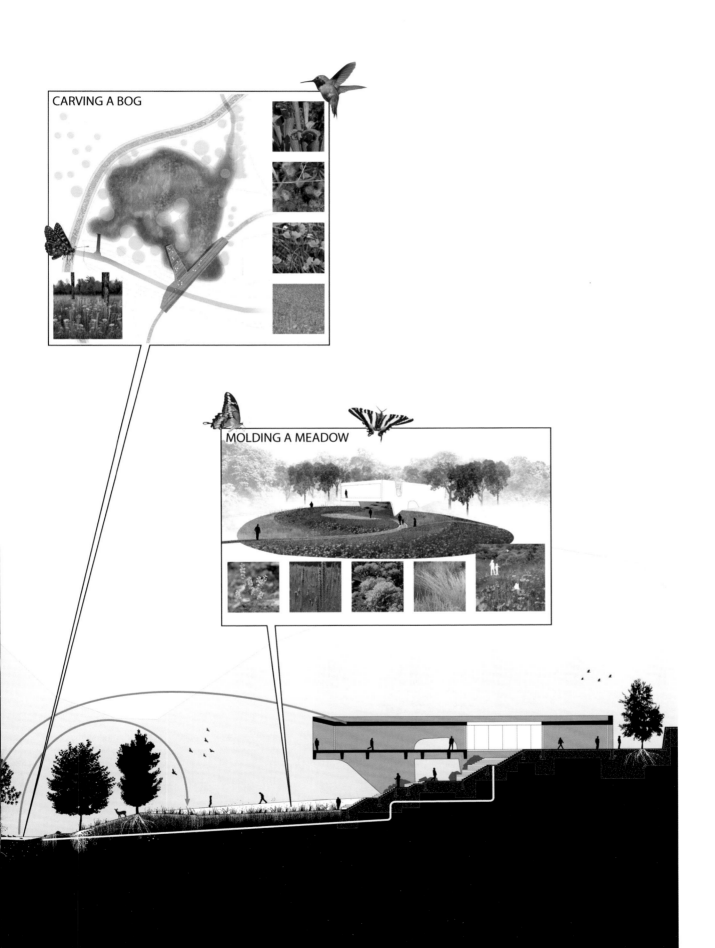

CARVING A BOG

MOLDING A MEADOW

SCAPE
Peder Anker, Louise Harpman, Mitchell Joachim

PA—Here we have a design firm that tries to be biocentric in the sense that they include not only the needs of human beings, but also the needs of various other species and the environment as a whole. Maybe the aesthetics take the backseat, but it is conceptually quite interesting and super green. If you want to think about the green design of the future, then you would have to take into account all the species which live in the area and in the surrounding environment. In that way, this is a truly inspiring project.

LH—I think that in its polemic, SCAPE takes up a position that few people understand, namely, that we are in a sixth wave of extinction. SCAPE posits that this an economical and ethical horror, but the lead designer, Kate Orff, also says that her role as a practitioner and an educator is to expand diversity as opposed to accepting the inevitable decline. She wants to embed biodiversity within cities because that is where we see the greatest reduction. The idea that nature is somehow "out there" in the "hinterlands" or outside of cities is an unfortunate distinction that we have to overcome. We have to, as Merleau-Ponty said, imagine an "elsewhere," but that elsewhere is here.

MJ—SCAPE is really using biodiversity as a hammer; in fact, they are centering the whole project on the beauty and the spectacle of biodiversity. These are things that we would find in different areas naturally and we are going to restore them and focus on it as the central visual asset. The virtue of biodiversity is justified in and of itself because it is a part of the Earth. It is not taking a landscape and framing it into artifacts, hills, or some sublime pastoral idea of beauty. Rather, it simply restores areas to a degree of what they were originally, almost enhancing them and fashioning them as the point. I don't know where to go beyond something like this genuine process-orientated bio-formalism realm; ecological succession as architecture. It's a curious point in landscape architecture. This is their high point of aesthetics; it is fabulous to see salamanders and rotting trees. This is what they see as beautiful since these forms were there in the beginning. The fact that we place them there is a bit odd, but we're actually replacing them there. We're full circle!

PA—There is an issue here. Will this project get LEED certification? LEED seems to be agnostic about design. It's all about awarding points based on carbon footprint and they are less focused on biodiversity. The Sustainable Sites Initiative would probably award this project with a certificate of some sort, and that's good. Yet this only confirms that there seem to be two systems for environmental impact certification: carbon footprint for buildings and biodiversity footprint for landscape design. I think it is great that Orff and her team are set on biodiversity as their core value, but why not also carbon footprint? And what about design for its own sake?

LH—Orff makes the point that aside from humans and mosquitoes, which are the only species expected to increase in numbers in the next one hundred years, we are losing diversity. The fact that we add more salamanders does not add to the diversity of species, but simply adds more salamanders. The architecture is probably the least compelling part of the proposal at this point. The environmental center stands very much apart; we still see a building juxtaposed with its landscape.

MJ—Could the center become more like Angkor Wat? A space that is overflowing with trees and foliage where it is impossible to find the borders between animals, buildings, and trees?

PA—Why not?!

LH—Fine, but at the same time, let's keep in mind the Masdar example. You can have a vision, you can hire the best architects, engineers, landscape architects, planners in the world, with the deepest possible pockets, but they still miss the goal to have an integrated, inter-speciated environment. Why not? First of all because Masdar is in the desert and second because it is not replicable. It stands alone. Will this be another partial or failed utopia? SCAPE at least addresses problems and sites that are typical.

MJ—This is terra-forming. It's not suffering incredibly, but it does not have the same diversity that once occupied it. Orff and her team's proposal is to bring it back by man, by our own hand and place it inside that site, give it new homes, and arrange it just right.

PA—I think architects and designers could harvest knowledge from Ecological Restoration scholars, which is an academic field in itself. I think this project is really promising and there is a lot to learn from it.

LH—But let's keep looking. At some point we have to get serious with thinking of green roofs as a "cure" for environmental woes. We need to be very skeptical of some of these proposals, when they become "greenwashing." Many major cities are developing "cool roof" and "green roof" initiatives. And yet without a more comprehensive building envelope upgrade, buildings still remain huge energy wasters. You can't address only the "fifth façade."

MJ—There are three thousand acres of unshaded roof space in the city of New York. It's a prodigious signal if we can create that change. On another level, from the plan view, it appears green, but from every other angle it is still business as usual. It's a good move, but it is in danger of putting parsley on the pig. It's a dash of green that ultimately does not change the animal. If a building has two cycles of heating and cooling, so basically winter or summer, a green roof will not stop the building from wasting energy.

PA—We have to start somewhere. You can't just dismiss a project because it is not 100% successful or the entire building is not green. You have to applaud small accomplishments like a green roof, and I think Orff would agree.

LH—There is a stitch between buildings in this project. The water that comes off the roof of the fire station feeds the community garden for the low-income housing next door. So the idea that they're already using an integrated mechanism means that there could be more stitching. The roof is good, but then what? Does it connect to the larger landscape? This project for the EMS station is done with an architecture team. SCAPE are the landscape architects working with the architecture firm Smith-Miller and Hawkinson. Doesn't this highlight the fact that we are all still in our distinct disciplines, with our very separate areas of expertise? Why aren't systems thinking and integration taught on a larger scale? The built environment encompasses landscapes and buildings. Bringing this type of integrated thinking together is my hope for reformatting architectural education.

SCAPE Kate Orff is a landscape architect and the founding principal of SCAPE, a landscape architecture and urban design office based in New York City. She is an Assistant Professor at Columbia University's Graduate School of Architecture, Planning and Preservation. Orff received an MLA from Harvard University's Graduate School of Design.

BJARKE INGELS GROUP

W57 | New York, NY

This building, located on Manhattan's West 57th Street, is a hybrid between the traditional Manhattan high-rise and the European perimeter block building. W57's distinct shape combines the compactness and efficiency of a courtyard building—providing a sense of intimacy while meeting demands for density and security—with the airiness and stunning views of a skyscraper. The form of the building shifts depending on the viewer's vantage point. From the West Side Highway, it appears to be a pyramid; from West 58th Street, a dramatic glass spire. By keeping three corners of the block low, while lifting the northeast portion of the building up toward its 450-foot peak, the courtyard opens to views of the Hudson River, bringing western sun deep into the block. The residential building contains cultural and commercial programs at street level and on the second floor. While the courtyard is a private space for residents, it can still be seen from the outside, creating a visual connection with the greenery of the Hudson River Park. The slope of the building allows for a transition in scale between the low-rise structures to the south and the high-rise residential towers to the north and east of the site. Every apartment has a bay window to take advantage of the site's spectacular views.

ARC WASTE-TO-ENERGY PLANT

This waste-to-energy plant is both a clean waste-to-energy conversion plant and a destination in and of itself. Located in the heart of Copenhagen, next to the marina, the plant produces CO_2 emissions in the form of bursting smoke rings. The plant aims to be a place of participation that encourages public engagement as well as entertainment. It will feature a ski slope, and the smoke rings serve to express to the public the extent to which we still face environmental challenges caused by CO_2 emissions. The ARC plant will replace the city's current waste-to-energy plant, and will provide about 97% of Copenhagen's homes with electricity.

ARC
WASTE-TO-ENERGY
PLANT
The new waste-to-energy
plant will feature a
comprehensive strategy
for sustainability, from the
level of building systems to
its broader communicative
role in urban and social
settings.

BIG GDNYU ELSEWHERE ENVISONED

MJ—Ingels's book *Yes is More* is on amazon.com's top-ten bestseller list for architecture and design. He produces buildings that have a very legible typology. They are very easy to decipher; the geometry is not exhaustive. There is some twist or a simple change that actually has a profound macro effect. Certainly with this project here we have to ask: is it a pyramid, is it a courtyard building, or is it a combination of both? It's actually tremendously clever. He consistently produces these direct and tranquil geometries that become his buildings. When he discusses them, he does it under this notion of deeply pleasurable sustainability as a way of getting us there. These are all things that are positive signals. As a communicator he sticks to that kind of directive as a guiding principle. His book *Yes is More* could not be more affirmative. In the same way that it communicates to people at all different levels, the format of the book is done in a traditional comic book fashion, which makes it incredibly informal to read. It's him as an individual that unpacks, explains, and narrates all the different aspects of his projects with unpretentious diagrams. Step by step, he brings you into the logic of the building.

LH—There are architects who have a love of obscurantism. They create their own language and diagrams and codes of communication. With BIG's diagrams, they go the other way and make their ideas hyper-legible, so that the solution seems inevitable. Ingels and his team are so clear and so procedural in explaining the formal diagrams that led to the design of W57. BIG is not trying to rethink urbanism in the twenty-first century; in fact, they are morphing the well-established courtyard and tower typologies in the service of housing. BIG is merging the types and thinking about how to activate the streetscape and the courtyard's interior, and how to bring light, air, and terraces back to a site that has been vacant for over thirty years. If we're going to inject life into the conversation about what is sustainability or what is green urbanism, we should look at somebody like Ingels who makes you feel that this is a better way to live, that good design is actually a value proposition as opposed to a technological fix.

PA—Yes, for sure, this is an important contribution to the architecture debate and sustainable design. Looking at his projects from Norway—where I am from—and comparing them to something like Snøhetta's Plus Building that produces energy and is beautiful, puritan, and has all the architectural values, it is clear that Snøhetta does not have the Danish flare of ".dk" and the hedonism that Danes are known for. They drink beer and smoke cigars during lunch in their offices and in meetings. The point is that Ingels, in many ways, reflects the Danish culture of embracing the pleasures of life. I think that it is an important thing to bring into the environmental debate, because it has been so puritan and lacking in this way.

LH—What's interesting about the environmental discourse over the last thirty years is that it has always been corrective. It says that "things are wrong and out of sync," and therefore we need to fix these things. Ingels says we should start from a place that he calls "environmental hedonism" which will make us, our communities, and our planet more healthy and productive. This might even be called "making good buildings," but it wouldn't get the media's attention!

MJ—Ingels is being joyous in his presentation. He removes ideas about doubt from his work. He does not make aggressive points in order to give a rationale for the building. He presents it with this kind of freedom of thought or ease. He relaxes us into the problem, as opposed to admonishment.

LH—Ingels cut his teeth doing housing design with Rem Koolhaas. While many people consider housing to be a kind of workaday building form, in fact, it is the fundament of cities and urban landscapes. The idea of building smart housing is where you can inculcate values into a population—where you can teach by living examples. Although W57 is a new building, Ingels often makes the point that cities are, for the most part, already built and need to be retrofitted. We need to become smart and effective actors within the existing built environment to upgrade, preserve, and expand for the next five decades. That view has a lot to recommend it

PA—BIG's pyramid in New York is a high-end residential building that may rub environmentalists the wrong way, since it caters to the rich. They have also done projects that have not catered to that audience. I'm thinking of their involvement in Superkilen, one of the most troubled regions of Copenhagen. Finally, we have to commend BIG for their new waste-to-energy building that is under construction, making an architectural object— indeed, a ski slope—out of a power plant in Denmark, a country known to have terrible skiers.

LH—The waste-to-energy building, Amager Resource Center, is a project that has captured so much attention. Not least of all because the design shows girls in bathing suits snowboarding down an artificial ski slope! Both the architecture and the way to "show" the architecture is provocative and pleasing, yet also smart. Has an incinerator ever generated so much positive press? The building is essentially a "jacket" around a needed community facility. The "dirty" incinerator is cleaned up by creating a sports center on the outside and a science museum on the inside.

PA—It is not a "building." It's more like a traditional plant nobody wants in their backyard. That BIG is packaging a waste facility so that people don't mind having it in their neighborhood is quite remarkable. And what's wrong with skiing girls in bathing suits?

MJ—Moreover, BIG is not Zaha. Their forms are more reserved, tightly knitted to context and less flamboyant. The court-skyscraper combination is rather unique given the typological history of tall buildings. Its slightly rotational exterior skin design is segmented into logically manufactured components. The pinnacle element is worth the most in property value, yet takes up the least space with the most views and natural light. He doesn't really desire to push the envelope as far as materials or structure or any kind of real architectural innovation. He may do it in the overall form, but his methods all fall into tried and true systems and ideas of inherent buildability. He is not trying to think outside the box. He works well within the degrees of safety to assemble things and get things built on time and within the budget. Ingels is not like Patrick Schumacher or the SANAA office, which would often experiment to a fault. He has not travelled into that territory yet. Maybe in the not so distant future, when he has a lot of projects underneath his belt, he could have the opportunity to explore and do something radically different.

BIG, founded by Bjarke Ingels, is a Copenhagen- and New York-based office practicing architecture, urbanism, research, and development. BIG is led by eight partners: Bjarke Ingels, Andreas Klok Pedersen, Finn Nørkjær, David Zahle, Jakob Lange, Thomas Christoffersen, and Managing Partners Sheela Maini Søgaard and Kai-Uwe Bergmann.

LATERAL OFFICE

MASON WHITE, LOLA SHEPPARD

THE ACTIVE LAYER
The installation invites visitors to experience the complex glaciated landscape of the Arctic condition, to be immersed in it, and to observe its complex patterns and terrain.

NEXT NORTH

The Canadian North is often viewed solely as a vast, sparsely populated, fragile, and sublime territory. Yet with one of the most dramatically changing climates on Earth and an estimated quarter of the planet's undiscovered energy resources, this Arctic region has emerged as a site of significant economic and developmental speculation. The balance in which ecologies and people coexist in this region, and the complexity of the interaction between national politics and local cultures, cannot be overstated. The region's unique combination of climate, culture, and geography produces complicated infrastructures, settlements, and sociopolitical negotiations. The melting of polar ice has given rise to territorial land claims, threatened ecosystems, uncovered new resources, and intensified interest in the northern frontier. The Next North project seeks to address the inevitability of the circumpolar frontier becoming, as the writer Charles Emmerson puts it, a "geopolitical flashpoint." The five themes that structure this research—Monitoring, Culture, Mobility, Ecology, and Resources—offer a chance to focus on key issues in this evolving region. Building upon these research threads, Lateral Office has developed projections that chart a new, alternative development method for the region. This project emphasizes looking at challenges in new ways, and developing synergetic solutions to diverse problems including health care challenges, the development of mobility and military infrastructures, and ecological concerns.

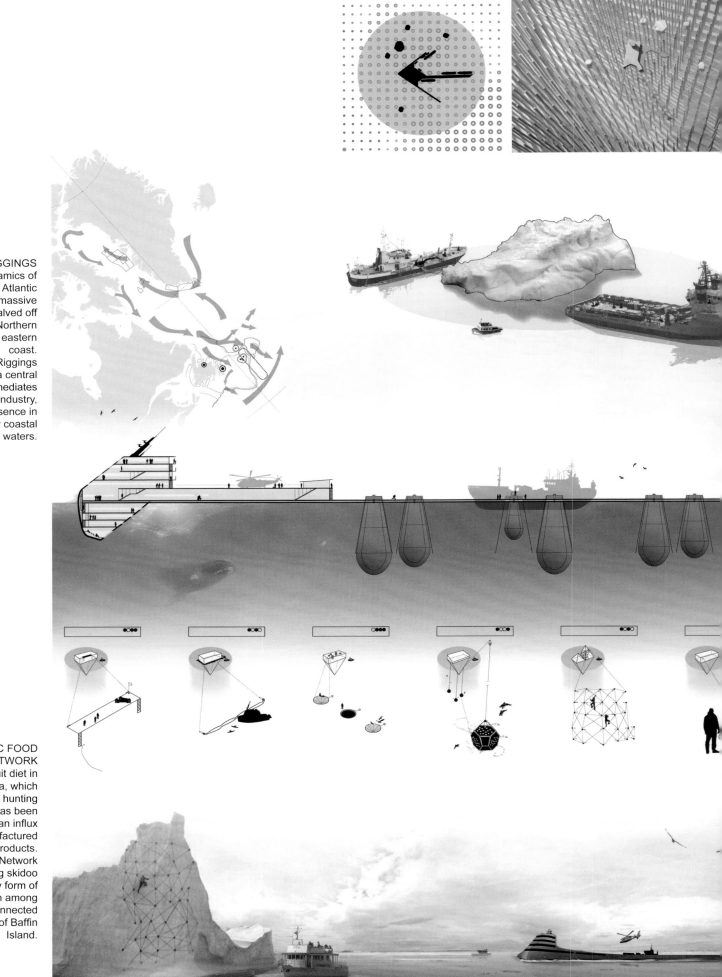

ICEBERG RIGGINGS

The hydrodynamics of the Canadian Atlantic circulates massive icebergs calved off Greenland and Northern Canada down the eastern coast.

The Iceberg Riggings project proposes a central rig system that mediates between tourist, industry, and military presence in the Iceberg Alley coastal waters.

ARCTIC FOOD NETWORK

The traditional Inuit diet in Northern Canada, which is centered on hunting and gathering, has been compromised by an influx of southern manufactured food products.

The Arctic Food Network utilizes the existing skidoo trails, the only form of ground connection among the eleven disconnected Inuit communities of Baffin Island.

LATERAL OFFICE
Peder Anker, Louise Harpman, Mitchell Joachim

LH—Lateral Office runs a research and design practice. This project identifies a contested natural environment, one that is being challenged by economic pressures which are opening the North to more exploration for oil and gas, but with very little regard for the environment or native populations. Lateral Office calls themselves speculators, but not in the gold rush sense. Instead, they try to imagine other ways to engage the competing demands of economic production and tourism, while also addressing global ecology and indigenous populations. They develop speculative proposals for engaging this challenging physical, social, and economic landscape. This is a landscape project that also responds to a very real set of demands from much bigger players—the oil, gas, and tourism industries— which are already altering this landscape for the worse. The most problematic images they show are the oil tankers and the tour boats, where nature becomes an entertainment commodity. On the other hand, Lateral proposes to set up a series of scientific monitoring stations and try to engage the architectural language of the nomadic local peoples in Nunavut and beyond. The local people are called Nunavummiut and number only about 30,000. I quite like the research and the speculation, but I also see that they hold back from taking a position either for or against the demands of tourism and oil/gas exploration.

PA—I feel like saying, if necessary with neon blinking lights, that oil exploration and tourism in these extremely vulnerable environments is not, in any way, environmentally responsible. There are moral issues here in questioning whether one should build at all in these types of environments, and I think they'd agree with me. What they're saying is, "if you must build in these locations, here is how to do it in a responsible way."

MJ—It's a curious project. They are doing these micro-interventions that made it to the cover of *Architect*. It's a curious little project where they show indigenous people in small, custom-designed huts or pavilions that do one specialized function, like fishing or gazing at the stars. They're working in a kind of vernacular that purports to be easy to assemble in the middle of nowhere in the Arctic. They're drawing on all kinds of connections to the lifestyles that these people have, whether it be their sleigh dogs or snowmobiles or fishing, in a kind of a fancy postmodern architecture that seems, without a shadow of a doubt, out of place, but plausible. I think that the evocative side of what they are doing is to create links in the food network, based on the ways that people in the area hunt for food, which they then combine with shipping lanes to drop off or add to that stream. I don't see the connections directly, except that they are taking on a vast area and trying to pinpoint very specialized zones and then get very detailed and concrete in their proposal. It is such a big task. They designed an installation to showcase this research. There was so much data-scaping that it wasn't really about architecture, but it was about taking all the information and, through many acts of mapping, saying this is what we know about the North.

LH—There is a whole part of their project that accepts tourism as a given, and seems to say, let's amplify the experiences and make more tourist opportunities. Lateral shows us a place where a helicopter can land on a polar trekking vehicle. To Peder's point, they are in no way critical of the demands and the real costs to the environment that are made by promoting this extreme tourist economy. I wish they came down squarely that this area and these people should be part of a preserved landscape. Shouldn't there be places that are *not* available to big icebreaker ships and their helicopter decks? In my view, this is an environment that needs protecting, not exploiting.

PA—There is a fine line between tourism and scientific exploration. Scientists love to go on these types of tours, to be explorers, to join the manly quest for the North, the "Shackleton factor" of the marine biologists. Climatologists have the same fascination with icebergs. The proposal feeds into that culture. There is nothing wrong with exploring the North and doing academic research; however, I'm not sure we need to build this type of infrastructure for it. The most Northern permanent research base I know of is in Spitsbergen. It is just a building, but it's not sustainable since the researchers have to travel there by plane and bring every bit of food and clothing and equipment with them.

MJ—There have been many images showing our failure as an industrial society to combat climate change or force the climate into a new direction. Al Gore's image of a polar bear floating on ice worked or at least resonated with certain groups of people. This project is a totally different approach. Maybe it is about being there and viscerally connecting to that polar bear floating on the ice. Maybe that is interesting to some people, but they want to see the evidence and acknowledge it themselves. For a university, maybe students need to go somewhere like this. It is one thing to study in Europe or China, which is slightly more exotic, but if this research station were built, we could go to the North Pole and see Texas-sized chunks of ice falling into the ocean.

LH—Making the crisis visible remains important. People need to experience that our planet is in peril. But maybe we don't have to go all the way to the Arctic. There is something here about data-scaping and the network thinking that I do think is exportable to another environment. Maybe we can accept that they're really looking for an idea about self-sufficiency in these Arctic food networks, an idea about producing power and food, and sustaining populations of a certain size. Maybe we have to approach our cities and towns like that, too. What is the right size? Is there a size that is too big, not to fail, but to survive? The megacities show that a massive increase in population promotes inefficiency and mounting social, health, political, and environmental problems. Maybe Lateral is proposing another model. What their data-scaping offers is information that shows where we cross the line, so we can see where the efficiency flattens and ultimately decreases. In that sense, I love that they might start to create a larger discourse about site, which is to say, with this limited population and in this extreme environment, can we hypothesize about what local self-sufficiency would look like? Could that translate to Washington Square? London? Istanbul? How do we understand population pressure, limited resources, and design with that information? Could this become a model for new settlement patterns?

LATERAL OFFICE, founded by Mason White and Lola Sheppard, is an experimental design practice located in Toronto. White is an Associate Professor at the University of Toronto. He has taught at Harvard, Cornell, and Ohio State Universities, and UC Berkeley. He received an M.Arch. from Harvard University's Graduate School of Design. Sheppard is an Associate Professor at the University of Waterloo. She has taught at the University of Toronto, Ohio State University, and California College of the Arts. She also received an M.Arch. from Harvard University's Graduate School of Design.

SPATIAL INFORMATION DESIGN LAB

Mobile air quality
monitoring system
for Beijing.

AIR TRACKS | Beijing, China
In order to better understand the localized effects of air pollution in Beijing, SIDL developed a mobile air quality sensor that registered particulate matter and carbon monoxide and matched those readings with a specific location. Partnering with the Associated Press, the devices were clipped onto the belts, backpacks, and bicycles of journalists and researchers as they traversed the Olympic city in 2008.

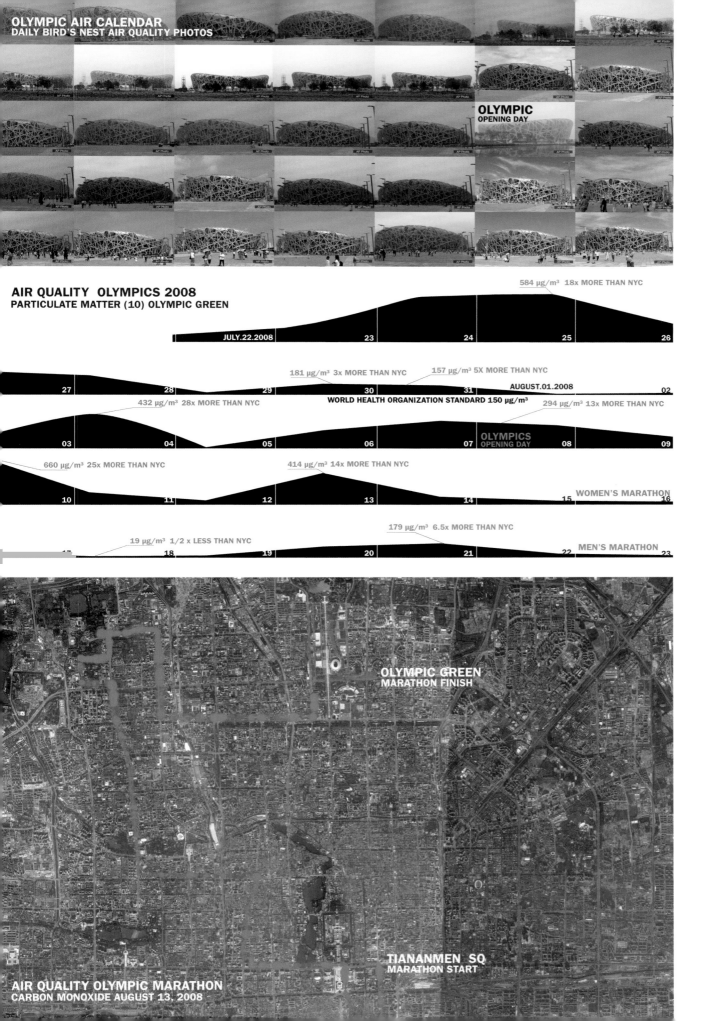

OLYMPIC AIR CALENDAR
DAILY BIRD'S NEST AIR QUALITY PHOTOS

OLYMPIC
OPENING DAY

AIR QUALITY OLYMPICS 2008
PARTICULATE MATTER (10) OLYMPIC GREEN

584 µg/m³ 18x MORE THAN NYC

| JULY.22.2008 | 23 | 24 | 25 | 26 |

181 µg/m³ 3x MORE THAN NYC   157 µg/m³ 5X MORE THAN NYC

| 27 | 28 | 29 | 30 | 31 | AUGUST.01.2008 | 02 |

432 µg/m³ 28x MORE THAN NYC   WORLD HEALTH ORGANIZATION STANDARD 150 µg/m³   294 µg/m³ 13x MORE THAN NYC

| 03 | 04 | 05 | 06 | 07 OLYMPICS OPENING DAY | 08 | 09 |

660 µg/m³ 25x MORE THAN NYC   414 µg/m³ 14x MORE THAN NYC

| 10 | 11 | 12 | 13 | 14 | 15 | 16 WOMEN'S MARATHON |

19 µg/m³ 1/2 x LESS THAN NYC   179 µg/m³ 6.5x MORE THAN NYC

| 17 | 18 | 19 | 20 | 21 | 22 | 23 MEN'S MARATHON |

OLYMPIC GREEN
MARATHON FINISH

TIANANMEN SQ
MARATHON START

AIR QUALITY OLYMPIC MARATHON
CARBON MONOXIDE AUGUST 13, 2008

SIDL GDNYU ELSEWHERE ENVISONED

LH—Laura Kurgan and Sarah Williams at Spatial Information Design Lab (SIDL), which is a unit within Columbia's Graduate School of Architecture, Planning, and Preservation, take as a starting point the collection of data. One project looked at the Beijing Olympics, where they planted a number of sensors in the backpacks of various people attending in order to map air quality and particulate matter. Data mapping has exploded and you can't have a conversation about the future without engaging Big Data. The problem is, to paraphrase Lord Kelvin, William Deming, and, most recently, Michael Bloomberg, if you can't measure a problem then you can't fix it. SIDL does a stealth collection project here, which is totally admirable given the levels of state control by the Chinese government. They brought awareness to the fact there was terrible air quality at the Olympics. This is a very short but powerful snapshot. They created a data set, combined it with a lot of open source information, and brought it forward in a visual way that can be used by planners and public health advocates.

MJ—Their work certainly challenges architecture and planning to become more like activism. The data and the synthesis of the data was meant to be very public, certainly at the international stage, and it received a lot of attention. It says something about America's relationship to Beijing that we're willing, if not openly so, to express a major fault in their key city during one of the most premiere moments. Even though the data is important, it must be embarrassing for both American and Chinese diplomats. They also make comments here about "shades of green," which allows us to know that there is no true green. There is no pure version of a successful, ecological, sustainable project. We don't have a picture of best practices yet. There are different ways of satisfying these demands without being as dark green or true green as they should be. We have come to some level of acceptance of these different shades. The topic of measurement and its relationship to these different shades of green becomes not a green issue, but rather a gray issue. It becomes very fuzzy defining what it means to achieve fitness with the Earth's metabolism versus doing just enough to be more responsible than some others. I think that is a really tricky place to be in, as well as a continuing problem.

PA—I must say I admire Kurgan's and Williams's activist approach in going to Beijing and exposing the terrible regime's pollution policies, or lack thereof. I'm wondering whether this project really belongs in the world of architecture and design. It is more about metrics than design. The problem becomes more apparent when you compare it to a similar project, MVRDV Metacity Datatown, from the late '90s, where they collected all kinds of data about how to be green and tried to design a city based on this data. The result was not that pleasing; in fact, it was quite ugly. If you take the slogan "if you cannot measure it, you cannot fix it," it implies something more than just measuring the problem.

LH—That is exactly right. I think bringing the metrics forward in a visible and communicable way is important, but not enough. Necessary, but not sufficient. I do think that some architects overly aestheticize things—so that's probably a legitimate criticism. But starting from the data allows us to ask about, and connect to, a building's performance. As architects, what are we trying to mitigate? What are we trying not to exacerbate? This is an important step because I think architects in the late '80s and early '90s were distanced from the idea of technical performance requirements in their buildings, and certainly there was very little discussion of landscape and systems. That was what "other people" took care of.

If we want to reformat architecture to be more inclusive and integrated, connecting to the work of teams like SIDL is a good place to start.

MJ—Urban ecology and, for the most part, ecology more generally, are by no means complete. Certainly urban ecology is relatively new compared to other sciences and does not have a definitive book of laws that define the tested and correct approaches to rethinking conditions in a city. Ecologists are still writing papers and making arguments and doing replicable test beds to prove some of their previous suppositions. If you go to urban ecology conferences, one scientist after another tries to show how close they are to creating the definitive "text" on how to make a green city. But ultimately nobody is able to hold up a book that would belong to every architect or planner, a text that would be absolutely necessary for designing a green city. The chapters in this hypothetical bible of urban ecology would contain facts, directions, and metrics in a very clear format that would explain how to make something truly green. It is not that these books don't exist, but the numbers are always in flux.

PA—As a matter of fact, we do have books on how to be green, and they're called LEED for buildings and Sustainable Sites for landscape. People register for these programs and get points and certifications, which they can put on their webpage to say "we are now green" because they have successfully followed all of the standardized procedures. On one level, it is often a huge accomplishment and takes a lot of effort—I support these efforts and I think we all should—but the essential thing that is lacking is beauty, aesthetics, or a sense of creating a building or a landscape that transcends the technical fix. In a deeper sense, that is what humans want: to transcend the technological-material world and reach for something else.

MJ—The LEED rating system was an achievement, and a shock. Nobody expected that it would be the topmost representative success story since Rio+20, as far as green design is concerned. Nobody thought that a set of rules and a points system with some different colored stars would be the thing that we would all celebrate as a green achievement. You are totally right that it fails to evoke beauty or any sense of aesthetic refinement. In fact, it is almost as if it has no design. That might even be the point. As Jesse Reiser rightly noted, if a Robert A.M. Stern building like the George W. Bush Presidential Library can have a platinum LEED rating, the same as the Thom Mayne building at Cooper Union, then LEED places no value on aesthetics. Even though one has columns in a neo-classical style and the other looks like a cleaved metallic cube, both of them received the same rating from LEED. It is completely neutral. This underscores the fact that the ratings systems are indifferent to style or design. That has probably given them the ability to ease themselves into the larger development world and gain considerable acceptance. One wonders if that means there needs to be another point system for style and aesthetics.

SIDL Spatial Information Design Lab, directed by Laura Kurgan, is a think- and action-tank specializing in the visual display of spatial information about contemporary cities and events. Laura Kurgan is an Associate Professor of Architecture at Columbia University's Graduate School of Architecture, Planning and Preservation, where she is also Director of Visual Studies. Kurgan received an M.Arch. from Columbia University. Sarah Williams codirected SIDL during the development of the work presented as part of Global Design NYU. She now is director of the Civic Data Design Lab at the Massachusetts Institute of Technology (MIT) and is an Assistant Professor of Urban Planning at MIT's Department of Urban Studies and Planning (DUSP). Williams received a Master's degree from MIT in City Planning and Urban Design.

SIDL GDNYU ELSEWHERE ENVISONED

RICHARD SOMMER

**JOHN H. DANIELS FACULTY OF
ARCHITECTURE, LANDSCAPE AND DESIGN
UNIVERSITY OF TORONTO**

Aerial view of industrial
waterfront in Belfast,
Northern Ireland.

BELFAST RECAST and CAMOUFLAGE URBANISM

The work shown here was undertaken by Richard Sommer in his capacity as the Gerard O'Hare Chair of Design and Development at the University of Ulster, Northern Ireland. The broad mandate of the O'Hare Chair was to engage with government agencies, academics, and other groups to develop concepts and proposals for the design of Northern Ireland's cities and towns as they emerged from "The Troubles." The two studies included, Belfast Recast and Camouflage Urbanism, employ a range of analytical, interpretive, and projective techniques, and bring them to bear on a twofold process.

First, Sommer and his students engaged a series of studies (historical, eco-topographic, morphological, economic, and cultural) about the divided territories. Second, a series of distinct urban, architectural, and landscape-ecological strategies, based on a new delineation of the territories in question, was proposed. The Belfast study attempts to project an alternative future by acknowledging how the city's rise and precipitous fall as a modern, industrial port city figures greatly in the continuing political and socioeconomic struggles between its competing Protestant and Catholic populations. The cross-border Camouflage study navigates and refigures a complex region with a history of agricultural and touristic uses that, until recently, fell between the cracks of Ireland's north-south partition.

RICHARD SOMMER **GDNYU ELSEWHERE ENVISONED**

RICHARD SOMMER

Peder Anker, Louise Harpman, Mitchell Joachim

MJ—Sommer's project is an all-inclusive soup of everything that you should do in responsible urban design. It's filled with all the right moves. It's a filter of reason that may unpack every chapter in Kevin Lynch's *Good City Form* to produce a scheme for a very large urban area, in this case, Belfast, Northern Ireland.

LH—What we see here is a faculty-led student design project, with many different teams of students working on transportation, infrastructure, ports, and the overall waterfront.

PA—To me it looks like Sommer is acting as the fountainhead of urban solutions. Where is the involvement from the public?

MJ—It's a phased and large-scale scheme that is attempting to deal with all of the potential issues that the city will be facing in the next fifty years. It would eventually be one scheme, but for now it is a compendium of suggestions and interventions that can be changed. It's a broad understanding of the relationships between these clusters of buildings and their functions, as well as their long-term uses and connections to the water and infrastructure.

LH—What's pushing this? Is it population growth? Is there population depletion? Why Belfast? Why now?

MJ—The city made claims that they wanted designers to research this particular area around the old port and bring it—kicking and screaming—into a vital part of the city.

LH—Architecture professors often insert themselves into public processes. We need to ask: what is the responsibility of university professors in a one-semester, possibly two-semester project, to make proposals for alternative futures? This is, potentially, a very important role for universities to provide research and resources that the cities themselves might not have. The professional community will jump in because there is work to be had and fees to be generated. But this represents a different model. The university research teams can and should take a much wider stance—zoom out, challenge accepted planning strategies, and also take risks. Engaged research projects such as this one can be tools for bringing students up to the current state of the art and possibly beyond it. In this case, we see a lot of students coming to learn various planning strategies and techniques, asking questions that are always asked. There could be a legal or sociological or historical overlay that we are not seeing. This kind of project is an important way to bring students into the discourse, but I wonder if there's more. Which is to say, I'm hoping there's more.

MJ—What's in this board is everything. Sommer claims there are only four possible tactics to develop urban design: identity, zoning, atmosphere, and infrastructure. On some level, setting limits and categories is the point of this kind of exercise. The teams have gone through every imaginable iteration and have looked at all of the scenarios. This project claims to settle on a few, but the job is to discard all the bad versions, get to some of the good ones, and then push the project ahead for somebody else to make the final decisions.

LH—But who is the "somebody else" here? Is it the professional town planners? The property owners? The longshoremen? We all know that "the community" in any city is never monolithic. Sommer needs to get out of the "studio" mode, to show that architects have other skill sets beyond design. They understand how to integrate ideas, how to balance conflicting concerns, and how to find solutions. The students need to find a way to share their research and nascent expertise.

PA—The closed quarters of the design studio brings us to the question of the gallery, of the closed world of the exhibit space.

LH—Do you mean: Is our energy properly spent in having architecture and design shows and symposia? What are the roles of galleries and journals, especially if architectural work is meant to engage a larger constituency?

MJ—Our Global Design shows in New York and London could be viewed from the street; they were totally open to the public and passersby; we hosted tours for all kinds of school groups through our shows. Our gallery shows created active and provocative spaces.

PA—Art theorists talk about entering a gallery or museum as walking over a threshold into a different space, a different world where art is for its own sake. *L'art pour l'art!* The gallery is separate and protected from everyday concerns. Both physically and mentally, you enter into a different space. The gallery can be a liberating experience in the sense that here we can do and say things that we cannot say other places. During the Cold War where there was a lot of political tension, the gallery was that safe space. I still think, when we talk about public outreach, it's ultimately the sign of a healthy political life when there is a space that welcomes controversy. It is not always possible.

LH—What is the difference between art and architecture in a gallery space? Our gallery was not showing art objects for sale. We were curating, deciding, and foregrounding certain projects and practices that we thought had something new and important to say about the built environment. We were not asking for open Rorschach-style free associations, but rather for a response. That's what I think the curatorial goal of a gallery is, or should be anyway. I think Peder is right insofar as the gallery is meant to be a space of risk-taking and discussion. My criticism of the time we spend in universities, galleries, and symposia is that we're in the echo chamber, still talking to ourselves. We have to get out more. This is a luxury of a democratic society.

PA—We come to gallery shows and read design books to open ourselves to other ways of seeing the world. But ultimately, we are once-removed. We need to always "check" ourselves with the natural and built environment, not just through images of it.

MJ—What's important is that we give the public direct information and resources to access the work further. We need to give architects and designers many opportunities to describe their process and their projects and to engage the various publics who will be directly affected by the work. The architectural students practice this "talking" throughout their studies. But when the language is so sophisticated and so based in one knowledge set, 99% of the world has no idea what's going on, and so have no interest in the built environment. This is one of the many things that needs to change, and this is what our Global Design initiative is trying to do.

RICHARD SOMMER is an architect and the Dean of the John H. Daniels Faculty of Architecture, Landscape, and Design at the University of Toronto, where he is also a Professor of Architecture and Urbanism. Sommer was formerly Associate Professor of Architecture and Urban Design at Harvard University's Graduate School of Design, where he was also the Director of Urban Design Programs. Sommer received an M.Arch from Harvard University's Graduate School of Design.

RUR ARCHITECTURE

JESSE REISER, NANAKO UMEMOTO

O-14 | Dubai, United Arab Emirates

O-14 is a commercial tower located on the waterfront esplanade of Dubai Business Bay. With O-14, conventional office tower typology has been turned inside out—structure and skin have been flipped to offer a new economy of tectonics and of space. The concrete shell of O-14 provides a structural exoskeleton that frees the core from the burden of lateral forces and creates highly efficient, column-free open spaces on the interior. A space nearly one meter deep between the shell and the main enclosure creates a "chimney effect," whereby hot air has room to rise and effectively cools the surface of the glass windows behind the perforated shell.

SHENZHEN INTERNATIONAL AIRPORT – TERMINAL 3 | Shenzhen, China

Instead of the bland monoculture of contemporary airports, RUR Architecture proposes spaces for travelers that are unique, yet globally coherent—spaces that humanize technology and are intimately attuned to the diverse needs, moods, and aspirations of the contemporary traveler. Shenzhen Airport proposes to employ a traditional yet modern material—concrete—but fabricate it using new concepts in engineering, including mass customization in formwork.

KAOHSIUNG PORT TERMINAL | Kaohsiung, Taiwan

For the Kaohsiung Port Terminal, RUR Architecture proposes a dynamic three-dimensional urbanism that takes advantage of the site's unique position related to the city grid. Existing pedestrian flows along the proposed elevated boardwalk are amplified by creating a continuous elevated public esplanade along the waterfront. Cruise and ferry functions are kept distinct to maintain secure areas for departing and arriving passengers.

RUR **GDNYU ELSEWHERE ENVISONED**

KAOHSIUNG PORT
TERMINAL
Kaohsiung, Taiwan,
Republic of China, 2010
Winning Entry,
Two-stage Open
Competition
Scheduled Construction
2014
Type: Cruise Ship Terminal
and Port Service Center
Structure: Multiple

SHENZHEN BAO'AN
INTERNATIONAL
AIRPORT
Shenzhen,
Republic of China, 2007
Invited Competition
Size: 400,000 sq. m
Type: International Airport
Structure: Steel Clad
Concrete Shell

RUR
Peder Anker, Louise Harpman, Mitchell Joachim

MJ—O-14 is a sexy contemporary building. The sleek, sensational, scripted exterior pattern detail features apertures reminiscent of Swiss cheese. It's appropriately cool, but that doesn't necessarily mean it's green. We are right in the middle of the argument about what digital design can produce and the promises it makes. We have been seeing these shapes since the '90s; this is "blobitecture 2.0." Somebody like Bill McDonough is their antithetical "other," as his work is less about gorgeous design and more about ecological systems, materials, behavior, and policy. It's the opposite of RUR's radicalized deviant form production. While the Dubai Tower is an exceptionally beautiful building, its main contribution may be to architectural aesthetics. Reiser and Umemoto do fabulous work. Contrarily, the McDonough projects are known for having light, air, views, orientation, understanding of the local, and inherent buildability. This Dubai tower is an expensive heroic construction. It's in the same league as the Sydney Opera House or the Sagrada Familia: it's a beautiful artifact.

PA—There is a line from Ibsen's play *Peer Gynt* which is relevant here. The Button-Molder comes to Peer Gynt and says, "You're not bad enough for the sulphur-pit, nor good enough for Paradise. And so, into the ladle you go!" The point is that a beautiful building is great and a truly ugly building also has its charm, while mediocrity is the worst. In terms of Reiser and Umemoto, the building seems driven by design, not primarily by environmental issues.

MJ—Though you can bring all this technical information into the design, what happens in terms of performance? We have many analytical devices and computer models that say "in fact, the external skin needs to be 17 inches away from the glass skin to allow proper airflow." This actually does work, and there is a cooling effect. And yet developers often run out of energy, enthusiasm, or money at the end and fail to implement performance criteria. Arup is known for these post-occupancy surveys, and they have found that again and again, the so-called savings benefits that are predicted or modeled ahead of time are not in fact ever realized.

LH—I think we have to look at the tower as more than a beautiful object or technological artifact. We can say that yes, passive cooling works. And yes, here's an example of the "stack effect" that architects diagram in their first year of environmental systems class. Christopher Alexander's *A Pattern Language*, which lovingly, sometimes obsessively, documents how passive cooling strategies have worked in many civilizations, in many places, over a broad expanse of time, is probably a reference Reiser and Umemoto would shun. The tower is beautiful, but the urban design is lagging. I would like a larger discussion about the incredible resources that go into making a spec office tower like this, with virtually no supportive urban fabric such as housing, schools, shopping areas, and so on. I would also like to see the post-occupancy studies about the actual energy savings.

MJ—I've seen studies that put a lot of doubt as to whether this is actually effective. There was a *Spiegel* article where the reporter got the energy bills for twenty double-skinned buildings in Europe. None of them met the performance criteria. They paid more for their energy in heating and cooling than buildings made forty years earlier without any of this technology.

PA—What's driving Reiser and Umemoto is not heating and cooling, but aesthetic form.

LH—But coming back to the claims about its superior performance, I would like to see external verification that this double-skin system really works in such an extreme environment. They have annual temperature fluctuations from 75°F to 105°F. Does this building assembly achieve more than internal shades could have achieved on their own?

MJ—They could have easily used cloth shades on rollers within the window frames. Amory Lovins would say building a double-skinned façade is like using a chainsaw to cut butter. The Swiss Re building, "the Gherkin" in London, is the classic example of the double-skinned façade with all kinds of claims behind it. But the building used to get so hot in the summer that they had to blast the air conditioning. The company was saving on heating, but getting crushed by cooling bills. The architects and engineers claimed it was a post-tuning issue.

PA—There's a political side to this project we also need to discuss. Bernard Williams addresses a similar issue in his book *Moral Luck*, which tells the story of Paul Gauguin, the painter who moved to Tahiti. Though Gauguin "went native," he produced beautiful paintings that we retrospectively admire. He was lucky to produce something beautiful, and we now can forgive him for what today might be considered immoral actions. There's a similar conversation here with Reiser and Umemoto. Maybe we need to hear more from them about what it entails to work with a dictatorship and how they use "guest" workers. RUR got lucky and made a beautiful building; unfortunately that suppresses the larger conversation.

LH—I recently moderated a panel on new architecture in the Middle East at the AIA, and this project was one of many being discussed. When you read the Human Rights Watch reports and start to understand the labor practices that go into constructing these buildings, you learn that there is virtually no enforcement of health or occupational safety regulations, no fair wage standards, and that workers are forced into housing in squalid camps, beholden to labor brokers who exact such a debt that their practices are lumped in with human traffickers. We have to ask: Is beauty enough? Are architects being used to prop up or validate repressive regimes? If a building is beautiful enough, will it mask all kinds of human suffering? We can assume that the slaves who built the pyramids did not forgive the pharaohs. If we want to stake out territory for Global Design, we need to ask: To what degree do architects, engineers, planners, and landscape architects have an ethical responsibility to understand the conditions in which their projects are realized? Who monitors wage, labor, and health policies? Sustainability needs to engage environmental performance, economics, and social justice. To go so far into aesthetics and not talk about social justice is a disservice.

MJ—We are sometimes willfully blind and surely seduced. But bringing social values, metrics, and science to the foreground is what we need to do with every project. O-14 creates a powerful image, a direct contrast to the Burj Khalifa, which you can see in the background.

PA—If you go back to the Bauhaus, you will see that a quarter of the curriculum was devoted to studying science. In the first year, students and professors would go out into the world, read science papers, and engage the scientific community. That was the foundation of the Bauhaus tradition. Walter Gropius said that without the merger of art and science there cannot be any culture. He was really into bringing science into architecture. What Reiser and Umemoto are proposing is not a radical break. It is more of suggestion to revamp or turn new soil and look back to the original ideas of modern architecture.

RUR ARCHITECTURE is a multidisciplinary architectural design firm that has built projects at a wide range of scales including furniture design, residential and commercial structures, landscape, urban design, and infrastructure. RUR Architecture was created by Jesse Reiser and Nanako Umemoto. Reiser is a Professor of Architecture at Princeton University. He received an M.Arch. from the Cranbook Academy of Art. Umemoto is a Visiting Professor at the Southern California Institute of Architecture, Los Angeles. She received a B.Arch. from the Cooper Union.

RUR GDNYU ELSEWHERE ENVISONED

AXEL KILIAN

DESIGNEXPLORER.NET

Operational chassis
prototype with eight
degrees of freedom.

ATHLETE CAR
The athlete car is a part of a larger project focused on car design and urbanism at the MIT Media Lab. This articulated vehicle adapts its stance to the road and acts as an extension of the body. This exploration attempted to break existing paradigms, not necessarily to improve specific design solutions, but rather to experiment with investigatating the consequences of changing multiple, system-wide design approaches simultaneously.

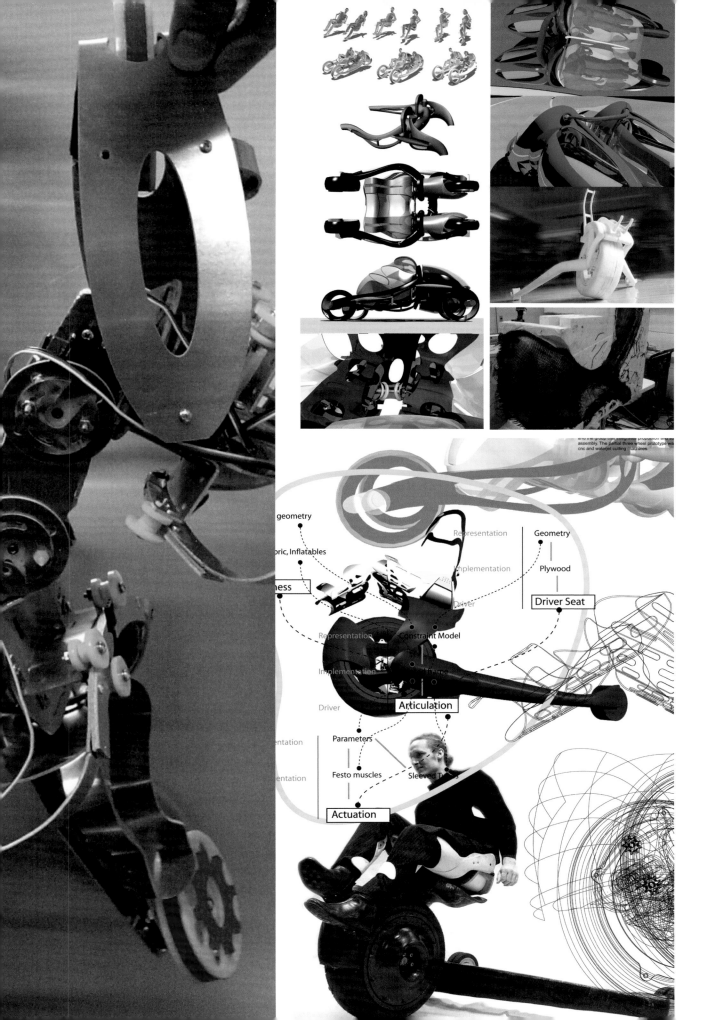

and the group that integrates propulsion and its assembly. The partial three wheel prototype was cnc and waterjet cutting machines.

geometry

bric, Inflatables

ness

Representation

Implementation

Driver

entation

entation

Representation

Constraint Model

Implementation

Driver

Parameters

Festo muscles

Actuation

Representation

Implementation

Driver

Geometry

Plywood

Driver Seat

Articulation

Sleeved T

WHOWHATWHENAIR

**PHILIPPE BLOCK, AXEL KILIAN,
PETER SCHMITT, JOHN SNAVELY**

Air-controlled movable
multi-story structure
prototype at full scale.

ACTUATED TOWER

The WhoWhatWhenAir project is a pneumatic muscle-actuated kinetic tower. The goal of the project was to experiment with full-scale structures equipped with sensors, which would become active structures that could cancel wind loads by leaning into them. The prototype followed remote control commands, but was useful in testing response times and the realistic range of motions achievable in the spine configuration.

STEERING OF FORM

The concept of form finding has been extensively explored, and there is a rich tradition of "compression only" forms in the work of Heinz Idler, Frei Otto, and many others. These studies were conducted using processes developed by Simon Greenwold to program a customizable design environment. The roof grid shown is inspired by the Mannheim Gridshell by Frei Otto and uses a standard length grid with the only variation in the joint angles. The color distribution shows the approximate force distribution, and the panel color shows the warp of the quad.

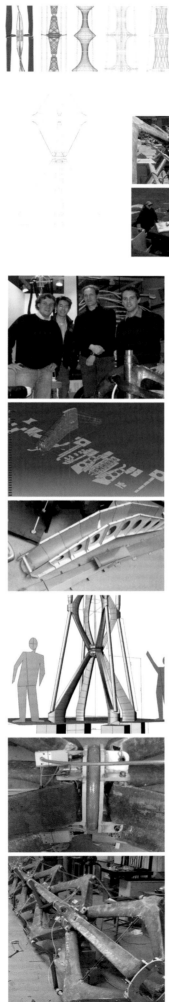

AXEL KILIAN
Peder Anker, Louise Harpman, Mitchell Joachim

MJ—We have here folks thinking about engineering science and how it relates to architecture as practice. They're moving into the field, creating designs, systems and operations based on computational models to produce figurations that are architectural. In many cases there is less design and more engineering. It is truly an integration of the two fields. The team that designed the Actuated Tower is thinking about efficiencies in curves. They are working with catenary chains—Gaudí used the exact same structures— and built a computer model that produces these chain structures based on a gravitational grid. This allows them to get super efficient vaults or domes. You can get an absolutely fabulous look using a code that they produced, which is certainly more efficient than doing it any other way. Gaudí used his bed sheets, some plaster, and fishing hooks.

LH—These guys are engineers from MIT, but what is driving their research group? Are they working toward a new kind of efficiency model, of somebody like Buckminster Fuller or Ove Arup?

MJ—Perhaps more like Frei Otto. This is an example of the university teaming up with corporations to pay for the science to create innovative structures, in this case, full scale. The idea is that the tower is a performance-based structure that can adapt to changes in lateral forces like wind loads; this shows how to solve a basic problem in tall building design. It is a kind of hackable structure that you can move in pretty much any direction, within twenty degrees, and still have incredible structural strength, which proves their hanging chain models. The car is more Axel's direct project.

PA—I'd like to add a critical remark to these excellent projects. You can start with data about efficiency, which is one set of environmental data relevant to structural engineering, but there is also a whole host of other data sets, ecological, biological, or whatnot. When we speak about the matrix of data, it is not so much a matter of incorporating science into architecture or design, but rather, which science and whose knowledge one should trust to bring into the equation.

MJ—What becomes the most important set of scientific or technical data?

LH—What is privileged and what is suppressed?

PA—We need to avoid the reductionism of only looking at efficiency data. I don't think anybody disagrees that this information is extremely important, but we have to be aware that the matrix we choose is a value judgment. If the goal is efficiency, especially efficient cars, then we have to question why they have chosen a specific set of data that assumes private cars and industrial society. They even accepted a "research" grant from the auto industry. There is nothing inherently wrong with this, but the process and results are controversial and should be reflected upon. There are lots of environmentalists critiquing this industrial understanding of efficiency. Why not bicycles? Why not mass transit?

MJ—What part of engineering science is more important than another? What you're saying is that there are many important fields that are fairly equal to one another.

PA—We are now living in a time where everything is reduced to an ecological footprint, your carbon footprint, while there are so many other environmental agendas, such as clean water or parks, that are pushed aside.

LH—I don't think we disagree on the importance of transportation, but it comes to this question of investment from, say, General Motors, or outside investment more generally. Research universities run on outside investment. One has to be aware of that and critical of it at the same time. At the end of the day, if you can invent the artificial heart, do you say no to Philip Morris who gave you the money to do that?

MJ—You don't. You just have to acknowledge it.

LH—I'm not so sure. But I want to bring up another issue. Architects look at project-based time frames—eighteen months to three years—to design and build a project, assuming the financing is in place. This time frame is absolutely antithetical to something like geological time or even primary succession in the plant world. Landscape architects look at twenty-, forty-, sixty-, and 100-year increments. City planners do the same. The question is, where do these semester-by-semester innovative research projects reside? Does the innovation move with the designers and researchers who did the work, or does it "live" with the IP agreement made between the university and the corporation? Every research university has a legal affairs office that spells out what can and can't happen. When those guys come in the room, are we really producing green design for them or are we just producing alternatives slowing down the process of change? Instead of moving us away from an oil-based economy, do they keep us busy or distracted while they continue churning out SUVs?

MJ—General Motors owns the car. If not General Motors, then it is owned by MIT in alignment with DARPA. Festo sponsored the tower.

PA—Do these sponsors help or hurt? Do they take the patents, say "nice idea!" and then shove the researchers aside?

LH—We have to see the incredible irony that the General Motors that sponsored the Athlete Car is the same General Motors that developed the electric car EV1 in the late 1990s. The EV1 was a success—it met California's zero-emissions mandate and people loved those cars. Yet there was a mandatory recall initiated by GM, who said there was "no market" for them. What do we know of the EV1 now? Not much. There's one at the Smithsonian. And we have a moderately successful documentary film, *Who Killed the Electric Car?* Where did all that research and development go? The landfill.

MJ—It is either that, or the research is used for pure evil. It becomes a military object. A skyscraper like this could have a machine gun mounted on its top! An autonomous vehicle that has eight degrees of freedom and can drive through any terrain is nice for a car or for a lunar module, but it would be particularly useful for Afghanistan! How about a Jeep that can find the enemy hiding out in different crags?

LH—There is a lot of room to invent another model for corporate sponsorship at a research university. I would like to know that my grant to design porous pavements or rainwater filtration systems did not come from W.R. Grace or Coca Cola or BASF. I don't think we're going to turn back the tide of sponsored research, but perhaps we can redirect it.

AXEL KILIAN is an Assistant Professor of Computational Design at Princeton University. He earned a Dipl-Ing. in Architecture from the Berlin University of the Arts and an SMarchS in Architecture Studies, Design and Computation from the Massachusetts Institute of Technology, from which he also received a PhD in Design and Computation.

RACHEL ARMSTRONG

AVATAR STUDIO

Unique protocell technology used to regrow the foundations that underpin the city of Venice, Italy.

LIGHT-ACTIVATED PROTOCELLS IN THE LAGOON

This project shows the solar energy falling on the surface of a lagoon. The color is removed to show energy "mapped" in relation to the proposed "activation" of protocell technology through sunlight. Protocells can be engineered to move away from light. This is a strategy that can be used to direct the protocells toward the darkened foundations of the city, where they deposit an artificial limestone shell to support existing building substructures, and attenuate sinking into the soft delta soils.

LIGHT-ACTIVATED SYNTHETIC BIOLOGY | Venice, Italy

This project is aimed at canal structures in Venice where wooden posts at the shoreline are decaying from weathering. Synthetic biology can be used to protect this interface and produce a protective living limestone deposit, performing a similar role to stucco/plaster over brick. This depicts the "resting" state for algae before they are programmed by light (algae respond to light via photosynthesis). This design proposes that a designed biology can be stimulated by light to engage in a process of construction, which builds an artificial limestone reef underneath the foundations of the city. This will spread the base on which the city is resting via wood piles to offload the point load and attenuate the sinking of Venice on the soft delta soils caused by the weight of the city and its increasing number of tourists. Augmented biological systems can be designed to protect, repair, and evolve the fabric of the city of Venice.

RACHEL ARMSTRONG **GDNYU ELSEWHERE ENVISONED**

RACHEL ARMSTRONG

Peder Anker, Louise Harpman, Mitchell Joachim

LH—Armstrong uses her training as a medical doctor and her PhD research in biology to look closely at biological forms and processes. She researches and designs microscopic systems with a view to altering and improving the structure of these naturally-occurring systems. One of her "test sites" is in aqueous environments, where building footings undergo deterioration.

MJ—What we are seeing are protocells under a microscope. They are not living things, but minerals that have reactions that lead to large-scale accretion that eventually makes a porous, rock-like material. They behave like or mimic things in life, but they are different kinds of natural oils and fluids that connect together rather quickly and form big reefs of rocky substances. She insists that this is an incredible technique to produce materials and make underpinning structures.

LH—Armstrong shows that by diving in (as it were) and looking at these underwater algae formations and veneers, humans can direct a biological process in order to stabilize the erosion of Venice's sinking foundations. She argues that these accretion structures could be used to offset this deterioration.

MJ—Here she shows them already beginning to work in Venice, forming reefs underneath particular buildings to maintain their foundations. It's a very small scale and a very long time frame for them to get to where she wants them to be. That doesn't mean we couldn't accelerate the process.

PA—Many environmental thinkers distinguish between anthropocentricity and biocentricity. This is one of the few designers I know who is truly biocentric. She puts the processes of the environment at the center of the design. That is the most radical step in her approach to architecture. Who knows what will come out of it? What's fascinating is the intellectual approach and how she is thinking about the world of architecture from that point of view. When she is turning her intellectual abilities toward underwater reefs for fish in order to build sub-sea architecture, these could become fascinating projects for food sources or saving species. Most of the ocean right now is a desert. If you can create artificial reefs based on these processes, then you can create more inhabitable space for endangered species. It is a different way of thinking about design that could provide a lot of innovation in the future.

MJ—She is thinking about minerals and rocks, and is trying to direct the landscape in order to support the undercarriage of the sinking Venice.

LH—There have to be unintended consequences here. How is she thinking about that?

PA—Should invasive species be removed or not? Do they really belong to the system? The answer has often been to remove these invasive species. To some extent she is bringing in new species and transforming the environment into something else, which could be damaging. There is a hubris issue here; you think you're doing something good, but maybe it will hasten the sinking of Venice. Maybe we won't have Venice in twenty years.

LH—If this is a demonstration project, you have to set up a rigorous framework, then try it , document it, and monitor it. You don't just throw in some algae or minerals to create a reef and then walk away. Research is what universities are good at. They can sustain long-term research projects with results that are replicated, then published. We need to see more about this project. Armstrong has been affiliated with major universities, so I assume the experimental model is there. This project reminds me of the UP series of films that started with the film *7 Up* in 1964. The premise of the film was to film a group of kids when they were seven years old and find out about their lives. Then every seven years there has been a new installment to see what's become of the original kids. The most recent film was in 2012, when the "kids" were fifty-six years old. It is a long-term labor of love. I assume that Armstrong has a long-view of this project. And she is very good about communicating her work to a large, non-specialist audience.

MJ—This is laboratory work under a microscope. If she doesn't alter this project genetically or solve the problem scaled up, then it might take dozens of years to grow in a natural state. Humans seed it, but eventually it will find its own path. It is hard to see this as architecture since it is a few microscopic elements having all kinds of interactions. It is vital research. It can go down different paths, but it would require a university or an independent consortium like Global Design Lab to make that happen. It is more biological or scientific than it is design, but the implications are exciting.

RACHEL ARMSTRONG is Co-Director of AVATAR (Advanced Virtual and Technological Architectural Research) in Architecture & Synthetic Biology at The School of Architecture & Construction, University of Greenwich, London. She is a Senior TED Fellow, and a Visiting Research Assistant at the Centre for Fundamental Living Technology, Department of Physics and Chemistry, University of Southern Denmark. Armstrong is a sustainability innovator who investigates a new approach to building materials called "living architecture."

RACHEL ARMSTRONG GDNYU ELSEWHERE ENVISONED

PNEUMASTUDIO

CHRIS PERRY, CATHRYN DWYRE

This project is a hermatically sealed ecosystem similar in scope to life-support operations on the International Space Station.

SPIRABILIS

Spirabilis utilizes NASA research on Closed Ecological Life Support Systems to propose ecological living where hydroponic plants produce the balance of nutrients and oxygen necessary for human life. Tubular algae cultivation provides clean air through micro-controlled output valves, as well as lighting and visual effects. The project imagines that laws of nature are newly shaped, complemented, and extended through technology. Habitation zones, rainwater collecting trees, and conduits of "heroic fluids" are joined with exuberantly growing substances in a new provisional architecture. The inspiration for Spirabilis can be traced to Diogenes of Apollonia, ca. 5 BC, who believed air to be the source of all being—the primal force that composed both intelligence and the soul.

https://www.hoverground.com

PNEUMASTUDIO **GDNYU ELSEWHERE ENVISONED**

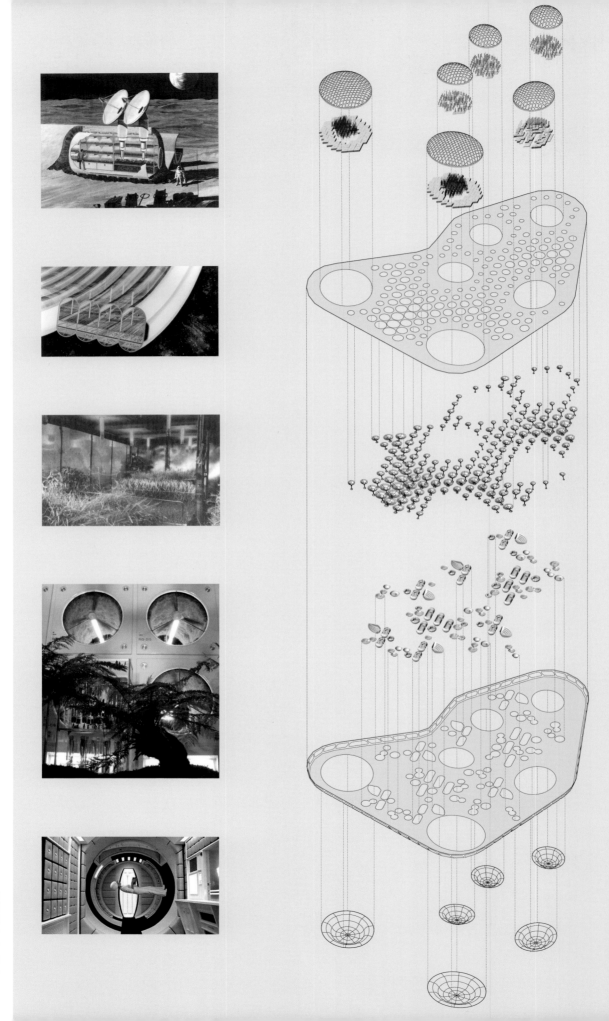

SPIRABILIS
The complete array of
phytotrons cultivate all
the nourishment, both air
and nutrition, required for
human life based on NASA
research.

PNEUMASTUDIO
Peder Anker, Louise Harpman, Mitchell Joachim

PA—This project comes out of a long history of NASA research on closed ecological life-support systems. The basic idea, from NASA's point of view, is that if you want to create a station on the Moon or Mars, then you have to be able to re-create a closed ecological system in order to live. The astronauts have to have enough food within the closed system. What Chris Perry and Cathryn Dwyre have done is to adapt this research in order to make a closed ecological system on Earth in which we live inside this closed dome à la Buckminster Fuller, where we can grow all our food and fulfill all of our living needs. This is a design that looks good, but I'm wondering what a closed system does to the social environment you are situating the building within and the natural environment. This building could be totally independent from both the natural environment you're trying to save and from the social environment you're supposed to engage. The project is basically saying "go to hell" to its natural and social community.

LH—We have to locate this within the category of failed futures of the past. Every generation comes to some bit of biological or scientific research anew and thinks of itself as fresh. In fact, I see this very strongly situated in the kind of post-Sputnik/post-Apollo thinking. I think that this place could be beautiful and that I'd like to go there for a weekend, but I see this as a piece of ecotourism. It excludes so many things that I care about, like wind and chance and other people. But maybe it needs to engage the site more directly. It could be part of a building envelope or be embedded in other structures or even in transportation systems, perhaps an underground system. The future of a project like this is to reside as "paper architecture" and provocation, or find a logical application.

MJ—I see it as a compelling siteless object. To me it is a spacesuit from a future past. It's about breathing, producing oxygen, using algae as fuel that also absorbs waste in one cyclical stream. It's an extended carpet, like spacesuit for a group of bodies as opposed to just one body. I see these kinds of things as deployable for colonizing other areas. I think it's a beautiful extraterrestrial artifact that could be inserted into some zone and you can confront it, like an emergency parachute. It definitely doesn't address anything beyond its own interiority. It is certainly a sealed bubble monoform and it makes no claim beyond that. I think it really wants to capture its constraints, reveal that it is intentionally limited in scope. The overriding principles are from the '50s, but are being recast here as visionary because we never really got to this in architecture. It's a Reyner Banham event about finding environmental services that would truly meet all the needs of the occupants of the building. It's so sensitive that the data it picks up makes you cold and me warm, because we're having different experiences at that particular moment. I love the project, but I think it is absolutely without a place or context.

LH—What is the next step for a project like this?

MJ—Perry just launched an entire program at RPI, a new master's degree in Geofutures.

LH—There's also a program at The Bartlett which is well established. And I expect we'll see more. Universities are very aware that this is a kind of research that attracts students and funding, and also that it might make a difference.

PA—As a model for the future I think this is solipsistic, because it does not reach out. There is a social movement saying that we have to generate our own food and resources instead of asking how we link in with the community and the environment that we are situated in. Having said that, I agree that this project is aesthetically beautiful, but as an intellectual project it puzzles me as to whether this is the right, or the left, way to go forward.

LH—I think this project situates itself more in the idea of the "techno-fix," a new terrarium, which people are right to criticize. And yet, Perry and Dwyre are trying to imagine what would happen if we could design an environment that could be tuned or catered to a distinct human population. I think it's a nice contrast with someone like Rachel Armstrong, who understands that there are natural processes that she amplifies. There are two different schools of thought. In Perry and Dwyre's case, if this becomes a research project that finds a larger audience, then I think it can become important outside of itself.

MJ—It could certainly link to people doing work on biofuels. If you have a known range and set of limits, this could actually allow researchers to extend beyond them and deal with people directly.

PA—There is a whole school of architects, such as Ken Yeang, who work in this way. He built "eco-cells" which are basically closed ecological environments. There are other people inspired by Biosphere 2, or also the autonomous house movements from the '70s. I see this as part of this history and I'm not sure I see the future in it; instead, I think I see the past.

PNEUMASTUDIO was founded by Cathryn Dwyre and Chris Perry and is an interdisciplinary design practice focused on the fields of architecture and landscape architecture. Dwyre currently teaches at the Pratt Institute School of Architecture in Brooklyn, New York. She received an MLA from the University of Pennsylvania. Perry is currently an Assistant Professor at the Rensselaer School of Architecture, where he is Director of the Geofutures Post-Professional Program. He received an M.Arch. from Columbia University.

PNEUMASTUDIO GDNYU ELSEWHERE ENVISIONED

DJ SPOOKY

PAUL MILLER

"ACOUSTIC PORTRAITS"
of Antarctica through
digital media.

TERRA NOVA: SINFONIA ANTARCTICA

The role of landscape in art evokes many collisions between art and artifact, between concepts of the natural and the manmade. Wilderness has a special hold on our imagination, and yet its very remoteness is part of its mythic construct. Paul Miller undertook a studio residency in Antarctica to engage some of these issues within the focus of climate change and data visualization. The aim of this project was to explore the process of documenting explorations of the continent's rapidly altering landscape, and to create acoustic portraits of Antarctica through digital media. Miller did a similar project on the environmentally devastated island of Nauru in the South Pacific. The Nauru Elegies and the Terra Nova Project see convergence between graphic design, music composition, and architecture. Digital media creates social spaces with the data we use to describe the world around us. In turn, these info-aesthetic motifs create acoustic and data-driven portraits depicting the urgent need to understand climate change as a modern anthropogenic phenomenon.

PAUL MILLER
Peder Anker, Louise Harpman, Mitchell Joachim

LH—At some point, designers and historians of the built environment have to understand that there are so many other players, factors, and conversations happening that we need to engage. Spooky is a graphic designer, musician, and activist who is focusing his energy and attention on particular environmental issues. He is a spotlighter, somebody who spotlights a place or an issue and brings attention and focus to it. Maybe he is not doing bioremediation on Nauru, but he makes accessible the fact that we totally degraded that environment for our shortsighted consumption practices. Where does this fit into the larger discourse about sustainability? He brings a pointed critique of so many contemporary practices that focus on the "first" world at the expense of developing economies. He directly challenges our focus on the developed world. He asks "at what cost" do we expand?

MJ—Miller and Bjarke Ingels are both great communicators, visually and in their texts. They represent a whole new internet-based generation that makes things as accessible as possible. They may not dig deep into original research—they never make that claim— but instead, they serve as a gateway into the big picture and produce graphics that are evocative enough to entice others to find out more about topic. Spooky will then go on to layer these graphics with all kinds of other discipline sets, which is what makes it so important and convincing. He is not coming from one particular side, but coming from many different perspectives at once. Spooky will produce a kind of a suite that gives you information about the topography of a place, the economy of the area, government and social issues, as well as what is beautiful. This is then transformed into music and graphics. It is kind of a performance-installation.

LH—Spooky also understands that there is a time frame and an immediacy to his way of working. If he commits to an issue, he will engage it by creating graphic design, composing a piece of music, performing it, and then releasing it over the internet for others to engage. This happens at a much faster pace than any urban design process could ever attain. As an artist and an activist, with an enormous reach through social media, he can bring attention to both standing and emerging issues, whereas long-term planning and problem-solving can take years, decades, and sometimes even generations. One of Spooky's great values is that he can marshal resources.

PA—You cannot argue with somebody who is a great communicator. These are good for any agenda, whether you are promoting a conservative Christian gospel or a green future. You need these communicators. Do these things make him a green communicator? I am not sure.

MJ—Spooky would never give one totalizing opinion. He is very smooth and adept, looks at many perspectives, and is ultimately holistic in his thinking. He is not this kind of monolithic single-minded communicator. He is an artist scholar, for lack of a better term. He is an offshoot and a cooler version of Marshal McLuhan.

LH—Among his many other initiatives, Spooky is also the executive editor of a magazine that is wholly funded by the Whole Foods corporation. Whole Foods it not wholly good. In fact, they have a lousy labor policy. When somebody like Spooky is so closely affiliated with a mixed-bag corporation, does he lose his singular voice?

MJ—He will do something like the Whole Foods magazine, but also be the first-ever "artist in residence" at the Metropolitan Museum of Art. They found him to be the most facile individual that can bridge all of their different departments. He was thought to be somebody that could spin, scratch, or remix the museum itself. That was his kind of uber function.

PA—Can he spin and remix academic disciplines? There is all this talk of interdisciplinarity and connecting disciplines to create this "ecology of knowledge," but when it comes down to it, professors of zoology don't really communicate with professors of biology or professors of architecture. We all just stay in our own little worlds. Spooky is perhaps the facilitator who can draw connections and bring people together to create this kind of environment.

LH—I think that is right. Most university professors don't do these kinds of things nearly often enough because they have other demands on their time. We are all aware of what it takes to be a "member in good standing" within an academic community. Should Spooky hold an academic appointment?

PA—He is more of an aesthetic activist, but there needs to be some kind of academic involvement. These people are hired for what they are good at, which is activism and communication.

MJ—I think these people are great for large institutions and/or universities.

PA—My point is that one of the accusations against environmentalism in the most general sense is that it is not scholarly, but rather merely an activist position. There is sometimes a disparity between being an activist for a certain point of view and being a scholar. The criticism against Greenpeace is that they are activists without any legitimate scholarship to support their cause.

LH—Every person who has participated in our Global Design exhibits or symposia has had some kind of teaching or academic affiliation as well. Here is where we might develop a platform that embraces the highest level of scholarship as well as activism. In traditional academic disciplines, you would submit work to a peer-reviewed journal; that's what makes it "scholarship." Built work or proposals for built work aren't often accepted in these forums. But I see these lines blurring. I think design research is emerging as another area of scholarship.

PA—The role of universities is twofold: research and teaching. That's it. There is not much beyond that. Perhaps service, but at the core it is teaching and research. One of the points of tenure is that you can say whatever you feel like without the fear of losing your job. In its early formation, the university and its scholars threatened the church, the Christian Bible, and even the notion of God. The university became a place that could protect those who spoke out. Maybe this "speaking out" is not activism in and of itself, but we do use defiant words against traditional logic all the time.

LH—The minute you make somebody like Spooky a tenured professor, you lose precisely the things you hired him for! He is meant to be really tentacular, very much spreading out and connecting and involved internationally.

DJ SPOOKY Paul Miller, also known as "DJ Spooky, That Subliminal Kid," is an experimental and electronic hip-hop musician, conceptual artist, and writer. Paul Miller is a Professor at the European Graduate School (EGS), where he teaches Music Mediated Art. In 2009, he presented "The Science of Terra Nova" at the American Museum of Natural History and was the first Artist in Residence at the Metropolitan Museum of Art. Miller received a BA from Bowdoin College.

DJ SPOOKY GDNYU ELSEWHERE ENVISONED

ARCHITECTURE RESEARCH OFFICE

STEPHEN CASSELL, ADAM YARINSKY, KIM YAO

Impacts of natural disasters and climate dynamics will be absorbed by a new wetland preserve in the Hudson River.

NEW URBAN GROUND | New York, NY

New Urban Ground was commissioned by MoMA as part of its Rising Currents: Projects for New York's Waterfront initiative, through which five design teams proposed interventions at specific sites throughout New York City to address rising sea levels. Taking into account rapid polar ice cap melt, scientists predict a six-foot sea level rise by 2100. A Category 2 hurricane would create surges twenty-four feet above the anticipated sea level—flooding up to 1% of Lower Manhattan. Like many cities whose sanitary infrastructure was built in the early twentieth century, New York City has a combined system that processes both sewage and storm-water runoff. New York City sewers are frequently overwhelmed by rainstorms, releasing an average of 500 million gallons of untreated effluent per week directly into the Upper New York Bay. This project proposes a system of porous green streets connected to a graduated wetland edge, reconceiving the city streets as a network of absorbent surfaces to accommodate the water overflow. This design converts the edge of Manhattan into a continuous, layered ecosystem that attenuates waves, manages the watershed, filters interior surface runoff, enhances biodiversity, and introduces a new form of public green space.

MARKET-PARK AT THE BROOKLYN-BATTERY TUNNEL ENTRANCE | New York, NY

This project creates a visitors' plaza, a farmers' market, and an elevated public park atop the Brooklyn-Battery Tunnel Entrance. The multi-lane entrance is located in the heart of Greenwich South, the 41-acre area in Lower Manhattan between the World Trade Center and Battery Park.

MJ—Here the boundary between urban or peri-urban becomes a soft zone for different types of vegetative species that allows the landscape typically occupied by humans to be taken over by water or flora and fauna that enter into the city and come out again. There is a kind of ebb and flow relationship with the planetary metabolism that isn't restricted by traditional boundaries between water and land. The boundary between the city itself and the elements that make up all of nature becomes very blurry.

LH—They say that hindsight is 20/20, but in this project foresight is 20/20. Five years ago, ARO was one of five teams commissioned by the Museum of Modern Art to look at rising ocean level scenarios that would affect New York City. ARO was asked to consider what might happen to Lower Manhattan after a massive Category 5 hurricane. Sadly, that's exactly what we experienced with Hurricane Sandy in 2012. They worked with structural engineer Guy Nordenson and Susannah Drake's team at dlandstudio, who are both architects and landscape architects. The team investigated New York City's resilience to tidal variation and made a series of compelling proposals for the urban edges. This particular project was a shelter for the Battery Tunnel that attempted to mitigate flooding at a critical urban juncture.

PA—This project is both utopian and dystopian. The dystopian element is the way in which this project, which was originally a product of the imagination, became real with the intense flooding of Hurricane Sandy. The utopian element is that ARO is trying to turn this disadvantage into an advantage.

LH—Here you see how architecture, landscape architecture, and civil and structural engineering are all necessary to make a proposal like this viable. For too long, architects have been educated and trained to perform very specific skills, yet interdisciplinary bridging is not taught within the standard accredited programs. Integrated thinking is long overdue.

MJ—We can thank MoMA for this.

LH—But it needs to happen more frequently, both inside and outside of architecture schools. This is fundamentally our Global Design proposal to reformat architectural education, so that we can become agents for the future we want to have. Today's designers need to have broad as well as deep exposure and expertise. And long-term vision.

PA—The idea of a long-term vision was fashionable in the '50s and '60s. Somebody like Robert Moses was seen as a master planner and was then criticized for his "meat ax" vision. Local projects then became fashionable and promoted short-term plans that could be realized in half a year. But now, long-term plans are being admired again. When we say, "Let's attempt to envision Manhattan fifty years from now," there is something scary about this endeavor; there are obviously many victims in this project, yet we endorse it. There is a dark side to this plan.

MJ—This, to me, is certainly long-term planning, but I'd prefer to call it speculation, which I mean in a positive sense. They're creating a fictional narrative, in this case of an apocalypse or an impending future that is based on some level of fear, but it promotes a grand utopian vision that will satisfy a future population and mitigate the doom that is portended. At the same time, it's actually not so much doomsaying, but science. There were many people in climatology researching these distressing problems; nobody thought their predictions would be so incredibly accurate and so soon, but there it is. Their speculation was definitely a kind of foresight that was incredibly important. I think the problem with utopia is that we never believe in it. Since Thomas More, we have always found some failure. I think that is my crucial position; I actually like defining utopia, and we are simply not finished with it as a brilliant research question. It represents the future of the human soul without having a marker or direction. Without this vision, what is the point of living? We are all trying to find or make a better life.

PA—Sometimes the utopia is incredibly conservative. This project is in many ways inspired by Eric Sanderson's Mannahatta project. All the plants here are native species, the Mannahatta of 1609. The future is very much the past, which contains a deeply conservative vision.

LH—I don't think the plant choices are the heart of the proposal. That's a very limited criticism.

PA—Instead of trying to re-create Mannahatta, one should focus much more on the plants that people will need, more in the direction of urban farming, rather than trying to re-create the nature of the past. The "native species" argument is too conservative.

MJ—Central Park has a long and similar history. Olmsted was arguing with landscape architects about the species that should be planted in Central Park. He was creating this large artificial environment, and the decision to bring in exotics and mix species was part of his vision. There was some argument that the plants would never survive, because you have to stick with the native species that have evolved to the local climate. Olmsted's position argued that these new species would change, evolve, and adapt to the climate. Some would die off, but others would create offshoots and thrive in the environment. He ultimately was correct.

LH—Coming back to you Peder, the idea of a sexy urban farmers' market for lower Manhattan is, to my mind, greenwashing. The vision of seasonal produce sold by local farmers on every street corner has become a trope, an image of abundance; it is a false god, a romantic vision. Designers need to look at production systems, transportation, waste systems, recycling systems, energy systems. The island cannot sustain itself in terms of energy, waste, or food. What we do have is money—and money buys things that we don't have. We have workers and money, but we don't have land or nearly enough rooftops on the island to feed ourselves.

MJ—I think that is right, but it is a vital exercise to imagine what a self-reliant version of New York might look like.

LH—This is what I think architects and engineers and sociologists and planners, working in teams, could be doing. If you truly want to have a different future, you have to set up a significant demonstration project, maybe a new building or a new section of the city, to ask: Can we be net zero? Can we be self-sufficient? This is what leading cities should be developing and showing to the world. Sadly, we don't see this happening in the United States.

ARCHITECTURE RESEARCH OFFICE is a New York City-based firm led by Stephen Cassell, Adam Yarinsky, and Kim Yao. ARO engages in strategic planning, architecture, and urban design. Cassell has held teaching positions at the University of Virginia and the University of California, Berkeley. He received an M.Arch. from Harvard University's Graduate School of Design. Yarinsky has taught at the Universities of Michigan and Virginia. He received an M.Arch. from Princeton University. Yao was Adjunct Assistant Professor of Architecture from 2001 to 2011 at Barnard College, Columbia University. She received an M.Arch. from Princeton University.

NEA STUDIO

NINA EDWARDS ANKER

LATITUDE LIGHT

With the onset of global warming, the increasing predominance of environmental technologies in architecture often comes at the expense of human perception, as well as local traditions, cultures, and environments. Standardized technologies tend to reinforce a narrow objectifying rationality. Latitude Light tries to address this risk by avoiding a global technological perspective, and by embracing instead a richer understanding of human experience. Geography thus conceived is not about mapping and planning the landscape from an external viewpoint, but about the individual understanding the surrounding world.

Latitude Light consists of three solar lighting designs developed from a basic module of interlocking cubes. The first is a solar lamp, at the scale of a tabletop object. The second operates at the scale of human inhabitation, in the form of a sauna accompanying a Norwegian hytte by the fjord, whose walls are formed by lighted screens. Latitude Light forms landscape installations for two waterfront resting areas along the Riverdale stretch of the Bronx Greenway bike path in New York City—heating loungers with back rests made of photovoltaic panels set into the south side of a hill, and a light installation in a grassy clearing at College Point, Bronx. The light installation belongs to a global system in which the structure can be adjusted to different places and climates.

LATITUDE LIGHTS
Landscape installation of
Latitutde Light along the
Bronx Riverdale waterfront,
New York.

NEA STUDIO
Peder Anker, Louise Harpman, Mitchell Joachim

PA—Nina Edwards Anker works on three levels: the object-scale, which are things like the lamp or furniture, the architectural, which is the building, and the landscape, which thinks about how to fit these things into the landscape. On all three levels, she thinks about how to create a global language for her work so that the lamp is situated according to a certain geographic position. The lamp has a solar cell that is tilted according to the location that you are in, which situates it locally, but it is also global in that it can be placed anywhere in the world. That goes for her architecture too, which tries to be local in the choice of materials, but also tries to find a language that can be used or placed anywhere in the world. The same goes for landscape. There is a sense of using both the local conditions and establishing this global language.

LH—nea studio's Latitude Light is one of the applied research projects coming out of this office. They are beautiful objects that have the environmental hedonism factor because of their materiality and formal sophistication. I really like that this object might operate at two, possibly three, scales simultaneously—as a table-top object, as a landscape element, and as a dwelling. The lamp could be in multiple sites, and its form is specific enough to be activated and effective in different landscapes. nea studio was commissioned by the Bronx Borough President's office to create an activated edge on the Bronx river, and we are seeing early design proposals here. This highlights the place where cities, municipalities, and leading-edge designers need to be in more dialogue. If we are going to see the most interesting and innovative green projects established by a community board or a local organization, then of course the question of a demonstration project comes back. How do we actualize these projects so that they affect conversations that are happening in design communities all over the world?

MJ—To me the complexity is in the individual lights themselves, which have a kind of built in parametricism in that they are angled to get the most amount of sunlight. They are based on the solar azimuth angles of where they are going to be placed alongside a meandering trail. They are this magnificent series of floating points that highlight the landscape, almost like will-o'-the-wisps.

PA—This is a low-income, socially depressed area of the city, so the idea is to make the river more enticing, and the waterway not so scary at night. As the sun travels during the day, the solar cells take in and store the energy and then release it to produce light at night.

LH—I think that a finely detailed, beautifully fabricated project like this blurs the boundaries between architecture and landscape architecture. This could be considered architecture, landscape, or industrial design. We start to see that the most interesting practices are uncomfortable in a single discipline; in fact, they are most comfortable when they branch off and embed themselves in other environments.

MJ—Can we say with this project that it is really landscape architecture? That it really is architecture? Or can we just say that it is really excellent industrial design that is considering the other scales? In other words, this is a light or this is a bench. It is certainly taking all the inputs from the site and it is extracting all of its information on how it should be assembled, deployed, and located. In most cases, this would just be considered really good industrial design.

PA—If you go back to the Bauhaus you see the same thing. They were crossing all the disciplines. They were architects as well as artists that created cups, plates, tea sets, and also buildings, as well as various industrial innovations.

This project is how I think we should think about the future of green design; we should not be so concerned about creating boundaries between landscape architecture and object-scales.

LH—Architects will be happy to call their work anything as long as they can get it funded. Many of the most interesting urban design projects in the past few years in New York City have come through the department of transportation, in part, because that is where the money is. Maybe landscape architecture has broadened its purview to include all of these elements, and the old-school architects are playing catch-up. Again, I want to make a push for an architecture and design education that is more integrated, across multiple scales. The departmental and degree-granting organizations may not be there, but the popular and leading thinkers already are.

MJ—Maybe the category or title for these kinds of studies is something like "environmental architecture" or "environmental design," something very broad that includes landscape, urban design, planning, industrial design, and architecture. The only thing that is consistent throughout all of these different categories is the environment itself. Maybe that is part of the job of our Global Design program, to be highly flexible and allow these disciplines to breathe.

PA—It speaks to globalization, to be sure. Here is an example of design where you can adjust the building to the specific location, whether it is New York City or Dubai. You have the same architectural language, but also the ability to "fit" into local conditions.

LH—I'm worried about this issue of branding, of the so-called Coca-Cola strategy where the brand is legible all over the world. I think there is an idea about specificity in nea studio's work. I wouldn't want this to become a franchise.

PA—There is supposed to be an element that you recognize and say, "Ah, that's an nea studio building."

LH—You know it when you see it?! That was Potter Stewart's definition of pornography in 1964! Are you sure you want to go there? I think the homogenization of the landscape is a legitimate concern. nea studio confronts this directly. I see the idea of tuning the lamp to a specific location as a way to get around this question of sameness. Not only at the scale of a lamp or a dwelling. Should something look the same in Shanghai as it does in Abu Dhabi? I don't think so.

MJ—Maybe it's more like an instrument that is played differently based on what the music calls for. It is certainly built to have that kind of delicacy, feel, and detail. It sort of feels like an instrument.

NEA STUDIO Established by Nina Edwards Anker, nea studio focuses on architecture, furniture design, product design, landscape and urban planning, and exhibition design. nea studio has offices in Oslo and New York. Anker received an M.Arch. from Harvard University's Graduate School of Design. She is currently a doctoral candidate at the Oslo School of Architecture and Design. Her dissertation bridges phenomenological theory and solar design.

SPECHT HARPMAN

SCOTT SPECHT, LOUISE HARPMAN

zeroHouse
Modular self-sufficient dwelling
unit for up to four people.

zeroHouse

The zeroHouse™ is a completely self-sufficient, off-the-grid modular house. Four people can live comfortably year-round in remote areas with no need for any utilities infrastructure. The high-performance dwelling is easily assembled and can be networked as needed, forming chains of voluntary "plug-and-play" communities. The zeroHouse is also suited to urban areas, with an electric intertie option.

prairieHouse

The prairieHouse™ is based not on a romantic vision of the American landscape, but on the reality of what is actually there. A Texaco station canopy is retrofitted for inhabitation, with living spaces tucked up safely under its broad shading plane and a tall-grass prairie on its roof. Reuse and repurposing of this ubiquitous, nearly invisible, and should-be outmoded structure is a most basic form of recycling, and one that may have greater impact than many active "greening" strategies.

windCatcher

The windCatcher™ addresses the reality of encroaching desertification that has come along with global warming. The modular, expandable system incorporates a number of interconnected passive systems, such as directed airflow, water collection, evaporative cooling, thermal massing, and selective vegetation that allow for habitation in harsh desert climates.

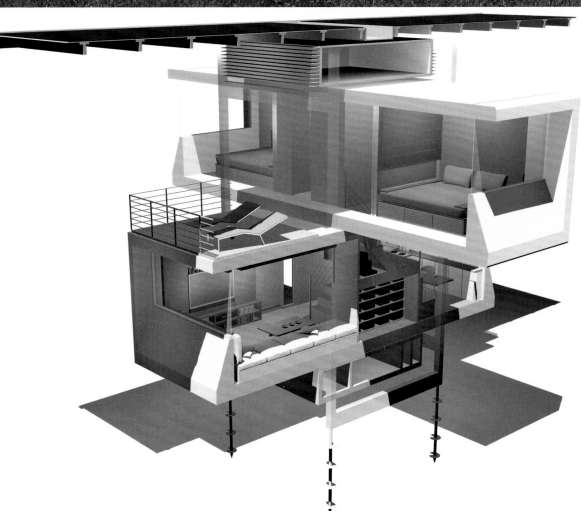

SPECHT HARPMAN GDNYU ELSEWHERE ENVISONED

windCatcher
Passive housing system.

prairieHouse
Retrofit of Texaco station,
with canopy for living
spaces.

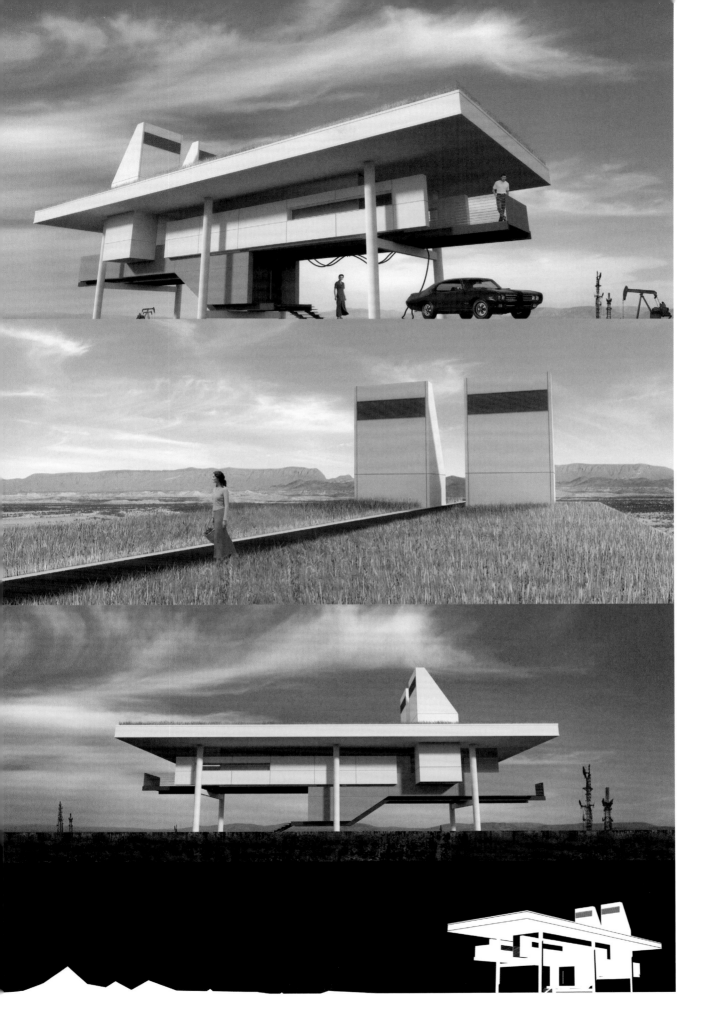

SPECHT HARPMAN GDNYU ELSEWHERE ENVISONED

SPECHT HARPMAN

Peder Anker, Louise Harpman, Mitchell Joachim

LH—zeroHouse is a design research project within our office. Architects are usually hired to provide services, and we thought what we really wanted to do was provide a product. We wanted to design the iPhone of modular houses—a beautiful, fully-functional, cool-ass living capsule. So that's how the zeroHouse came into being. It is solar-powered, collects its own water, and processes its own waste, so people can live off the grid entirely. This was also a project about comfort. So many prefab houses, like trailers or trendy container houses, carry this idea of roughing it. The zeroHouse tagline is "live comfortably anywhere." It is 650 square feet of interior space, with four outdoor living spaces. We worked backward from average sun days in a wide range of latitudes to figure out what our maximum electrical load could be. The interiors were designed around the limitations that went along with these calculations. We can run all the basic house loads with the existing solar array. There is a gravity-fed water system, a pump, and a composting toilet. There is very much a technical side to this project, but promoting comfort and highlighting the aesthetics were always part of the thinking.

MJ—I can see that it's modular, but is it meant to collapse? What happens during storms?

LH—In coastal communities there will be hurricanes, but the building will not fail until winds surpass 130 mph, at which point it twists. We worked with a structural engineer to design a series of studies to see how it fails. The exoskeleton doesn't come off or overturn, but bends to the point of failure. In structural tests you want to find out exactly where the building fails. Does it fail in overturn? Bending? In shear? This failed in bending, interestingly enough.

PA—Allow me to be the devil's advocate. The virtue is that this building is not situated to a particular landscape, but this is also its problem, because you can just drop it anywhere. It becomes a foreign object, completely detached from the landscape as opposed to being built into it. The other problem I could see is that it does not seem to link to social or natural structures. It is encapsulated within itself, which adds to the sense that it's a foreign object.

LH—We see the house as a way to showcase integrated technologies that, in fact, do link to every environment, because you need power, water, and waste management for every kind of human habitation. If you can actually integrate those systems in the most efficient package, you solve a huge host of problems. There are many other formats of the zeroHouse that we've designed—smaller units, linked units, service facilities, multi-family residential. In terms of emergency management, FEMA, UNHCR, and the Red Cross are dealing with mobile populations that are not mobile by choice. We see a logical link to these organizations and those specific environments.

MJ—Every time I see the zeroHouse, it is always shown as this lone, powerful object in the landscape. I haven't seen any images where it shows up in a suburb or a town, or in multiples. That is something that I really want to see, how these would feel in those situations. My feeling is that since there is a very high modern appeal, so many of them in a row would be a bit robotic.

LH—I worry about that, too. It could turn out to be similar to the Dymaxion house, which looks foolish in the suburbs! The idea of living comfortably anywhere means that people are willing to give up their ranch house, their center hall colonial, their two-car garage, their ornamental lawn, and lots and lots of stuff. We are heartened to see that what's trending now is the micro-loft or the twitter apartment. The zeroHouse technology becomes more efficient as the units are put in proximity to one another.

PA—We could contrast this to the prairieHouse project, which is actually my favorite. This kind of building answers my concern that the zeroHouse is not situated. prairieHouse is very much situated. It takes over an old gas station and can generate energy from the local environmental conditions, which is the wind. It is situated in a particular landscape and addresses the unique concerns of those landscapes. This building has a relationship to the larger modern tradition and language, but also is successful in answering to local conditions and issues.

MJ—I think it's great and iconic. And playful and smart. I never knew it was a gas station. Once you make that statement and rethink that house, knowing what was there before is just fabulous. It has its very kind of classical modern moments with the staircase entry, the Corbusier colors, and Myron Goldfinger wind catchers. This thing—this vestigial piece of infrastructure—is being reused and made into a very beautiful home. It is very rich and quite beautiful.

PA—Every green project has to ask: how can we reuse old structures instead of tearing them down? Here is an answer. When you think about green design, it very often involves building from scratch and making brand-new buildings. This project takes seriously the question of what to do with old structures. It turns them into something usable, innovative, and beautiful.

LH—This occupation isn't limited to outmoded gas stations. This could be the ubiquitous mini-mart on the side of every interstate highway, which if activists took over, we would be able to see what we have somehow blindly accepted as necessary. Why is this necessary? We need to encourage the canopy dweller as well as the tree hugger.

MJ—There is this super opulent, incredibly decadent grassy roof that is absolutely minimal, almost privileged, which gives the person who occupies the house his own plot of land to occupy the big sky. It's very American that way.

LH—The desire to activate the roof plane, the so-called fifth façade, is very common in the architectural/engineering conversations, but has yet to actually seep into the public discourse. zeroHouse captures sunlight and rainwater on its roof. prairieHouse has a green roof. How is it that we've given up this much real estate for so long?

PA—When I look at windCatcher, I see very simple technology or hardly any technology, but really just a building that catches wind. It is not talking about tools and pumps.

LH—That house is all about passive cooling. If you bring hot air over a body of water, it cools. This has been done in traditional north African communities for centuries, so this is not about new technology. The formal logic, the understanding of shade, the breezes, and the sculpted environment are what we consider the primary design elements. The basic building, however, requires a sizable investment in concrete, which is problematic.

PA—I wouldn't be so harsh on concrete as a building material. There is a lot of research happening right now on how to make concrete green. There is hemp concrete, which stores carbon in the system. The concrete industry is a multi-billion dollar industry in the slow process of developing new green materials.

SPECHT HARPMAN, founded by Scott Specht and Louise Harpman, is an architecture, urban design, and research-oriented practice. Specht and Harpman received their M.Arch. degrees from Yale University. Harpman is an Associate Professor of Practice at NYU's Gallatin School of Individualized Study. She taught previously at Yale, Penn, and the University of Texas at Austin.

SPECHT HARPMAN GDNYU ELSEWHERE ENVISONED

THEVERYMANY

MARC FORNES

POLYPESQUE

The project is an investigation into linear paths, planes, and warped surfaces made possible through a digital design interface. Each of the panels can be deformed to maximum deflection and connect with adjacent panels to create a continuous set of surfaces that defy description as either interior or exterior. This project represents a search into a non-linear overall morphology—from genesis to form description—and prefigures important successive work, including installations and pavilions for Centre Pompidou, Art Basel Miami, and for the collaboration between Louis Vuitton and Yayoi Kusama.

MJ—Fornes is essentially about fabrication and coding; that is his practice. He is not rewriting code, but he is making incremental steps in an existing code to produce very complex geometries that mimic something biological. He absolutely refuses to say that it has anything to do with biology. He makes no connections to biomimicry; to him it's just the expression of form. I think that's actually something really important: it's not about the idea, but its expression. Anyone could have a good idea, but to him it's about the real ability to make it physical. These things do evoke concepts of corals or microscopic creatures, but it is a long process that he has been using over and over again to get very self-similar results that each time improve upon the preceding attempts. It's about expressing the tolerance or the limits of the laser-cut material just before collapse, or ultimate curvature before it bends and breaks. The panels are held together by rivets. It's very time-intensive to assemble by hand, but he does installation after installation. It is kept at this scale.

PA—Could it be something larger? Could he move up into the architectural scale?

MJ—Probably not with this method. If he went up in scale to building size, the rivets would be the size of eighteen-wheeler trucks.

LH—We had two different projects of his in our New York exhibit, but only one here in the book, this seductive green and silver panelized pavilion that is made and unmade every place it goes. The piece might be described as a proto-geo-hydra or even a sheet metal anemone. Fornes exemplifies what it means to be a fabricator. He posits an idea about architectural and design processes that have to do with refinement—doing something again and again, building in new knowledge at each step. This iterative process of design is something that Fornes shows very dramatically through his work, but it is not unique to architects. Programmers and coders and industrial designers work this way, too. You may say that we see this with writers also, and that it's called "editing," but I think something else is happening here in his work. We see a type of Steven Johnson-style emergence. My question is this: Is improvement built into the system? Can it learn from itself? Or does the knowledge of this one project just carry over into the next one?

MJ—Would you say most architects do this? I thought architects usually do one building and then move onto another building that uses a totally different set of solutions for façades, flooring, or staircases. This is as if he is experimenting with one staircase again and again. Even though the macro-language changes, it is the same method, so we can see incremental improvement. So many of the characteristics are identical to the previous ones.

LH—I wish Fornes were more explicit about his process. Is he developing or testing a theory? Or does the work stand on its own? I think either position is totally tenable, I just wish I knew more about his intentions.

MJ—He is a maker and fabricator. He has been told many times to make this process into a chair or a table in order to find different ways of releasing the project. He said no, because these processes wouldn't work for a chair. You would not be able to sit on the chair, because it would break. He is working for the optimal amount of surface to get the most amount of volume. It doesn't need to be a chair.

LH—It is certainly true that technical precision, fabrication, 3-D printing, and other types of digital skills need to come into the global design dialogue. Whether it is computations with big data or precision fabrication, I don't think these are separate from the larger project of an integrated design curriculum. Students will find their way into this discussion about fabrication, but it cannot end here. We must see this as more than "playing with big toys." If there is a criticism, it is that the projects close in upon themselves without linking to other demands about functionality and use.

PA—Isn't this sort of a masquerade? He uses all of these computational techniques and digital processes, but ultimately it looks like an aesthetic project or a sculpture. These projects seem to be largely driven by aesthetics. The computation then becomes a technique to achieve an aesthetic. I kind of like that, but he doesn't seem to articulate this very clearly.

MJ—On some level that is absolutely right. The material is techno candy-colored; he switches between greens and silvers, golds and bronzes, whites and blacks. There is a lot of contrast and shimmer and evocation of light around it. It is very beautiful and lush, like a Jeff Koons.

PA—Hey, I much prefer Fornes to one of Koons's puppets, not to mention Ilona Staller.

LH—Lance Hosey and David Rothenberg write about beauty and aesthetics as value propositions within the environment, both natural and built. Their books are important to this conversation. We have to find a way to bring aesthetics and beauty back into the discussion of green architecture. So, on the one hand, we can criticize this as an aesthetic that closes in on itself and is somehow not accessible, but I think the fact that it is so tactile and luscious gives it value. And because Fornes makes pavilions, people can enter them, rather than only look at them. They provide an experience.

PA—It is not merely aesthetic, but a deeply aesthetic project. Aesthetics is what drives the project, and he has found a technology to achieve what he wants to do. In that way he is a sculptor and an artist. I admire him for doing that.

MJ—I think he would be most proud of the optimization issue. He designs and builds things to their maximal limits to get these eye-catching surfaces, while achieving this with the minimal amount of materials and connections. He is also showing all kinds of variations in both form and process. If you talk about the raindrop versus the snowflake, he is actually both at once. The raindrop is the most optimized structure for gravity delivering the right amount of water to the surface of the Earth and finding its way almost aerodynamically through the sky. The snowflake is just the opposite. It works against gravity and has infinite varieties of form. Most of it is about being fabulous, beautiful, and unique. It is certainly not optimized in any way to deliver the right amount of snow. Marc shows that there is a connection between the two.

LH—Every leading-edge design school has these "digerati" on the faculty. We already have a whole generation of students with access to this knowledge. How do we expand the discourse to include more students across a wide swath of disciplines?

THEVERYMANY Marc Fornes is the founder and principal of THEVERYMANY™, a New York City-based design studio and collaborative research forum engaging in the field of architecture. Fornes has led workshops and appeared as a guest critic at the Architectural Association, The Royal College of Art, Pratt Institute, Columbia University, and the University of Pennsylvania. He received an M.Arch. from the Design Research Lab of the Architectural Association in London.

THEVERYMANY GDNYU ELSEWHERE ENVISONED

RUY KLEIN

DAVID RUY, KAREL KLEIN

PANGAEA | Proposal for Nodeul Island, Seoul, South Korea
Pangaea, a proposal for a performing arts center in Nodeul Island, South Korea, consists of a low-lying structural mist in which artificial landmasses drift together in the Han River. Pangaea provides a system through which a synthetic geology of organic and inorganic materials can be cultivated. Seeking to manufacture a territory neither natural nor urban, geometries are used to facilitate change over time, creating a cyclical, perpetual making and unmaking of the island.

ARTIFICIAL SKY | Proposal for The Sheep Meadow
The Artificial Sky is an installation project designed to evolve with the changing seasons over the period of one year, after which time it can be dismantled. It has an internal lightweight cable structure that is designed for ephemeral effects. The organization is dynamic and evolving, producing zones to create artificially-induced weather, lighting effects, clustering, accretive systems, and ambient sounds.

KNOT GARDEN | Proposal for PS1 Summer Pavilion
This project is an entanglement of rope forming a hanging garden of exotic knots. Made from the fibers of the banana plant, 18,000 linear feet of sustainable rope is knotted using variations on just four simple knot types. The Knot Garden produces a suspended mat that simultaneously functions as canopy, structure, and ornament.

RUY KLEIN **GDNYU ELSEWHERE ENVISONED**

ARTIFICIAL SKY
Implicit surface of structural
network with unstructured
gridding.

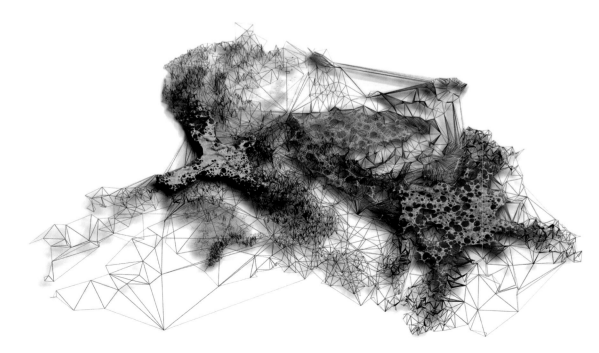

KNOT GARDEN
Algorithmic instructions
and macramé model.

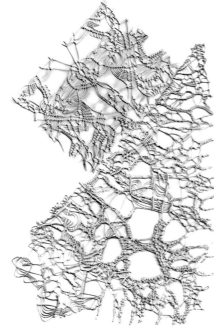

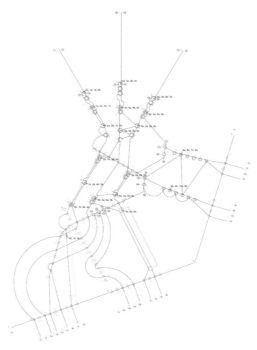

RUY KLEIN **GDNYU ELSEWHERE ENVISONED**

RUY KLEIN

Peder Anker, Louise Harpman, Mitchell Joachim

MJ—Ruy Klein is a leader in computational design, and they developed a script for creating knots. The proposal here, Knot Garden, for MoMA PS1, was to lay down this under-grid, find areas where the most amount of activity takes place, and then let the system create the highest number of knots in those spaces to provide shade from the sun. It's a kind of summer pavilion/party space.

LH—PS1/MoMA in their annual competition for the "warm up" series provides a very valuable urban lab. The Guggenheim LAB does something different, but both museums activate specific places in the city, or, in the Guggenheim example, several cities. There has to be a place or series of places in a city where this kind of creative risk-taking can happen. The city and its "creative class" need to demand this. We need to support projects like this that can be played out in public—like public experiments that are visible and available to be critiqued and experienced. Ruy was one of the first generation at Columbia when they went to "paperless studios." He moved into digital design and, in a way, developed his own language. Aesthetics figure very seriously in their work as well. They want it to be beautiful and lush, and I think it is. It feels like Belgian lace. I would love to see this built.

PA—Ruy Klein blurs the boundary between what is inside and outside, artificial and natural, by creating these boundaries where sun and wind are partly coming in and partly not coming in. I like this from a philosophical point of view, because we need to open our spaces to the environment and our way of thinking about embracing the natural. From a practical point of view, you get shade, wind, and all these other benefits. We know from anthropology that the boundary is where the most interesting work is being done.

MJ—The Pangaea project is also about exploring new kinds of grids. The knot project was this very informal way of producing a grid using the peripheral geometry of a given space, and then exploding inward. Here they are using the close packing of circles to create a grid. The larger open circles represent one kind of space, while they get smaller toward the edges, where more detail and refinement is needed. Larger circles could also serve as macro-grids with smaller circles inside of them, and the grid proliferates. They seem to be searching for a new way to define and create a system of points or even a system itself before it becomes architectural. It is a very sophisticated process to not accept the traditional gridiron in an attempt to find other ways of working.

LH—This project is called Pangaea. So one wonders if there is a historic or nostalgic attitude at play here with this proposal for a performing arts center in South Korea. As for tectonics, Ruy Klein does imagine a system can remake and unmake itself, which is intriguing. And the problem of waste is foregrounded here, since the interstitial spaces do not become wasted, but actually become programmatic. That is what seems to be happening with the formal logic of the circle. It is preliminary, but it is also interesting to think about what he calls the "discrete landscape" that comes from the circle-packing algorithm. Think about packing bottles of soda into a box. All of the space in between is wasted, but in Ruy Klein's proposal, it's not.

MJ—This grid that he is evoking with the closely packed circles, whether he notes it or not, looks like a Gustav Klimt painting. It is the kind of mosaics you would find in *The Kiss*, which has the mosaic blanket that wraps the lovers. It has those entrancing colors, effects, and geometries.

LH—It could also be a tribute to Yayoi Kusama. But we digress. How do you position this idea of a pure geometry? Do you go back to Buckminster Fuller? Do you go back to Keith

Critchlow? This idea keeps coming back, since we are always trying to understand how to maximize area with minimal material. How do we minimize waste? We always seem to go back to these geometric models and some fallacious idea that geometry will save us.

PA—Lydia Kallipoliti has been documenting these kinds of movements on her website www.ecoredux.com. In her documentation of these alternative experiments from the mid-1960s to the 1970s, you can see a lot of play with Platonic forms in order to optimize the ideal structure. There is sort of a Platonic longing in this desire to reunite with the environment, which is fascinating.

MJ—There are now entire groups in major offices that study just this. There is the architectural office itself, and then there is the internal geometry group that looks at the base methods for optimizing whatever is going to be built. It is becoming more and more commonplace. Now the architect and the engineer are working to replicate and verify their independently arrived-at solutions. They each produce their models, then look at the benefits and constraints; they are each doing the same thing. It is nice to see that the architects can do it, but originally you would pay the engineers to solve these problems and the architects would just accept the solutions.

PA—The architect was always the idealist coming in with his beautiful drawings and telling the engineer to figure the rest out. That was the traditional division of labor.

MJ—Now it seems they are getting to be equal. The real-estate developers are also on board and hire the same people to do the same work and they also use the same software.

LH—There is, in some places certainly, a common language, but there is reason to worry when the software drives the design. Google SketchUp has infiltrated design schools across the country. The program privileges extruded, orthogonal forms. Why? Because they're the easiest. Higher-level students then jump to parametric modeling with Rhino, because it's "cool" and sexy. And yet there's a huge degree of copycatting. I worry when Zaha's students only design Zaha-looking things. And the industry has embraced Building Information and Modeling (BIM) systems, which allow for a higher degree of accuracy with quantity surveying and costs. With BIM, architects are actually trying to claw back some authority, taking the lead on cost management, sequencing, and scheduling, which has been possible through the development of new software programs. But big picture: these programs don't make you a better architect, and they don't make better buildings. They solve certain problems but ignore others. I think that the language question is important. We can all be in the same conversation, but that doesn't get you to the deeper thinking of, say: should we even build an entire off-the-grid city in the desert like Masdar? We always need to evaluate the tools.

MJ—Totally agree. Don't be seduced by your hammer, because it is just a hammer. It might be complex and do wonderful things, but at the end of the day it is just a tool and doesn't do the thinking.

RUY KLEIN is a New York design practice directed by David Ruy and Karel Klein, which works at the intersection of architecture, nature, and technology. Ruy is an Associate Professor in the Graduate School of Architecture and Urban Design at Pratt Institute, where he is also the Director of the Network for Emerging Architectural Research (NEAR). Ruy received an M.Arch. from Columbia University. Karel Klein teaches at Columbia University's Graduate School of Architecture, Planning, and Preservation, and at Pratt Institute. She received an M.Arch. from Columbia University and a degree in Civil Engineering from The University of Illinois, Urbana-Champaign.

INTERBORO PARTNERS

**TOBIAS ARMBORST, DANIEL D'OCA,
GEORGEEN THEODORE**

Imaginary landscape
of downtowns, slums,
suburbs, beaches, and
gated communities.

THE ARSENAL OF EXCLUSION & INCLUSION

The Arsenal of Exclusion & Inclusion is a series of drawings and forthcoming book about "weapons" that architects, planners, policy makers, developers, real estate brokers, community activists, and other urban actors use to restrict or promote access to the space of the city. Inspired by Pieter Bruegel the Elder's painting *Netherlandish Proverbs*, the Interboro mural depicts the book's 101 weapons of exclusion and inclusion, operating in an imaginary landscape of downtowns, slums, suburbs, beaches, and gated communities. Interboro enters into the contested space or "war" between the forces of integration and segregation, between NIMBY (not in my back yard) and WIMBY (welcome in my back yard). The friendly graphic language belies a sharp social critique. Examples of many everyday acts of exclusion are posted regularly on the blog of the same name.

INTERBORO
Peder Anker, Louise Harpman, Mitchell Joachim

PA—Interboro conceives its role in architecture as radical community engagement. They are developing tools and a program for how to reach out to various communities and engage them in architecture and urban design. The designers at Interboro go out and interview community members in order to find out what they want, whether it is objects or solutions, and then make proposals to try to get things to happen. Their approach is very different from the usual client/architect relationship.

MJ—This to me is the example of how far you can get away from architecture. Interboro is so clever because they absolutely ignore, almost to a fault, any kind of form or tectonics or even spatial relationships—their entire project is sociology. They are out there conferring with the community, finding out their needs, and delivering objects through their work. They take an almost journalistic stance towards design, showing their technique, letting everybody know their process and their way of thinking about urban design. In some ways, it's absolutely valid. If you look at it through the lens of architecture and urban design, it is very new. If you look at it through the lens of planning, it is a fifty- or sixty-year-old concept and not new whatsoever. They've got these cartoon graphics that piss on the holier-than-thou aesthetic that many architects produce. Interboro produces statements about the community that get their message across by engaging communities in a literal way, such as through billboards, signs, and leaflets.

PA—… so you get all this feedback from the community, but do they know best?

LH—One of the things I think Interboro does is couch social protest in these friendly, child-like graphics. They show a whole series of complaints that are lodged within what we think is a happy graphic regime—thought bubbles, flags, little text boxes, nice colors—but in fact, they're actually coming in the back door and showing all the entrenched interests that keep communities down. At the top there are these friendly text bubbles, but at the bottom there is a withering critique of failed urban design. In that sense, they are activists and also have a very serious commitment to education. Democratizing design is clearly part of their mission.

PA—I frankly disagree with the premise of "give the people what they want" with no regard for expertise or "best practices" from other places. If we go to a community and ask them what they want, you might just get another McDonald's or a Starbucks.

MJ—Perhaps, but no one wants an art museum that's hemmed in by a fifteen-foot concrete wall. Art for many people is already so distant, elite, and irrelevant. Interboro is just trying to bust down that wall.

PA—You can say the same thing about "green" initiatives, which can be seen as just as artificial and distant for people trying to survive. If you are struggling just to put food on the table, then green design is very distant.

MJ—The uncompromising world of green policy is fairly unreasonable with respect to economic development. Any time when you come upon a conflict between green and job-based economy, green principles must make a compromise. It is seen as totally elite and part of a faction of crazy environmentalists who don't know what they're talking about. I think Interboro is in the category of trying to balance the world of the elite with the world of the everyday.

LH—They have developed an inclusive process, and it will be interesting to see what happens once they've refined and tested their process in different neighborhoods with different goals. Can they duplicate the results? Can they be measured? How does a practice like this evolve? Who does it inspire? Does Interboro ultimately transfer their skill set to the community itself? Do they empower community members to become advocates or agents of positive change? They are certainly a practice to watch.

INTERBORO, led by Tobias Armborst, Daniel D'Oca, and Georgeen Theodore, is a New York City-based architecture, urban design, and urban planning office. Armborst is an Assistant Professor at Vassar College. He received a Dipl.-Ing.in Architecture from RWTH Aachen, and an M.Arch. in Urban Design from Harvard University's Graduate School of Design. D'Oca is an Assistant Professor at Maryland Institute College of Art, and a Design Critic in Urban Planning and Design at Harvard University's Graduate School of Design. He received an MUP from Harvard. Georgeen Theodore is an Associate Professor at New Jersey Institute of Technology's School of Architecture, and the Director of the Infrastructure Planning Program. She received an M.Arch. in Urban Design from Harvard.

TERREFORM ONE

MITCHELL JOACHIM, MARIA AIOLOVA, MELANIE FESSEL, NURHAN GOKTURK

One Day Tower made from twenty-four hours' worth of compacted waste in New York City. Trash is perceived as a constant upcycled nutrient, not a detriment.

RAPID RE(F)USE

New York City disposes of 38,000 tons of waste per day. Most of this discarded material ends up in Fresh Kills landfill. This project supposes an extended New York, reconstituted from its own landfill using robot 3-D printers. Eventually, the future city makes no distinction between waste and supply.

BIO CITY WORLD MAP

The Bio City World Map is a forecast of the world population density in the next hundred years. It has been modeled by combining all the world cities together as one continuous growth system. The current phenomena of explosive growth—the "mega-city" (Shanghai, São Paulo, Mexico City, Lagos) and the "instant city" (Dubai, Abu Dhabi, Zhengzhou, Ordos)—merge together into a continuous urban construct. As the human population expands, Terreform ONE sees it as one single macro city spread across the continents. Other cities, mainly in the developed world (Detroit, Leipzig, Manchester), demonstrate the opposite tendency, because they are shrinking at a significant rate. The world map suggests that most nations cannot view the effects of planetary population density through the lens of just one city or region. Instead, the map aims at revealing the long-range effects of massive human population in areas of present and future urban intensity.

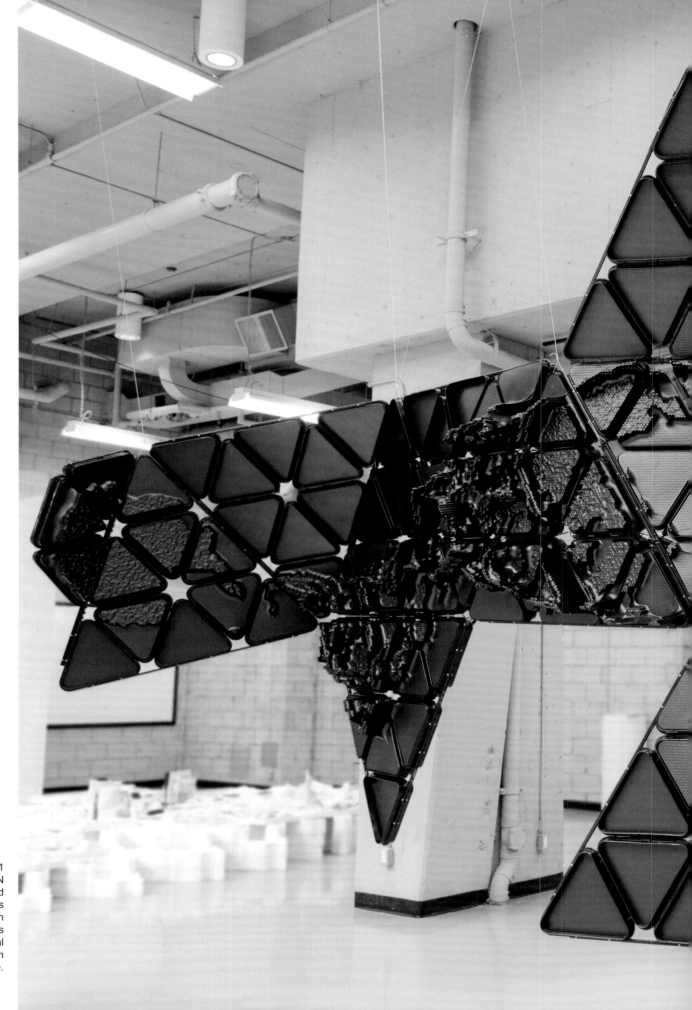

BIO CITY MAP OF 11
BILLION
Global networked
habitat: topological forms
illustrate the shift in urban
population density across
continents as a biological
habitat for eleven billion
people.

TERREFORM ONE **GDNYU ELSEWHERE ENVISONED**

PLANETARY ONE

MARIA AIOLOVA, CARLOS BARRIOS,
ALEX FELSON, NURHAN GOKTURK,
MITCHELL JOACHIM, DAVID MAESTRES,
WALTER MEYER, JASON VIGNERI-BEANE

Transitions of infrastructure between water and industrialized landscape. Self-sustained working dry docks for clean industries that are incubators for new technologies.

SUPER DOCKING | Brooklyn Navy Yard, NY

As a form of urbaneering, this project explores the possibilities of the architectural retrofit. On an urban industrial site in Brooklyn, New York, Super Docking imagines a self-sustained working waterfront as a center for clean industries that are incubators for new technologies. The designed landscape is adapted to local climate dynamics and is outfitted for a living infrastructure to seamlessly connect land and water. The project interfaces the historic dry-docks, which are retrofitted into five distinct research and production facilities with massive 3-D digital prototyping and scanning, replicable test beds for studies in freshwater limnology and restorative ocean ecology, freight delivery of raw materials and finished goods, automated shipbuilding, and plant remediation barges for sewer overflow. The surface of the site mitigates architectural space and water flows. It supports programs to clean polluted water and sets the terrain for privileging pedestrian movement throughout the site. The project docks are highlighted by shapable deployable structures and membranes. Planetary ONE imagines an industrial ecology landscape established to manage both human and natural systems, with reinforced land-use needs. The urgency to aggregate areas for innovation with social and economic diversity is in demand. The project encourages research, both as an industrial activity and as an ecological intervention. If realized, the proposal will promote new products, jobs, green office spaces, and areas of exchange.

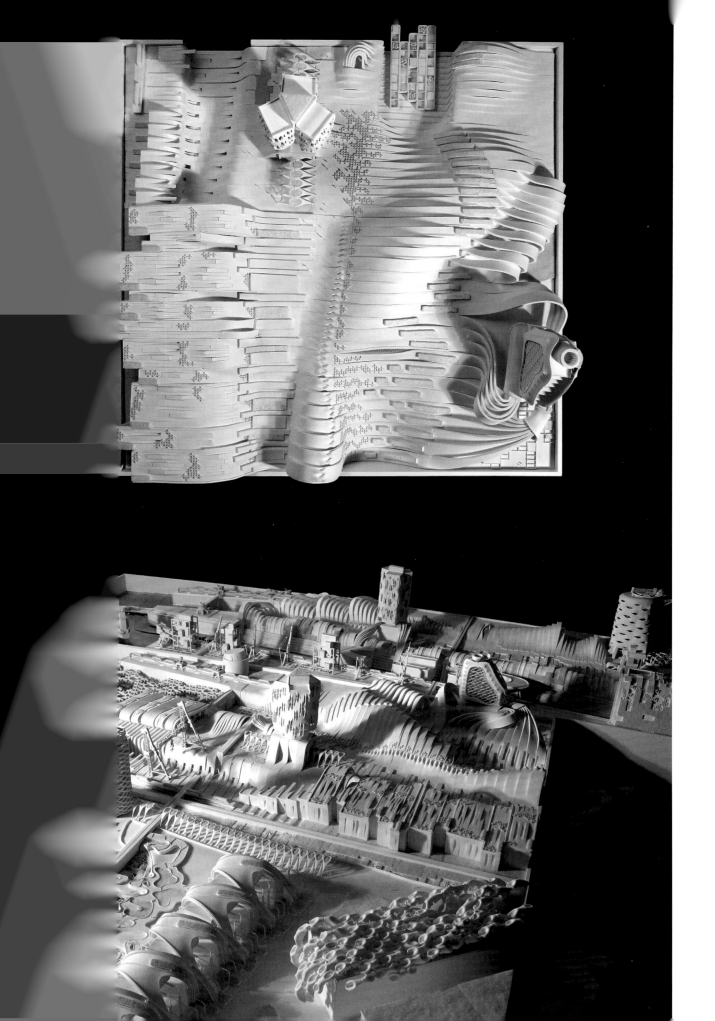

MJ—Gertrude Stein once said, "There is no away, away has gone away." We were thinking about what would happen if we ended waste, where everything would be constantly upcycled or recreated endlessly—then there would be no such thing as waste. This tower illustrates twenty-four hours' worth of waste in the city of New York. It would fill up the entire Statue of Liberty with compacted refuse in one hour. The project is a fifty-three-story skyscraper comprised of 36,000 tons of trash collected over a single day. Traditionally, this garbage was delivered by barge to Fresh Kills Landfill, but now it goes to Ohio by train. That is why there are cargo and freight boxes on the surface of the building. The idea of waste in and of itself is one of the seminal problems in environmental design. We should not have the term waste. We're not destroying matter, we are recreating it. This project recognizes the amount of waste produced in the city of New York.

PA—In most of Europe, landfills don't exist anymore. Garbage is instead burned, and the energy is used. There are ashes and metal that is being recycled coming out of it. Isn't that a solution?

MJ—That process tends to produce dioxins. The newer form of plasma gasification is probably more efficient, especially when regulated. There are ways to filter out the ultra-poisons, but America has mostly steered away from trash incinerators.

LH—I think the trash tower becomes provocation. If this is just one day's waste in New York City, then what? Is the proposal that if we can show a year's worth of waste—365 of these towers—then people would wake up? Data visualization is very powerful. I think that's where a project like this might reside. I think it's great that you and your partners are working this way.

MJ—We cocreate large composite visions of what a city might be. This showed that we must rectify a world of waste while addressing other environmental issues like food, water, energy, mobility, air quality, and the like. The tower is specifically about the waste component, to connect with our vision of the whole city and its networked infrastructure.

LH—Helping people visualize a problem is a terrific contribution. There is real value here in helping people understand the scale of these massive problems. I think this work is in good company with Bruce Mau, Edward Tufte, Nicolas Felton, and many others.

PA—Not only them. This follows modern architecture back to the Bauhaus. Herbert Bayer, Walter Gropius, and others: they all emphasized not having one sign or one homogeneous way of communicating huge numbers. I think it is important to visualize and communicate data in this way.

LH—I see your team created the Bio City World Population Map. What does it represent?

MJ—In the next hundred years, we can expect the human population to reach eleven billion. What does this rapid increase in growth look like? We used the Buckminster Fuller Dymaxion Map grid to communicate an all-encompassing view of the world population. The map visualizes the Earth as one entire urbanized place, as opposed to a number of unconnected and disparate towns, municipalities, and regions. Our Bio City Map displays population density as a parametric graph on the front. The back focuses on numerous mega-cities, designed and grown inside petri dishes. Our approach experimented with hundreds of thousands of bacteria colonies. We chose colonies of E. coli as a method of analog computation using synthetic biology. Population density was represented in two different forms of bioluminescent E. coli under UV light. Glowing red E. coli represented future census projections, while green represented existing demographic conditions you would find in cities. We used the dilution method in biology to show the range of densities of E. coli populations in each petri dish. Stencils derived from CAD files would shape the E. coli into specific geometries that would show or display the current conditions in cities.

PA—The initial map designed by Buckminster Fuller during World War II was designed so that its users could piece the triangles of the globe together according to their own geographical perspective on the battlefield. This jigsaw-puzzle approach allows a local relationship with the global, which I think is important. For Bucky it was a question of trying to understand the global battlefield from different military and political perspectives. Perhaps you could assemble your world map differently depending on where it's on display? It's a gorgeous map. Who was involved in making it and why?

MJ—This is an interdisciplinary team with cartographers, urban planners, biologists, and architects all working together to think about how to make a map of human population projections. We argue that most nations cannot and should not view the effects of population density through the lens of just one city or region. Like the Dymaxion Map, we try to show the world in all its interconnectedness. We aim to reveal the long-range effects of massive human population growth in areas of present and future urban intensity. Moreover, we expanded the technique of "bacteriography" to shift scale and underscore the highest zones of growth. Ultimately, the bacterial shapes grow to reveal patterns in urban regions.

PA—Let's turn to planetary ONE's "super docking" model of the Brooklyn Navy Yard, which to me is an artistic visionary plan beyond the scope of anything possible, while at the same time firmly grounded in a desirable future we should indeed try to realize. Tell me more about it.

MJ—We wanted to know whose job is it to create a city. Our intent is to jump-start a new heterodoxy that can reinvent and negotiate the complex mix that embraces urban territory. We have outlined a radical new vocation to regenerate, pioneer, and sustain the future urban domain. These groundbreaking multidisciplinarian activists are called Urbaneers. The strategy for the Super Docking project was based on urbaneering. This includes the replacement of dilapidated structures with vertical agriculture and housing merged with salubrious infrastructure. Former dry docks become snaking arteries of manufacturing spaces embedded with renewable energy sources and productive green zones. By reengineering the obsolete military framework, we can install radically robust and ecologically active pathways. These operations are not just about a comprehensive model of tomorrow's city coupled with a cyclical resource net, but are an initial platform for discourse.

TERREFORM ONE Terreform ONE [Open Network Ecology] is a nonprofit design group that promotes smart design in cities. Mitchell Joachim is Co-Founder of Terreform ONE and an Associate Professor of Practice at NYU's Gallatin School of Individualized Study. He is a 2011 TED Senior Fellow and received a PhD from Massachusetts Institute of Technology, a MAUD from Harvard University, and an M.Arch. from Columbia University. Maria Aiolova is the founding Co-President of Terreform ONE. She received an M.Arch. in Urban Design from Harvard, and a Dipl.-Ing. from the Technical University of Vienna, Austria and Sofia, Bulgaria.

TERREFORM ONE   GDNYU ELSEWHERE ENVISONED

FRANÇOIS ROCHE

tBWND
Laboratory of light.

theBuildingWhichNeverDies (tBWND)
The "Laboratory of Light" is an ongoing speculative research project that links the health of the planet to individual human health. The building envelope holds markers to show the weakening ozone layer, the penetration of UV light through the Earth's atmosphere, and the human circadian cycle that is dependent on light. By day, the building's exterior collects the sun's energy with phosphorescent pigments and photovoltaic cells. At night, the phosphorescence indicates the intensity of UV sun radiation. In the interior, the project sets up a physiological study of how light intensity affects human metabolism.

OLZWEG
The project is a museum for experimental architecture with an interior labyrinth. It is a random and uncertain aggregate of glass elements constructed by robots. Visitors are forced to find their position in the glass maze using specificities of the exhibition.

"I'mlostinParis" HOUSE | Paris, France
This dwelling is located within a Parisian residential courtyard. Imagined to be like an urban duck blind, the house contains 1,200 ferns supported by a hydroponic system, bacterial cultures, and a mechanized system for collecting rainwater and providing nutrients to the organisms.

R&SIE(N) **GDNYU ELSEWHERE ENVISONED**

"I'mlostinParis"
1,200 hydroponic ferns,
bacterial cultures, and a
mechanized system which
collects rainwater and
provides nutrients.

OLZWEG
Museum for experimental
architecture with an interior
labyrinth.

R&SIE(N) GDNYU ELSEWHERE ENVISONED

LH—My understanding of theBuildingWhichNeverDies is that it is meant to be an active and direct interface between the human body and a building, and that the building is an interface between itself and the planet. I love the idea that Roche is designing a building that creates an active, positive response for its human occupants, promoting health and well-being. I don't know how serious he is about this therapeutic proposition, but I think the idea is quite beautiful.

MJ—This project, like most of his projects, has this kind of unbelievable acid green sensibility. They are not necessarily intended to exist in the real world, but to be instigators or a form of agitation to push what we understand as the limit of building and the limit of green technology. The glowing ethereal images are science fiction; they are beautiful and evocative. His visions are done so well—they're for the history books, the paradigm for this kind of work. Who knows whether or not the façades of theBuildingWhichNeverDies can pick up UV lighting, or if a robot arm can actually build an entire city? His work is impossible to grasp in any one single image. For the house in Paris, he uses plants as camouflage for the actual architecture, which I don't think he really considers very important. The house is probably very conventional at the end of the day, but here he invents this wonderful mixture of plant life and blown glass tubular jars that serve as hydroponic elements. The plants encapsulate, if not take over, this entire site. The whole city block is one grown-over mass.

LH—Does Roche position himself as an art practitioner? A provocateur? Would he like to see this built? Does someone like Patrick Blanck steal his thunder? We have been seeing grow-y walls all over the place for years now.

MJ—He is an anti-architect architect! He puts these ideas out there and lets others run with them. He is first to the plate with a lot of these projects.

PA—I see something here that I have not seen in many other green architects, and that is a green architecture that really puts human experience and sensibilities at the center. Other green architects may work really hard on other aspects, such as ecological footprint or saving a certain species, but what is going on here is an attempt to be green yet still make the environment beautiful and exciting for human beings. It reminds of Sylvia Lavin's book about the architect Richard Neutra, *Form Follows Libido*, where she uses affect theory to reinterpret Neutra and show that he was really about creating the right psychological environment for the welfare of human beings. Neutra's agenda was to save the environment in order to save our own humanity. There is a similar project happening here. You see that an individual's experience of the natural world, perception, touching, smelling, sensing, is a way of helping humanity by being green. I am, however, struggling with, I must confess, the robot component. Honestly, I could do without it.

MJ—Using robots in green design is a huge movement. There is a group that we can call Rob-Arch, robot architecture, which begins with Gramazio & Kohler at ETH Zurich, quasi-architect engineers that are looking at repurposing obsolete factory robots. You can buy them cheaply off the internet for about $50,000, which is not bad considering they're probably about $2 million brand new. Architects and engineers are beginning to test what the possibilities are for construction techniques, especially green design. What the robots provide is an unbelievable sense of craft, precision, and speed.

LH—To what end? Does this get us closer to using mass production to solve, say, the affordable housing crisis? I think Gropius and Wachsmann's book from the 1940s, *The Dream of the Factory-Made House*, is still relevant. We haven't solved this. Donald Albrecht wrote about so many postwar failed experiments in his book *WWII and the American Dream*. Do you think we're just making the same mistakes all over again, just more expensively and extravagantly?

MJ—I think what the robots represent is the leading edge of craft and precision. From all the results I have seen so far, the more exciting stuff is in quad-rotors, things that fly and things that have more freedom. The robotic arm is really limited to one specific mount, and I find that the people who continue to do this research are ultimately secondary followers to the work that was done at the ETH Zurich, which really looked at sprays, bricks, concrete, and stacking methods.

LH—We are already seeing that digital design and fabrication offers more territory for design innovation. But back to Peder's point, Roche's work promises a lush environment that we want to occupy. Lance Hosey talks about the psychological benefits of beauty and the environment.

PA—Look, a robot is a tool just like a hammer is. He uses it well, there is no question about it, but his program is not about the robot. Instead, it is about the immersive human experience of the environment.

LH—Maybe Roche's work has an embedded reference to the 1960s and Leo Marx's *Machine in the Garden*. How do we start to understand these conflicts that we set up between, on the one hand, industrialization and mechanization, and, on the other hand, the idea of a "pure" pastoral landscape? I think we wouldn't go so far as to say landscape is somehow pure and therefore better. It, too, is constructed, and we need to accept that we live in a constructed environment.

MJ—I think Louise hit the nail on the head. This is clearly part of that narrative where Marx discusses Hawthorne in some sylvan glade near Concord, Massachusetts, trying to escape the world of the built, the world of man, trying to find a connection to nature. He goes into the forest to disappear, witnesses the sun gleaming through the trees, and hears the singing of the birds. Then, off in the distance, he hears the troublesome whistle of a coal-powered train. Even though he cannot see it, he can feel the smoke bustling out. He argues that there is no distinction between city and nature, that this is all part of the natural world.

PA—Roche celebrates this.

LH—He is amplifying that response. He takes an established residential neighborhood in Paris and plants an idea as much as a process. It's messy and unpredictable, but potentially marvelous.

PA—Our old-growth cities need to embrace these informal, experimental places and practices. When humans decide to build a "duck blind" in a place, birds and other creatures are attracted to that habitat. Adults and children play there, with unintended but desirable consequences.

R&SIE(N) is an architectural practice founded in Paris by François Roche. The practice has been run in collaboration with Stéphanie Lavaux, Gilles Desevedavy, Olivier Legrand, Alexandre Boulin, Jean Navarro, and Kiuchi Toshikatsu. François Roche is currently a research professor at Columbia University. R&Sie(n) is part of Roche's architectural organization, New-Territories.

WORK AC

DAN WOOD, AMALE ANDRAOS

Experimental housing
typologies that rotate for
best sunlight and views.

PLUG-OUT TOWER | New York, NY

Commissioned by New York's Downtown Alliance, WORKac proposed a series of experimental new housing typologies for a vacant site in Lower Manhattan. The housing and associated programs are stacked in a segmented forty-five-story building, each with a rooftop that contains its own ecosystem. Each housing type rotates around the building's core, with each cantilevered section offering increased access to daylight and views. The concept of the "Plug-Out" is that a single building can provide the necessary ecological infrastructure for a neighborhood, allowing it to "plug out" from the city grid while performing "urban dialysis"—filtering and cleaning its own water, managing its own waste, and providing its residents with energy, the excess of which is then fed back into the surrounding district.

WORK AC
Peder Anker, Louise Harpman, Mitchell Joachim

PA—The "Plug-Out" tower seems to draw inspiration from Ken Yeang. Yeang thought of a closed ecological system within a building, so that the system is autonomous where food and water is produced and recycled. It's clearly designed in that utopian vein. Yet at this point, we see a huge monolithic building that is detached from the city itself, from the life you want to protect. It is closed within itself. This is what Yeang calls an "eco cell," a closed compartment underground or within the building.

MJ—I don't see this as a Ken Yeang project. If it were a real Ken Yeang project, the transition elements between the exterior and the interior would be more obvious and emphasized with gardens. There would be more balconies, with opportunities for exchange and flow of air throughout the building. The aim is to get natural ventilation in tandem with other controlled systems such as lighting inside the building. The "Plug-Out" tower is meant to be a vertical street with different programs hanging or flying off it. In one image, it shows Brooklyn brownstones with backyards stacked up as a vertical street. There are some more intriguing programs like hot yoga, a caldarium and tepidarium, and a fish farm somewhere on the fortieth story. Also, there is a hydroponic farm and a waste-to-energy incinerator. There are all kinds of infrastructural programs stacked vertically, and spinning off of it are these more regularized spaces for housing or work. It is an exciting project, and it is certainly in the vein of Archigram. There is a lot to glean. I actually don't even care if this is possible; it is an exquisite corpse of radically different programs. It is vertically supported on almost unbelievable cantilevers. Structurally and programmatically, it's radically ambitious.

PA—It is important that architects, especially ones who teach, put up suggestions like this, not because they are going to be built, but because they show things we want to do. Each of these are little programs that show what could be done. Technically, most of it is probably possible. Getting it together in one project is perhaps impossible, but still, every unique element is fascinating. These are ideas worth exploring in themselves.

LH—This "Plug-Out" tower is hyper urban-hybridity. It starts to aggregate all these things that we are used to seeing in disparate locations—urban agriculture, aquaculture, waste management, composting. It is systems thinking about cyclical events in order to sustain human occupation. What I would love to see is how much space is given over to human occupation versus how much is given over to human consumption (waste, energy, water). As a series of diagrams, I think it is very provocative and beautiful. I don't mind that aesthetically, it's a stepsister to Archigram or even the Metabolists.

PA—This harkens back to the MVRDV project from the 2000 World Expo in Hannover, in which they stacked all these programs at different levels. That project was built as a sort of experimental pavilion, and WORKac is developing this idea even further. There is nothing wrong with that. Architects inspire each other all the time.

MJ—I think this is WORKac at their best. This is a firm that moves between theoretical and research-based work, as well as built projects. Here, in the diagram for the "Plug-Out" tower, it starts with a novel wet stack as a core. Once that is solved, they add a lot of interesting programs. Surely this is profoundly investigational, but it makes a lot of sense, as it evokes deeper analysis. Only certain developers could afford to build this. Developers are going to consider the amount of airspace and these huge shelves that produce dark spaces and shadows.

LH—But if you look at this work as design research, this is precisely the kind of experimentation that twenty-first-century cities should be undertaking. All cities should commit to building net-zero buildings with integrated programs, including offices, residences, schools, energy co-generation, waste management, and food production. Maybe we need an X Prize for this building type. But for now, this project wraps big thought bubbles around lots of interesting ideas and communicates them really well. The fine grain and detailed thinking that would come after a diagram like this is exactly what we should encourage. MJ—WORKac has done a lot of significant projects over the years that are small-scale but remarkable. They won the PS1/MoMA Young Architects Competition in 2008 and did a project called PF1 (Public Farm One), which was a small-scale containerized upright urban farm idea.

LH—But don't forget the Home Grown urban farming project that won the Architectural League's Envisioning East New York competition back in 1995; this kind of thinking has certainly been in the mix for some time. I really like that these "greening" projects capture a moment in New York's evolving idea of itself. Dickson Despommier and his Vertical Urban Farm certainly grabbed the public's imagination in 2008 when he was profiled in *Time* magazine. I only hope that we will see more of these projects built. WORKac's Edible Schoolyard project is certainly another one to admire.

WORK AC, located in New York City, is run by Dan Wood and Amale Andraos. Wood received an M.Arch. from Columbia University. Andraos received an M.Arch. from Harvard University's Graduate School of Design. She is the Dean of Columbia University's Graduate School of Architecture, Planning and Preservation.

AUM STUDIO

ED KELLER, CARLA LEITAO

DNA-like components of
living tissue, geometry,
program, and culture
connect with other bodies
in the city's game board.

ENANTIOMORPHAO

DNA-like components of living tissue, geometry, and culture connect with other bodies in the city's game board. Video and audio installations use the wall system as a set of quasi-public projection screens, which function as a new type of plaza. With occult scale shifts, site super-scaling, dimensional alteration, and pattern iterations, it addresses the molecular as well as the macro-scale in the city.

nudiflorum

pachysandra terminalis

AUM STUDIO
Peder Anker, Louise Harpman, Mitchell Joachim

LH—I think of AUM as stealth actors in public spaces. For our New York exhibit, they created a version of their SUTURE installation. They're showing that design matters, that it activates a space. On the one hand, public space can be read as an interactive and unscripted space. But AUM challenges this, making a space look open and relatively free of constraints, but then you realize something else is going on; they bring a specific narrative to their work. They are playing with both interior and urban design: their work animates and activates an otherwise silent space, but also they bring a narrative overlay, which in our show had to do with film. Film is another way in which we experience urbanism. Most people can name ten films where the city is a character.

MJ—SUTURE is an installation with pressure sensors, which essentially allowed people, as they walked through the space, to set off different signals in relation to the sensors that send out a connection to the projectors to change a selected film sequence of various images from different points in a city. I think this is a mediated/interactive architecture space that they have been working on for some time. AUM is working on how people can be more immersed in an experience and really feel connected. It's difficult because people don't see invisible things—they need a tactile connection. In our show, folks didn't realize they were actually in the project. I think that was the point, that by walking through the space you become aware that you are linked to a machine. It is a sensory experience that is very subliminal, not necessarily overt. It's unclear what the operations are supposed to mean or intend.

LH—One of things that happened in their environment is that it heightened awareness. Because their systems are mysterious in the "special" space of a gallery, it makes us aware of how conditioned we are by the everyday systems that structure our daily lives, like traffic signals, ATM networks, or cell phone/Wi-Fi receptivity. I think AUM created an interactive/immersive environment in a gallery space where we expect to be challenged. Yet the experience was strong enough to survive outside it, too. We realize that, on the city streets, we are in a totally other kind of conditioned environment where we don't have that many ways to push back. The installation piece, especially in a ground-floor gallery space, was really successful because we have this idea of the gallery, which is a different, set aside place, in opposition to the city, which we somehow didn't think about in quite this way before.

PA—I was actually spooked by the installation, getting a feeling of surveillance, tracking, and recording. Every movement of mine was not only monitored, but the system reacted to my movements by following and tracing me. AUM created a cunning and uncomfortable space. It gave me a sense of paranoia. So if it reflects the cities we are living in today, so much the worse for them. Keller and Leitao may perhaps feel cool about this wired world. As its creators they control it, and as tech wizards they are capable of understanding large-scale technological matrixes. Or they have convinced themselves that they understand these things. I say that because I think we were all taken by surprise by the revelations of what the National Security Agency has been up to. It was a fantastic installation, but I don't miss it for one second. Good-bye and good riddance. Perhaps this is exactly the type of reaction they were hoping for.

MJ—I know that these guys live in the world of the humans 2.0. They're very interested in the trans-human, in our bodies being manipulated or changed by microchips. This is directly coming from films like *Minority Report* and out of the MIT Media Lab, where a number of research groups are looking at this landscape that is constantly wired and connected to our smart devices. There is another layer of projection on all kinds of systems. It is a smart veneer that interacts with windows, mailboxes, or sides of buses. The landscape is much more digital. The chance for interaction and the unbelievable chance for advertising, hopefully the chance for communication, will be much more an everyday event. I don't mind the world of *Minority Report*, although slightly Big Brother.

PA—Slightly?

LH—This suggests, and I experienced this, the idea of collective action. When you have two or three people interacting in the space, you begin to get different collateral/collective experiences. You don't experience the space as "me and my data point," but as an "us." You could get the screens to go all black, which I thought was pretty exciting. You also may be able to overload a system, which is interesting too. Do Keller and Leitao think of themselves as activists? Are they hackers?

PA—If they were hackers they wouldn't tell. But you are right about them giving the audience agency to hamper their installation. The tension between human will and that of the machine was there, though who's in control of whom was perfectly unclear. I guess that was intended. We could also step out of the installation at will, unlike the cities and societies we live in. The title "enantiomorphao" is a clever combination of the Greek words *enantios* (opposite) and *morphe* (form), suggesting to me that they have tried to make a digital mirror image of whoever enters the installation. I hope they will ultimately fail in doing so, but am afraid they might just succeed.

AUM STUDIO was founded by Ed Keller and Carla Leitao. The New York City-based practice designs environments that integrate new media, art, urban interactivity, and smart surfacing within private and public spaces. Keller is an Associate Dean and Associate Professor at Parsons The New School for Design. He received an M.Arch. from Columbia University. Leitao received an M.S. in Advanced Architectural Design from Columbia University's Graduate School of Architecture, Planning and Preservation.

BLOOM:
THE GAME

ALISA ANDRASEK, JOSE SANCHEZ

Repeated interconnected module as a game of assembly in a public space.

BLOOM

This urban toy, a distributed social game and collective "gardening" experience, seeks the engagement of people in order to construct fuzzy Bloom formations. The game begins when designers, ordinary citizens, parents, children, and passersby join together a massive population of cells known as a "portal." The collective act of coming to one place and building something becomes a shared experience for each person in attendance. None of the pieces can do anything on its own; only by putting together thousands of them can a Bloom garden emerge. Bloom cells are all identical, but by making use of their three unique connections, a limitless number of different formations can emerge. Simple combinations between cells produce different sequences. Only by playing and discovering does the actual "design" emerge. The final piece is a collective act of imagination, searching, and play.

BLOOM
Peder Anker, Louise Harpman, Mitchell Joachim

PA—Bloom has designed what they call a "game." The game pieces are identical, easy-to-hold pieces, with slots and tabs. The materials they use are 100% recycled plastic with some pink dye in it. Yes, you need heat and so on to make these forms, but it is not like they take new plastic. You can take all the plastic and recycle it. It is not an ecological scandal, despite its looks. It looks artificial, and that is part of the game, to make something that looks artificial at first glance. I appreciate that this is very much a public toy in which people can come and engage, build, and have that Lego experience. People get to have fun together in the city or wherever they are doing it. We have to admire this aspect. Finally, the structures that evolve are fantastic: maybe horrible, maybe beautiful, but certainly entertaining. And they create this sort of biological-looking space.

LH—One of the things that Alisa Andrasek and her partners in Bloom are doing by setting this up as a game is that they have found a way to engage the broader public. They are expanding the design discourse to be more inclusive. It is not just architects talking to other architects. Bloom was actually commissioned to play their "game" in public parks in London and in different communities throughout England. The office staffers start the setup, and that is what attracts other people to join in. Imagine seeing this pinkness show up in your local park! The pieces are rounded and smooth and easy to hold; kids and grownups come together and make these fantastic constructions that look like skeletal prehistoric creatures you might have just found. I also think that once you start playing the game, as we all did, you realize that this system starts to suggest other uses—for me, it's an idea of more permanent habitation. Could they invent a new, smart system? Is this in the lineage of construction experiments where the panel and the joint are integral, with no need for other fastening devices? The fastening is part of the conception of the panel. Is this like Gropius and Wachsmann's General Panel proposals for affordable flat pack housing? Does this anticipate new designs for UNHCR emergency housing, like what we're seeing in IKEA's Refugee Housing Unit? That is what I start to think about. When you look at theverymany and the work of Marc Fornes, especially the project he built with us in New York, it, too, is a type of habitation. I start to want more—to see what else this system can do. There is so much demand for emergency shelter, for low-income housing, and for temporary housing. I feel like this game has a very serious side to it as well.

MJ—This project is fabulous to look at; it is very pleasing, certainly attractive, gets people active in the performance of making something. I think its point is to discover the happy accident, to assemble these things together, make some mistakes, or see the end result as being something very different than what you thought you would get. It is playful. It is a great way to activate the public in the conversation of what we call tectonics, the systems of assembly that build or make things. This is a reduced and simplified tectonic. It is one object that you can connect into four or five different slots. It makes reference to complex algorithms and different forms of computation to produce these kinds of geometries or grammars for assembly, but it does it at a very reductive and simplified position.

PA—I would like to reemphasize the social importance of this. Here is an example of something we can all do together. We can be creative and let loose a bit.

MJ—David Rockwell produced a similar project out of EVA foam bricks. His blocks are blue. It is for toddlers to play with and adults to assemble. It is a kit of parts at the scale of the hand. They are big enough to make structures and all kinds of different projects.

LH—He calls them Imagination Playgrounds and installed the first one in a park near South

Street Seaport on the Lower East Side in New York. Now it's a playground kit you can buy. This idea of the spectacle and the temporary has value. People come together, there is a curiosity, an attraction, and there is an, "Oh, I can do this!"

MJ—Leisure, making, and enjoyment.

LH—What you're both getting at is that there is an act of renewal, but also the idea of agency. One can actually do this. You can take over and transform public space. You don't need permission. Maybe we are too distant. How do we bridge the unfortunate gap between people and the landscape or the environment that we create? We are not passive actors.

PA—Public sculptures normally commission some famous guy and place their art in the middle of a public space. In this case, people come together and make their own sculpture. I like that.

LH—We should have something like this, some design event, as part of our next GDNYU exhibit. Maybe we should propose a competition?

PA—Bloom encouraged us to take pieces home, to continue their projects in new locations.

BLOOM The lead designers for Bloom are Alisa Andrasek and Jose Sanchez. Andrasek is an architect and curator. She is a founding principal of Biothing, operating at the intersection of design, complexity, and computer science. Andrasek teaches at The UCL Bartlett School of Architecture and has also taught at the AA, Columbia, Pratt, UPenn, and RMIT Melbourne. Sanchez is an architect, programmer, and game designer based in London. He is founder of the Plethora Project, an initiative to accelerate computational literacy in the frame of architecture and design. He currently teaches at The Bartlett School of Architecture and at the Architectural Association.

BLOOM GDNYU ELSEWHERE ENVISONED

ABERRANT ARCHITECTURE

KEVIN HALEY, DAVID CHAMBERS

Ad-hoc tiny travelling theatre for an audience of up to six people for intimate one-off performances.

TINY TRAVELLING THEATRE

The Tiny Travelling Theatre gave its debut performance during Clerkenwell Design Week. The mobile theatre toured Clerkenwell for the duration of the festival, occupying multiple sites—including Clerkenwell Green and St John's Square. Inside, an audience of up to six people enjoyed a series of intimate performances.

In 1678, Thomas Britton turned his rooms in Clerkenwell into a concert hall. Although situated above a coal shed, the Small-Coal-Man's Musick Club became a wildly popular venue that attracted performances from all over Europe—from first-time amateurs to Handel. The Tiny Travelling Theatre draws on contemporary accounts to replicate some aspects of this ad-hoc music venue. The stage door is opened by use of a boat handle, and a "coal scuttle" roof references Britton's former profession. Audience members are seated in extruded seating boxes, and an assortment of musical instruments and other props allows them to join in the performance. A large sound funnel gives passersby a taste of the activity within, while folding tables and ice buckets on the exterior allow visitors to enjoy pre- and post-performance drinks at the impromptu bar.

ABERRANT ARCHITECTURE
Peder Anker, Louise Harpman, Mitchell Joachim

LH—This traveling theater is a project about engaging public space, which is, in fact, a project about the idea of social equity and justice. It is green because of its focus on people and engaging disenfranchised people. How do we activate public spaces so that the public realizes that this is their "right to the city," to paraphrase David Harvey?

MJ—This is a kind of theater, but the intention is to break the spell. Everybody walks through these kinds of public spaces without thinking twice. They are automatons stuck in the doldrums of the everyday and do not appreciate the kind of activities that are there. Then, wham! Some kind of giant fluorescent object appears!

LH—My thinking is that a project like this can address another scale of green architecture. If architects typically think of themselves as designing buildings with leftover space around them and in between them, then this promotes an active disregard for the "rules" of streets, sidewalks, and plazas. This project is an activator in the same way that an architect like John Hejduk thought of his projects as activators. This is a small project that just shows up and is strange and interesting. With plays and theater people. I think that you can come back to Walter Benjamin and understand the city as a space where people perform rituals of self-making. In cities, we actually identify ourselves and remake ourselves by our actions in them. The theater is explicit about that. It is a place to have speculation, it is an object of provocation, and it moves. It doesn't just live in one place, but it brings up questions about mobility, which comes back to the theoretical underpinnings of some of the 1960s avant-garde architecture groups that focused on just this. You had the idea of the "walking city" from Archigram, architecture that moves and does not just reinforce the existing socio-political economy. The movement itself is provocative.

MJ—There is a sense of performance, of breaking down the boredom and repetition that one has every day. This gets people to rethink the logic and structures around them and to have a sense of appreciation for their environment. It motivates people to become part of the stuff of life. It is a moment where art, theater, and architecture combine with action to engage the public. It is extremely important. Certainly the twenty-first-century city has to be involved in getting people to wake up and appreciate the grand cities that they are in, appreciate the folks around them, and take time to experience the little things. These are projects that are small but aggressive in scale and in their juxtaposition with the surrounding context. Most people will have a strong reaction and will probably either hate or love this kind of thing. You have to be dead inside your soul to walk through this space and not have any kind of opinion. Part of the mission of twenty-first-century designers is to move away from "shock and awe," and to demand that people wake up and realize that there is a world around them that they have to participate in.

PA—What should be included and excluded under the umbrella "green"? What about spiritual spaces like cathedrals and churches? Or other cultural spaces? We can all applaud these spaces and say that they're wonderful, but how is a project like this green?

LH—I don't think this is anything like a cathedral!

MJ—Where do you see the link to spirituality in this project?

PA—I'm thinking about religion as part of culture—and this is certainly a cultural statement. There are millions of cultural statements that we can celebrate. I think this is a wonderful cultural and artistic project, but why should it be under the umbrella of "green"?

LH—For me, it's the relationship is in its use of public space, spaces that are not named or claimed, as well as in the disruption of daily life. There is a curiosity factor. I see this and I wonder, what is it, what does it do? I think a lot of people have no idea how decisions are made in a city. Ordinary people rarely get the chance to affect urban design. This project says otherwise. It is all about community engagement. Normally in a plaza like this there would be a fountain that would be looked at. This project is anti-fountain. It asks to be engaged with, to be looked at, to be played with. Active performances are scheduled here. It puts a magnifying glass over what we think of as public space. It shows that public space is open space—physically and programmatically. This is about bringing some lungs into the middle of the city. This project promotes social equity, which is a key part of the green or sustainability discourse.

MJ—What are the limits of green? Does this fit within the boundaries? As an example, I'd say if out of a giant speaker or cone came the sounds of bird songs from the Amazon, maybe that would be some connection to another place or some connection to ideas about the environment. Maybe if out of that giant speaker came a Depeche Mode album from the 1980s, a bunch of dance music, that too would provoke people to say, "Wow! This city is filled with everything but nature!" and realize that there is a peaceful world outside of the city that might be spiritual, one that might be filled with respite, one that might be the kind of sanctity or otherness that contrasts with the city itself. In that sense, the individual would be polarized to escape the area. Something like that could be so aggressive, so mechanistic, so much about the celebration of the urban space that it would get you to reevaluate and appreciate the openness, the accessibility, and the reason that you're in the city in the first place. The point is that there could be any number of contrapositive models that could justify whether or not this is green. It is a difficult question.

PA—Yours is basically an "anything goes" attitude with respect to being green. I agree that such anarchism has its charm.

MJ—I think that is intentional. Anybody could write something to defend this as green.

LH—If this were made out of bamboo or reclaimed barn siding, would you feel differently?

PA—I would.

LH—I think that is a fallacy of green, that you have to be a card-carrying tree hugger to say that only some work belongs in a discussion about sustainability. I think we have to expand the discussion, not narrow it. This is how our conversation began, that is, by asking about where the boundaries and peripheries of green are. I don't think we are trying to set these restrictions, but saying that "one must have X" is the wrong way to go. That kind of thinking only gets you to a LEED checklist, or some tired mantra: "If it ain't bamboo, it ain't green!" I disagree with that. It is too narrow.

ABERRANT ARCHITECTURE Kevin Haley and David Chambers are partners at Aberrant Architecture, a multidisciplinary studio and think tank that operates internationally in the fields of architecture, design, contemporary art, and cultural analysis. Founded at the Royal College of Art and based in London, Aberrant Architecture is inspired by the way contemporary lifestyles are evolving, and imagines new ways that our environments can respond to these changing trends.

FRIEDRICH LUDEWIG

Building cells represent the collective nature of the UN identity: each one is inhabited by a different function, ranging from exhibitions to education facilities, conference rooms, offices, restaurants, and public viewing platforms.

UN MEMORIAL | Chungju, South Korea

The United Nations Peace Park master plan is designed to encourage tourism in the city of Chungju, South Korea, the birthplace of Ban Ki-moon, current UN Secretary General. The new UN memorial building will include a UN assembly hall that seats up to 1,500 people, two conference halls, a theater, and an exhibition space, and will be prominently featured within the UN Peace Park. It will not only be a local landmark, but also a building of national and international significance. This building will be a fitting memorial for the work of the United Nations—bringing together many nations as part of a united whole while preserving their individuality. Each building cell serves a different function, ranging from exhibitions to education facilities, conference rooms, offices, restaurants, and public viewing platforms.

RHINE VALLEY BRIDGE

This bridge in the Upper Middle Rhine Valley—a UNESCO World Heritage Site—provided an opportunity to investigate how to use infrastructure to improve the surrounding natural landscape. The design reduces the visual impact of the structure by omitting pylons and cables above deck, reducing the bridge's engineered appearance. The openness of the landscape is maintained and the bridge seeks to create continuity with the existing characteristics of the valley. To emphasize the differences of both banks, two distinct landscape typologies are introduced. The south bank is designed as a flat, terraced surface using slightly kinked slate walls and rows of trees. The north bank is quite different, taking the existing open space as a basis, and creating a landscaped park.

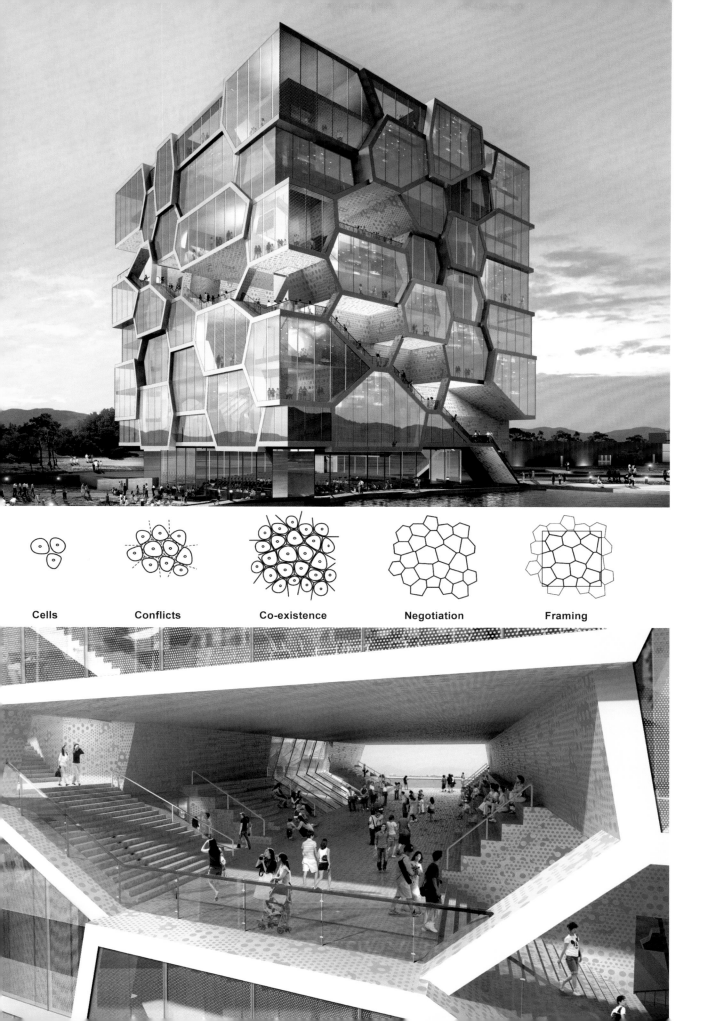

Cells   Conflicts   Co-existence   Negotiation   Framing

ACME GDNYU ELSEWHERE ENVISONED

The bridge and new landscape parks have become integral, sculptural elements of the Upper Middle Rhine World Heritage Site, unifying structural, cultural, economical, and ecological demands in an exemplary way.

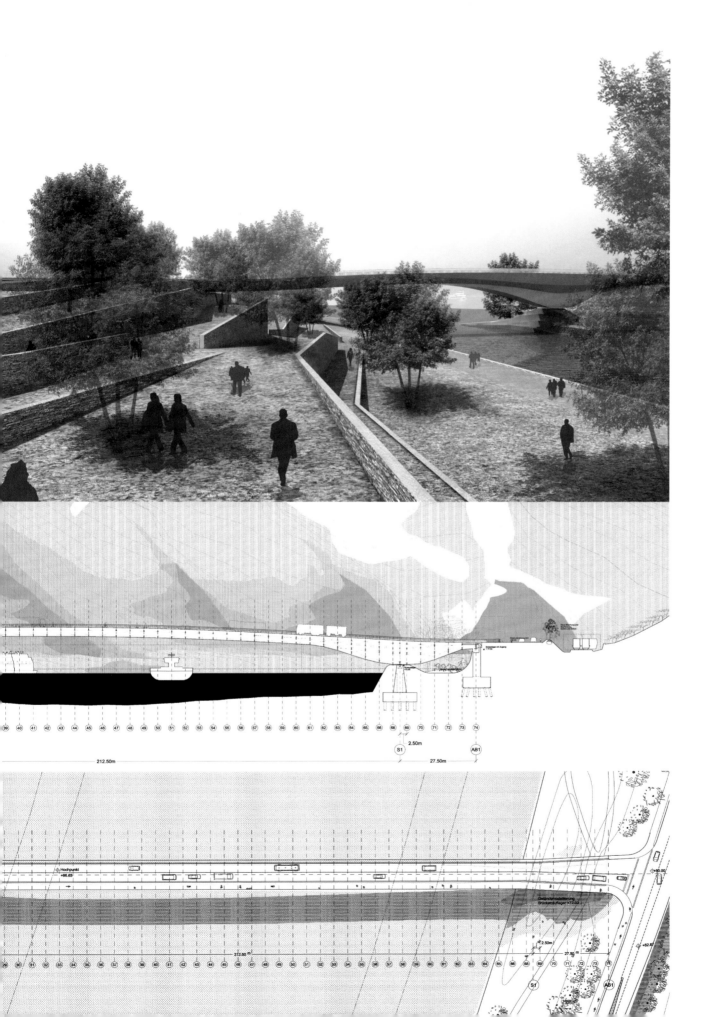

ACME
Peder Anker, Louise Harpman, Mitchell Joachim

LH—The principals at ACME position themselves as "stealth activists." Their new building for the United Nations is like a three-dimensional version of an El Anatsui tapestry. If our current understanding of the spatial regime of the UN is this secretariat with everybody sitting around in a circle, ACME is thinking about it differently, more like a hive or a network.

PA—There is a long history of green thinkers, especially during the Cold War, who look toward the UN as institution that can save the Earth. Through the UN, which brings everybody together, we have better chances of collaborating to save the planet. The most important environmental institutions, including the climate panel, are based in the UN for exactly that reason. It is thus appropriate, I think, that a UN building should be an uber-green building, because that's the place where green debates often occur.

LH—This project is speculative, to be sure. But I want to think it's more than an object-building in a park. I think if you squint your eyes, you start to see that the diagram is anti-hierarchical and it promotes different kinds of communication/connection. Again, it is a diagram as architecture, but I also think, as a model, that it is provocative and potentially very productive.

PA—If you go the UN in New York City, you enter through a gate into a different space and it is sort of a mental bridge from a singular nation into international territory. That goes for all of the UN buildings. I'm always struck by how you go from one space to another. I think this building welcomes this transition from a national into an international space. It may allow for reflection on our global problems.

MJ—I think you're seduced by the UN program. I think it is a fabulous program, one of the most important things humanity has contributed to itself. It is hard to argue with it as an idea; but it fails in many ways and is not perfect. There is room for improvement. This building is a memorial to the failures of the UN. It is a single artifact, a building, or rather, a cube in a field. It has just the right amount of "clunk" not to be clunky. There is no perceptible regularized geometry that would say that these are honeycombs. It is kind of a polygonal solution coming from some CAD software. I don't want to get into a critique of the building itself, but it doesn't say to me anything beyond that it is a cube that is just on the edge of being too clunky. As for green, I don't see any integration into the landscape, no connection to anything around it or any mention of materiality that would make it green or not.

PA—I think their Rhine Bridge project will fit beautifully into the landscape. It is a UNESCO World Heritage Site in the Upper Middle Rhine Valley, and they are trying to create a non-intrusive bridge. However, it evokes the whole German tradition of the autobahn. Hitler would build environmentally friendly outdoor autobahns that are still celebrated today as being situated correctly in the landscape. I'm wondering, to what extent can the autobahn or the road, in Germany or anywhere else, be environmentally friendly?

LH—I think that is exactly the right question. These images don't give us enough information, but do put up some red flags. The Rhine is one of the longest rivers in Europe and flows through six countries, so we can't say this is just a German bridge. Maybe they are proposing a series of bridges, or a "language" of bridges. But, unfortunately, the landscape probably looked much better before the bridge showed up. Why should we privilege the car? If they were to say that this is a pedestrian bridge and it is helping people get to their jobs or that it has a light rail on it for public transportation, then I could swallow the project more easily.

PA—The response will always be, "But we have to build this bridge! People need it. And the money is in place." So then what do architects do?

MJ—In so many cases, architects and designers are not involved in bridge-building and municipalities will just go ahead and build. In this case, hopefully, they are asking people with some level of sensitivity to do something that would mirror or reflect the landscape in a way that would contribute to it in a positive manner. It would be great if the bridge was connecting two pieces of landscape together, so that flora and fauna would have ways of merging, whether it is seedlings or small animals. Perhaps one side will contribute to the other. This might create a reconnection of the mosaics of the landscape, something that would be more about local animals or the plants than the drama of the human will, which is about getting to work faster.

LH—They say that they're trying to enhance and support the differences on either side of the bridge. And they are also trying to reduce the negative visual impact of standard bridge building. The pylons are really very minimal.

MJ—You are offending every bridge engineer that ever lived! There is a fantastic pedestrian bridge at Squibb Park in New York that goes from Brooklyn Heights down to the Brooklyn waterfront. It is gorgeous. It is an all-bamboo structure and was built at the lowest possible level of embodied energy.

PA—Why not try this for roads, too? Now that we've moved to another cultural artifact, the road, the conversation is returning to green materials again.

MJ—There is a whole field called "road ecology" that researches the road itself and its relationship to, and impact on, the environment. People have traditionally viewed the road as a line of demarcation between a particular study site and the rest of the universe. But the road itself is a connector to points along its route as well as its crossings.

LH—In the larger ecological debate, we start to talk about not just bridges and roads, but riparian corridors and watersheds. Does this bridge expand the corridor? Does it interrupt or disturb it? Is this a potential passage for certain types of species? In an abbreviated format like an architecture and design exhibit or book, that conversation doesn't have space to happen.

PA—That is an excellent point, and these types of concerns must be brought into the debate. The fact this bridge is built within a road culture with a Nazi history does not make it a Nazi bridge. That should be made perfectly clear.

LH—ACME may not locate their project in the same way a historian might. But they're not yet trying to layer or hybridize transportation programs, either. I'm seduced by Norman Foster's proposal for a SkyCycle above the train lines going in and out of central London. I would hope that rural projects could benefit from this kind of thinking, too.

ACME is an architectural, urban planning, interior design, and product design practice whose work engages private, corporate, and public clients internationally. ACME is based in London and has worked on numerous cultural, commercial, and residential projects.

ACME GDNYU ELSEWHERE ENVISONED

ATMOS

ALEX HAW

WORLDSCAPE

Worldscape is a vast dining table seating eighty people around a geometrical representation of the Earth. Worldscape's structural landscape factually accords with the world's geographic geometry, and operates both as furniture and as a social instrument. Worldscape is based on the Equidistant Cylindrical map of the world, a map dating back to AD 100, and NASA's current digital map of choice, in which all degrees are equal lengths in both directions. The table is divided into a grid of thirty-five modules, with each section on the grid representing an individual landmass that is then linked with the others to form a collective landscape. Diners sit inside Worldscape's representation of the sea—astride a bench that is interlocked with the tabletop and situated beneath the ocean surface—and eat off the sea-level coastline, the image conventionally recognized as a world map. The main surfaces at sea level are striated by longitudinal lines and perforated with the patterns of global cities. Each table has multiple light sources illuminating these urban constellations. The view from above Worldscape thus replicates a satellite view of the Earth at night.

THE MOBILE ORCHARD

The Mobile Orchard is an inhabitable public art installation and a tribute to the urban fruit tree. Its design offers a labyrinth of complex and inviting spaces that celebrate the formal structures of nature and the social structures of cities. The Mobile Orchard is centered on a sculptural timber structure and can be used as seating, shelter, stairway, or sky-throne. A lightweight latticework of curved and folded aluminum unfurls from the laminated plywood to support a canopy of laser-cut leaves—each blade cut in the shape of a London borough. The installation for the City of London festival holds five hundred real apples, replenished each week, and one hundred live fruit trees.

ATMOS **GDNYU ELSEWHERE ENVISONED**

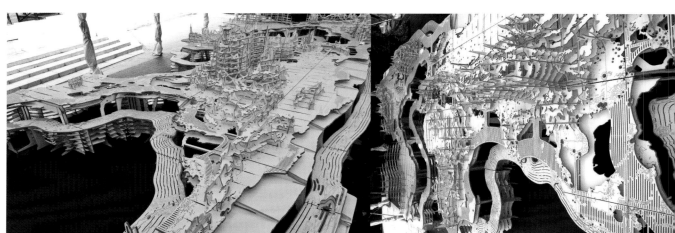

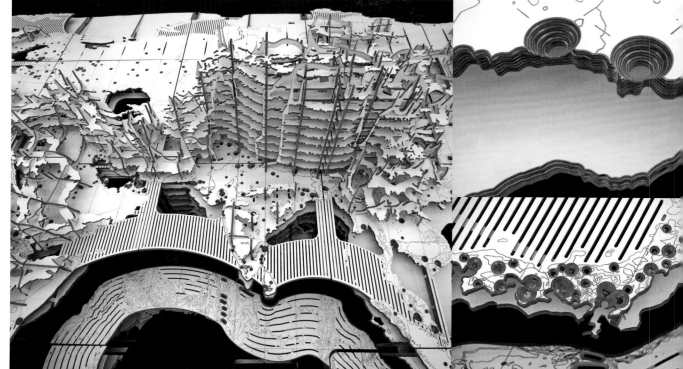

WORLDSCAPE
Combining table and bench, its deeply sculptural landscape uses all the world's contours to create a smorgasbord of unique inhabitable spaces—faithful to world geographic geometry, yet deeply unfamiliar as furniture.

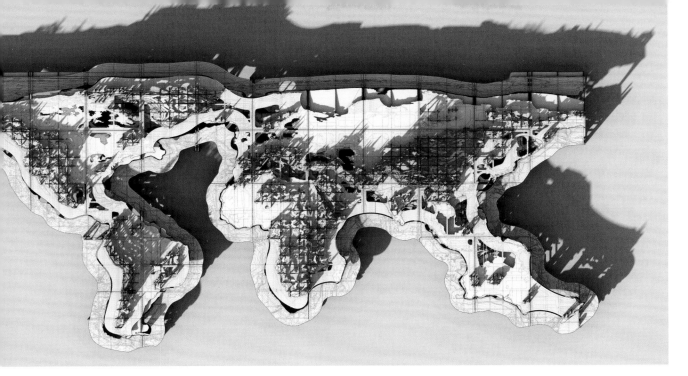

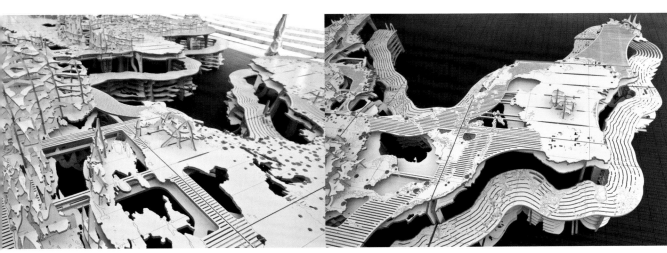

ATMOS
Peder Anker, Louise Harpman, Mitchell Joachim

LH—ATMOS won a commission as part of the London Olympics to design a project that would somehow engage the world through food by hosting dinner parties every night of the Games. They featured cuisine from different places in the world, by latitude. ATMOS scheduled, for example, a 38-degree North Latitude dinner, and so every city or culture along that corridor could be connected through that country's particular cuisine. Visitors could sign up for the different dinners. They were wildly successful, and everybody sat around this big table that ATMOS called the "world table." Part of the project was designing a physical model that could also serve as the table for the dinners. The model is interesting, because it is topographic but does not recognize individual countries. It also doesn't accept a static shoreline, which is no real line anyway. It is Pangaea, where all the continents are merged again, and seems to promote the idea of a one-world. It is a very hopeful idea about bringing people together.

PA—This is at once a wonderful and problematic project. Wonderful because the table model of the world is beautiful, as well as fun and entertaining. All that is good, but there is also something troubling about all of us sitting and eating on the Earth, especially in Britain, with its imperial heritage. When I think of this project and Alex Haw, the famous line by Bill Marsan comes to my mind: "The British Empire was created as a by-product of generations of desperate Englishmen roaming the world in search of a decent meal."

LH—I can see what some of your problems are, from a formal design point of view. This model, like other urban design models we've seen, is monochromatic, which homogenizes everything: it's all white. The world is white. So, if we extend your argument, one of the differences between the British and the people they colonized is that "natives" were non-white.

MJ—I see this project as a kind of Lewis Carroll fantasy of scale displacement, with rabbits and giant mushrooms. It is a convivial engagement on extraordinarily heavy issues. Maybe that is OK, the idea that you can become convivial at dinner, that there is some level of pacification that takes place when you're eating food, so you can talk about big picture issues without really getting too contentious.

PA—The point here is eating together and eating food from around the world. Eating is important for mutual understanding and the whole feeling of being together on the Earth. Haw travels around the world organizing the Latitudinal Cuisine, which is a sort of communal food road show, including once in my apartment here in New York. It was an unforgettably fun event, and we have been friends ever since. Buildings and fine design don't bring people together in the same way a meal does, so to me his food-work is taking architecture to a new level.

MJ—Hey, I'm not arguing against the pleasures of eating.

LH—This project both privileges and suppresses certain readings. It privileges an idea about continuity and adjacencies. It is also trying to understand interdependence and shared objectives. But, at the same time, it suppresses or erases sociopolitical conflicts and divisions. That is probably at its peril, but perhaps it could be repurposed for use at the United Nations. As architects we get used to seeing these site models from overhead—look but don't touch. I like the fact that this one actually wants you to sit on it, mess it up, spill your red wine on it, that it is not so precious. You could actually say, "We sat back to back when you were in Brazil and I was in Ghana." There is a productive dialogue that can come from an experience like this. I really appreciate that they tied program to the model.

MJ—It is no different than a game board. If I was to put a tablecloth where we are sitting now, that had a picture of a world on it, and we placed our coffees in Africa and in Anarctica, I don't think that would change our conversation. It has some influence, but it is a minor gesture and perhaps really belittles the big problems. I don't think they are making any claims that dinners at the big table can solve big problems. On the contrary, ATMOS is making claims that this is a project about entertainment and eating and enjoying life. For that, I can completely respect the ritual implications.

LH—The World Table proved wildly popular and was provocative enough that people accepted it more than criticized it, so I think that is an important position to recognize. This means that ATMOS can do more and push harder; they have visibility and an active following.

MJ—Probably 90% of the dialogue, if you aren't given instructions or there isn't a curator serving the appropriate dishes and hosting the event at the table, would be commonplace. If we were to have globe-shaped chairs and desks all around the office, would we start thinking more globally? Maybe it's also an act of intimate theater. But I will agree that an installation of this quality and craft and beauty is one successful way of engaging people in important topics in a radical yet genuine way.

LH—It shows that architecture or installations need to be programmed. This table doesn't come without its programming; in fact, I think the programming preceded the table, which is to say, how do I create an engaged environment? How do I make the environment support the conversations that I want to have? It is sometimes silent and other times very active.

PA—The mobile orchard is another public installation from the ATMOS team. They made this for the City of London festival and I think it is fantastic. As a child I climbed trees all the time, and then I somehow lost interest. Thanks to Haw and his team, I feel like climbing again, as it's such a welcoming structure for fun and reflection, including hanging apples in the "branches" for people to pick and eat.

LH—If you're walking down the street and come upon this, it is, on the one hand, totally extraordinary. And lush. And fantastical. But then this brings on a profound sadness, too, when you realize that many people have never picked a ripe apple straight from the tree and that urban fruit trees don't produce apples you'd want to eat, anyway. They are cutting down a lot of trees and then reconfiguring them in CNC-milled tree-like forms. I think the orchard operates on more than one level, to be sure. It shows a supreme level of human ingenuity, and a sense of loss for the natural environment.

ATMOS, located in London and founded by Alex Haw, is a multidisciplinary art, architecture, and design practice that works across scales—from small-scale product design to large-scale master plans. ATMOS's core architectural work has centered on innovative residential designs, while its core artistic work has focused on a mixture of lighting, interactivity, and data visualization. Haw received an M.Arch. from Princeton University.

ATMOS GDNYU ELSEWHERE ENVISONED

ALESSANDRA CIANCHETTA, MARC ARMENGAUD, MATTHIAS ARMENGAUD

Observatory along
the banks of the Seine,
with a view toward
Villa Savoye.

PAVILIONS AND FOLLIES OF THE "PARC DES BORDS DE SEINE" | Carrières-sous-Poissy, France

The planning and design practice AWP collaborated with Swiss architects HHF to win the competition to design this public park along the banks of the Seine near Poissy, in northwest Paris. The project includes the landscape master plan as well as all the infrastructure buildings for this 113-hectare (280-acre) public green space near the terminus of the RER train line A. The park includes a new visitors' center, observatory, restaurant, and a dozen smaller structures. The public green space is being designed by French landscape architecture firm agence TER. The site provides visitors with land- and water-based recreational opportunities. Existing boat docks, mooring spaces for barges, pontoons, lookouts, and cantilevered terraces are incorporated into the landscape plan to highlight the relationships between human and non-human park users.

AWP **GDNYU ELSEWHERE ENVISONED**

MJ—I see this is an extension of postmodernism. They're using the image of a house, an idyllic house, a monopoly game-board icon of a house, and they're making statements using that imagery by inserting it into a public space, raising it off the ground. There is an element that rallies others to go there or attracts them to the area. The symbol of the house becomes a spectacle.

LH—The project is credited to HHF and AWP together, so we probably need to say that outright. What I find interesting is that AWP is very active in civic, large-scale projects, where we see them trying to bridge the gaps between what we consider landscape architecture, architecture, and infrastructure. They position themselves as a kind of collective, with a wide range of expertise. They put together mega-teams that rethink what a river is. What is the course of a river? And what does that mean for agriculture? For recreation? For wildlife? How do all these questions come into a discussion about how we understand an environmental education center? Their projects actually do what we think twenty-first-century cities should do, which is to understand that systems are not unique and bounded, but they are branching and interwoven. The team approach does that. We can focus on the iconic building structure—the raised house form—but there's much more going on here. One photograph cannot show everything involved in bringing back a river's edge. Photography isn't very good for that.

PA—I don't think the postmodern label is fair here. I think AWP and HHF might come out of that debate, but they have gone way beyond it. Yes, there are historical references to traditional building typologies, and this image has a sort of Rousseauean reference to the cottage in the forest or a tree house. What I find fascinating is that they really try to take the landscape seriously and interconnect architecture and landscape, making it into one unit.

LH—There are a series of pavilions that are part of this park. The one you're focusing on is the Observatory.

MJ—Still, I see a house raised off the ground in a public space made out of wood and glass. I see no reference to the landscape—in fact, the only reference I see is "I'm bigger than the landscape, separated from it, raised off of it." It is the object of focus, the spectacle, and I see no connection to the landscape. They look like they are just plopped down in the land. From what I see here, the houses are treated like toys and there is nothing ecological about them that I could possibly read.

PA—It is perhaps not ecological, but visual. The landscape becomes a place of spectacle. You have views and can see things at different levels from the house. It is not so much about ecology, but about views and horizons.

LH—Would you go so far as to say they are using the landscape as an excuse to do their very willful architecture? That they are using this overlay of environmentalism just to get their postmodern projects out of the back of the drawer? I disagree with that.

MJ—I think that the operations on the landscape are not visible.

LH—Landscape is slow! What are you going to do? Watch the grass grow?

MJ—There are landscape architects that have decided to make ecology visible. They show off the functionality of an event as the design intention, like runoff from a parking lot, instead of going into a sewer, goes into a bioswale. Then it becomes the center of the design and they could foregorund those images as the functioning piece of how the landscape is fixing an environmental issue. These pavilions are concentrating on house forms. It is not that I don't like the raised house. It is absolutely dreamlike and memorable. You cannot forget the raised house project, and I'm sure it does some kind of amazing things for that public space. The raised series of cabins are perhaps about nature in that you can be inside those spaces and can take privileged views of certain vistas or areas. The views might create a response as the body moves through that building and bring a different sensibility about areas in nature. I could see that being the point.

LH—We are much more comfortable criticizing projects that register as architecture than those that register as landscape. I wonder whether a gallery show or even a book is the right way to show landscape projects? We are always several degrees removed. We are looking at the photograph of a thing or a place. We are never there, yet we are much more comfortable talking about architecture in this way—at this distance. I suppose that's because we are more familiar with it. Landscape discourse has not yet advanced in the general public or in the academy. How do we understand how things go together? Or master plans that are realized over thirty years? In thirty years that building will degrade, but the landscape will come into its own. That is an interesting sense of time. Universities, especially American universities, think in semesters. Boards of Directors think in quarters and "returns," driven by the thinking of Wall Street. That is why landscape and the longer-term thinking that goes with it is never going to get the attention it deserves unless there is a new generation of students and activists that show the way.

PA—We have to distinguish between landscape and environment. Environment you can actually measure on a semester basis. For example, that air pollution has gone up or down, this year we had a good year in terms of growth of forests or grass or whatever you can measure. Landscape has a much longer maturation and therefore is harder to measure or put into a plan. Maybe the way to deal with landscape is to think about it in terms of the environment and not as landscape.

LH—Because we want the numbers. There's that now-familiar saying, "If you can't measure it, you can't fix it." New York's Mayor Bloomberg was always saying something like that.

PA—Power of numbers! He knows what works and what doesn't. We can wish that we would think in a thirty-year perspective, but reality is different, and thus counting the environment by the numbers might be a better way of analyzing our surroundings.

MJ—The comment about not being able to see the landscape in the same way we see architectural artifacts is true. As a society we're trained to see things as machinists or carpenters. A child could pick out the coolest cell phone, but could not distinguish between two species of plants. I think we need more botany in our lives.

AWP is a Paris-based architecture, landscape, and urbanism practice, as well as a center for the study of current and prospective architectural trends. AWP is led by partners Alessandra Cianchetta, Marc Armengaud, and Matthias Armengaud. Cianchetta holds a Master of Architecture degree from Università degli Studi di Roma "La Sapienza" + ETSA Barcelona. Marc Armengaud holds a Master of Philosophy degree from the Sorbonne in Paris. Matthias Armengaud holds a Master of Architecture degree from the Ecole Nationale Supérieure d'Architecture in Versailles.

CREUS E CARRASCO ARQUITECTOS

JUAN CREUS, COVADONGA CARRASCO

Coastal pavilion and public
space enmeshed into the
local geology.

HARBOUR REMODELING | Malpica, Spain

This harbor redevelopment project aspires to create a new public space in the coastal town of Malpica. With its historic fishing industry and spectacular views, the harbor holds particular appeal for visitors and locals. Ramps, stairs and balconies provide a unique vantage point over this vista, while the distinctive horseshoe shape of the harbor supports multiple lookout points by a promenade resting on rocky outcrops and the sea wall. An intermediate layer of necessary infrastructure upgrades is camouflaged from both the walkways and the harbor. Murallón Lookout extends toward the harbor and is separated from vehicular traffic. Along the southern edge, selected buildings were demolished to allow space for a new promenade to Punta de Piancha, which continues along the stone face of the harbor's edge, at a constant 4.5 meters above the harbor platform. This project demonstrates the potential for redevelopment in many Galician fishing villages. By integrating architecture, engineering, and site design, these often hidden or neglected landscapes can be made desirable. This type of project can generate a different, unstructured kind of beauty, which reflects the local geography, people, and culture.

CREUS E CARRASCO ARQUITECTOS **GDNYU ELSEWHERE ENVISONED**

CREUS E CARRASCO ARQUITECTOS

Peder Anker, Louise Harpman, Mitchell Joachim

LH—This project is the reconstruction of Malpica Harbor in northern Spain. The architects came into a fishing village to redesign and reinforce the shoreline, making what should be a public space more public. The large-scale harbor redevelopment was a project of the local port authority.

MJ—This is a delicate, caring, responsive way of taking in the existing terrain as a mechanism to spark how the form flows and weaves in and around this particular area. It does a great job of offering many different views and exciting points to either see things or experience more of the landscape or rest.

PA—This project is surely a beautiful one. Yet I can't help being critical. This project will create stunning views and a romantic, solitary Rousseauean walk through scenes of nature. It is great for tourism, but I don't see this as an ecologically sound project. It is using concrete, which leaves an immense footprint. Tourists are flying into the area, leaving a footprint as well, and I'm not sure this helps the fishing industry or the harbor or the environment around it by having people walking on these concrete paths and ramps. Although it is attractive and architecturally as well as technically impressive, I wish it was taking green considerations more seriously.

LH—I don't think they give us, as remote viewers, quite enough knowledge. What is the character of this town? When the architects say, "we're demolishing these other buildings," what is lost? What is gained? Who wanted this? Was the harbor in decline? Was it an infrastructure project that was going to happen anyway, using the local equivalent of the US Army Corps of Engineers? I want to think that Creus and Carrasco brought elegance and sensitivity and delicacy to what would have been just a basic seawall reinforcement project, that also needed to "camouflage" an unsightly wastewater duct. This is the part that we don't know. I think architects and designers do themselves a disservice when they don't do more to contextualize their projects.

MJ—It was probably a fencing mechanism to stop erosion, to stop falling rock, a series of problems. Nobody spends this kind of money to establish a piece of infrastructure in an area unless there was a series of very important needs. There would be issues of accessibility, wear in the landscape, and road building that would have been done with a brute force technique even for Spaniards.

LH—I think that we are going to see engineering taking the lead in more and more shoreline projects. If we zoom out and look at other resilience efforts or waterfront developments around the world, we will see projects, like the Brooklyn Waterfront Park, that create active public spaces while also meeting demands for resilience. The new edges will support both active and passive recreation. This project in northwest Spain focuses on passive recreation, and creates a space to stroll, or meander, and engage a series of different publics. There is an area for rock climbing, too, but this is not a space where you go and play football. But if you are old or young or on a date, this looks like a really romantic and beautiful place to go. There is always value in places to just go for a nice walk. It is a public infrastructure project realized at a high degree of elegance . . . I support it.

PA—I admire its design, but where is the architecture for non-human beings? Is this good for all the other species? We don't know. I'm sure there are tons of other species that live in the area that were affected by this project. I want to know more. Sorry, but I just can't see this as a green project.

LH—Compare this to SCAPE, if you will. In their presentation they talked a lot about process, what was at stake, what they were seeking to ameliorate, and what new techniques they were bringing to the table. In this project, maybe we see too many pretty pictures and not enough about the research. In the twenty-first-century city, we need to collaborate on what we call "replicable best practices." My point is that this could be a model for a best practice, because we are going to see eroding shorelines in many places throughout the world. How do we engage those processes that are going to be led by a crew of civil engineers? How do we bring in the ecologists? How do we bring in the architects?

PA—An eroding shoreline is not necessarily a bad thing! It is simply what nature does and maybe we should accept that the shoreline changes over time.

LH—There will always be places with high population centers on the waterfront, and places where the culture values proximity to the water. We certainly saw that in the US in New Orleans with Hurricane Katrina and in Brooklyn with Superstorm Sandy. These low-lying areas may be undesirable from an emergency management point of view, but for the people who live there, it's their home. A recent World Bank report showed that the "top ten" cities most at risk from coastal flooding are Guangzhou, Miami, New York, New Orleans, Mumbai, Nagoya, Tampa, Boston, Shenzhen, and Osaka. I wonder how many Americans are even aware that five of the "most likely to face disaster" cities are in the US? Manila, Ho Chi Minh City, Bangkok, and Kolkata are among the Asian mega-cities at greatest risk. There is another list for South America, and still another one for Africa. This is a problem that is more global than local. Which is why the global/local discussion is so important to have.

CREUS E CARRASCO ARQUITECTOS is directed by Juan Creus and Covadonga Carrasco. Creus is the Co-Director and creator of the art and architecture magazine *O Monographs*. He has taught at the Superior Technical School of Architecture at the University of Coruna in Galicia, Spain. Creus earned a doctorate in architecture from the University of Coruna. Carrasco attended the Superior Technical School of Architecture at the University of Coruna. She has taught at The EASD Ramon Falcon art school in Galicia, Spain. Both were founding members of the Association "O da Deboura Cerne," involved in studies for architectural preservation.

CUAC
ARQUITECTURA

JAVIER CALLEJAS, TOMÁS GARCÍA PÍRIZ,
JAVIER CASTELLANO PULIDO,
FERNANDO A. CIENFUEGOS

TETRABRIK PAVILION
Guinness World Record
for biggest structure made
with recycled material.

ABOVE CORDOBA | Cordoba, Spain

The proposal for a new headquarters for the Foundation of Contemporary Architecture in Cordoba establishes time as a primary design factor. The building and site offer a strategy of urban intervention that recognizes the vast history of the city of Cordoba. Like any metropolis, the city of Cordoba is in constant flux and is a product of successive layers of history. This history necessitates an approach to design that is respectful of the past and views the many versions of Cordoba through the years as deeply interconnected. Thus, modern-day Cordoba is not a singular urban center, but a series of superimposed cities— versions of Cordoba from past and present that are combined.

TETRABRIK PAVILION

The TetraBrik Pavilion project focuses on the recycling of a standard milk carton—the Tetra Brik. The project creates a spatial experience that explores new possibilities for the creation of structures made from recycled materials. Approximately 1,320 people (1,200 students for the collection of milk cartons and 120 for the construction) collaborated to create the Pavilion. CUAC constructed the TetraBrik Pavilion as part of a local campaign to raise awareness about recycling plastic containers—work that earned the Guinness World Record for the biggest construction made of recycled materials. Through an information campaign staged at several high schools throughout the city of Granada, CUAC received approximately 45,000 containers for the realization of the Pavilion, which was constructed exclusively with this element. After two weeks of display and enjoyment, the final part of this project was the deconstruction and removal of the Pavilion. The materials were transported to a recycling plant with no environmental footprint left behind, demonstrating the truly sustainable nature of CUAC's design.

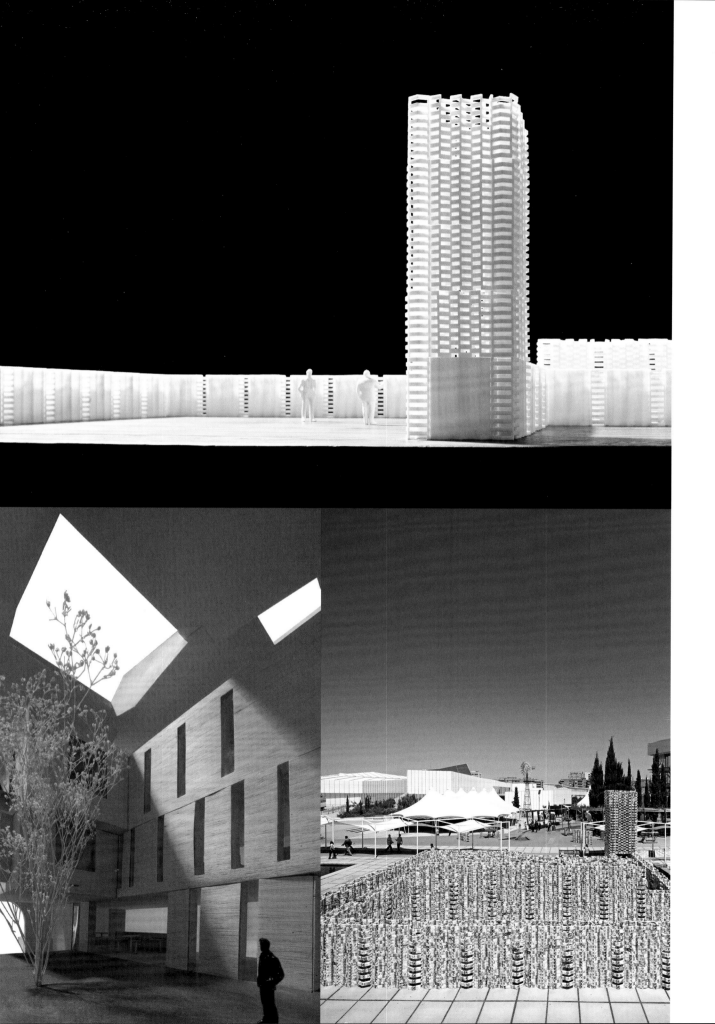

CUAC ARQUITECTURA **GDNYU ELSEWHERE ENVISONED**

CUAC ARQUITECTURA

Peder Anker, Louise Harpman, Mitchell Joachim

LH—The project we are seeing is an architecture museum, but they are actually looking at the city as a museum. They are looking at old growth cities and very much pick up on the idea of the palimpsest. They show that the place we inhabit now is one of a succession of layers within the city that is made and unmade over time. Active erasure, the idea of tabula rasa, is something that CUAC is opposed to. Is there a way to somehow acknowledge the history or prehistory of a site when creating a new building? For them, there is an idea about excavation, but also an idea about illumination. They are literally trying to use light to bring the sub-surface layers and the history of the space into view. As part of the sustainable agenda, the most sustainable thing you can do is use what you already have. I think this is a first principle of sustainability, which understands that there is a legacy to places. Rather than erasing, one can use the history for inspiration or as a platform to imagine the old and the new in conversation.

PA—This is all good, yet I feel like they have not been digging deep enough. I think the original landscape where these cities were established is not part of the equation. They only seem to be looking at the buildings and the people. A contrast could be Eric Sanderson's Mannahatta project, which is interested in the landscape that Manhattan once was. CUAC has not gone that far in discovering what type of landscape this city was once established on, or investigated ways to incorporate and build in those lost landscapes.

LH—I agree. In a way, it is an established cityscape, but if they were true to their mission then they would have to look at much more. They come into a space that is a courtyard and reveal the walls that have been covered up on the adjacent buildings and then insert a jewel within that shell. I like the architectural strategy of withholding, that they withheld their new building from the existing buildings in order to make evident what is old and what is new. I think it is a fair criticism to say that they do not go far enough in looking at questions of ecology or human use.

MJ—Sticking a tree underneath a super roof with one cut-out window is absolutely ignoring, I would say attacking, something ecological. It is a paved open space that they've now completely covered. They've trapped the tree, and have given up all opportunity for the normal arc of daylighting to have this symbolic oculus with a tree poking out. It looks like the tree is being choked. If you want to respect life, then respect life! Don't create a super mat or a folded slab over it and try and stick trees in it. The image suggests that this is something that would be delightful. It is empowering as far as an architectural expression goes, but there is such a severity and containment of natural processes, that any chance for vegetation there is truly problematic.

LH—We have to check ourselves a little bit. This is in Spain. Maybe they get plenty of light and can have the ornamental tree garden. Do we know this? There is a deep history of gorgeous interior courtyard gardens in southern climates. Are we just too northern?

MJ—I'm pretty sure the crowns of the trees need access to as much daylight as possible. This is a very diagrammatic and schematic design. There are certain intentions that we can read and certain speculations that we can make. We can find something appealing in the façade, but then we see an ornamental tree in a dark shadowy landscape. The tree they're showing is dead. Either they need to be better at Photoshop or they need to be more serious.

PA—Come on, Mitch, some trees do like to be in the shadows. And creating a beautiful courtyard with a tree in its midst for humans to enjoy is not a bad thing.

LH—What does the roof do? Right now it is connecting with the walls to make a formal entry, or to enhance the frontality of the plaza. The roof also engages the back side of the plaza, making another kind of public space that promotes permeability in the city. As an urban design strategy, I don't think any of us will fault that. Maybe what we are asking more of from a building like this is for it to commit to other systems of integration, not just public gathering spaces. We want to see what is ecological? What is green? What is sustainable? This is a programming and materials question as well.

PA—Planners thinking about how to build, sustain, or revamp areas can learn a lot from this project. They can learn how to reuse buildings and appreciate the way to engage both natural and social history in a site. I question, though, the use of what to me looks like concrete, a not very sustainable material seen from an emissions point of view.

LH—Every place has a social history. Even college campuses have social histories. At NYU, we have the Triangle Shirtwaist Factory fire as part of our campus history, but what do we really know about that? We merely have a plaque on the side of a building. We have to resist the erasure as well as the memorializing of all places.

PA—How far do you want to go? Take the Harvard Yard. Should we bring back the cows?

MJ—I can't possibly judge this scheme by that lens; it would be ridiculous to do that since there is so much that it is doing that contributes to the city. It has the right scale and mass, an enormous sensitivity, doing wonderful things with the aperture of the façade. It is very evocative.

PA—CUAC is not only evocative in its work, but also playful. Their Lego-esque building made of 45,000 used milk cartons should remind us all not only of the importance of recycling, but also of making sustainability into something exciting. Let's hope there is an environmentally minded Ariadne out there guiding visitors with hints and threads to explore their labyrinth-like pavilion.

CUAC ARQUITECTURA, located in Granada, Spain, is comprised of photographer Javier Callejas, architect Tomás García Píriz, architect Javier Castellano Pulido, and graphic designer Fernando A. Cienfuegos.

DAVID KOHN ARCHITECTS

DAVID KOHN

CLOUD PAVILION | London, England

Shortlisted for an open competition to transform London's Olympic Park post-Games, Cloud Pavilion was inspired by the history and experience of the Lea Valley site. Traveling east out of central London, the overriding impression is of an abundance of sky. In 1802, amateur meteorologist Luke Howard was so taken by the Valley's skies that he went on to invent modern-day cloud classifications—cumulus, cirrus, and stratus—on his walks through East London. The Cloud Pavilion proposal features cumulus, cirrus, and stratus landscapes with a cloud-like pavilion floating above. Underneath the billowing roof, a series of rooms, each with its own distinct character, are designed to house a variety of programs. These include a small auditorium, a multipurpose hall, a café, and a winter garden housing a prayer room. Wherever possible, the proposal uses recycled material from the Olympic site. New landforms would be constructed from fill originally excavated to build the post-Games venues. Water collected on the roof would supply water for restrooms. Calibrated fritting on the ETFE envelope allows filtered daylight in all the rooms; the thermal mass of the precast concrete and brick floor slabs holds heat and re-radiates it in the cool evenings. Both of these construction strategies reduce the energy required for lighting and heating.

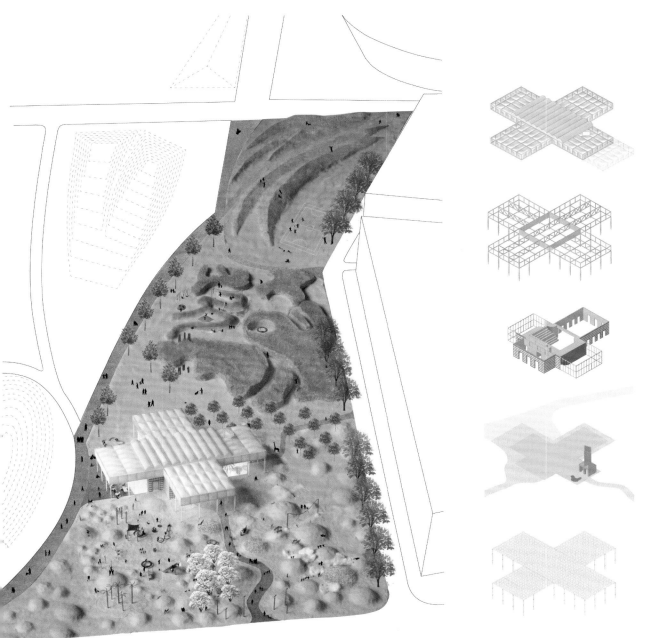

DAVID KOHN ARCHITECTS **GDNYU ELSEWHERE ENVISONED**

DAVID KOHN ARCHITECTS
Peder Anker, Louise Harpman, Mitchell Joachim

LH—The Cloud Pavilion was a proposal for the London Olympics' Legacy Park. Kohn's idea was to reuse and recycle parts from the different temporary structures that had been built for the Olympics. The aluminum gets recycled into the frame for the system, the ethylene tetrafluoroethylene (ETFE) panels become solar collectors, and there is a water collection system that services all of the toilets for the pavilion. The goal was for the pavilion to become a social space, a gathering space, but one that also has this pedagogical waste upcycle story. This project didn't get built, but I suspect we will see many other levels of innovation coming from this office. He is a younger architect who's doing lots of interesting work and has come up with a compelling financing scheme for middle-income housing in the UK.

MJ—This is a super delightful project.

PA—I'm a lover of clouds, I think clouds are beautiful. The only architectural project I can think of that successfully mimics the beauty of clouds was Diller and Scofidio's Blur Pavilion. I can't imagine how Kohn's proposal will even remotely evoke clouds. It's basically a roof made of plastic bulbs. Can you mimic nature and be faithful to it at the same time? This is an example of not being able to do so. I don't think trying to copy the environment is the way forward. I do recognize the fact that he has used recycled materials and that is something we should admire. In terms of an architectural statement, the building is actually not bad. It is interesting and has a social agenda to it. In terms of taking inspiration from clouds, I cannot see this as successful. Sorry, Mitch.

LH—I wouldn't read this project as biomimicry. A cloud is something the public can name and be familiar with. He tells us what his inspiration is, and I don't think he is trying to fool us into thinking that this looks like clouds. The idea of somehow completely discounting his inspiration or the idea that we can understand natural systems in an integrated way, I think that is throwing out the baby with the bathwater. I think that this project showcases a lot of research at the structural level, at the material level, all places where I think a lot of innovation starts to happen. If you're caught up in the name, Kohn tells us that it comes from the meteorologist Luke Howard, who developed the cloud classifications—cirrus, cumulus, stratus—in the early nineteenth century when he was walking in the area.

MJ—I think he is using some kind of poetic license and named it Cloud Pavilion. I don't think he literally means cloud. The issue of mimicry is a fascinating one, and any time you want to mimic nature you have got a problem. You want be able to understand nature and work within its confines and nudge it or reproduce it, at least for research or other products that are useful for people. We are not there yet. I think the idea that you just make it as a decorative or ornamental element is problematic, especially in this century. This building is fun and playful. It comes from the school of thinking that includes Renzo Piano's IBM Pavilion, which is clearly making some kind of commentary on Jean Prouve's tropical house, modularity, and lightweight assembly systems with some kind of connection to the local context. The performative aspect of ETFE foil pillows, they are something that can expand and contract with different heat gain issues or light and ventilation issues depending on how they're deployed. It is a wonderful, water-based, super lightweight material that really captures a lot of space without using a lot of embodied energy or needing a lot of structure to support it. Birds, sound, and rain easily penetrate it, but it is just a pavilion, so it is nice to use a really lightweight material.

LH—His proposal was to use the ETFE panels for solar gain and for energy generation. He also has a water collection strategy there, too, so if he can get to net-zero energy use and solve the water demand by collection and filtration, then two really basic needs are met. Moving toward this kind of systems integration is exactly what I think new buildings should strive for. One of the great backstories here is how the London Olympics and Legacy projects engaged the design community at so many different scales. Young architects with smaller offices were very much involved, and remain engaged with the work. The London Legacy project seems to have been as richly conceived as the London Olympics themselves. All of the relevant regulatory, professional, and environmental bodies got together to think about this. That shouldn't be the exception, but the rule that we expect from twenty-first-century cities. They need to think about meeting immediate needs, but also include propositions for what happens in five, ten, and fifty years down the line. We don't see this enough in terms of physical planning.

MJ—Part of the study should look at master plans for Olympics, world expositions, and all of these large instantaneous projects that require a lot of backing and money that have appeared and will appear in cities. We can do a kind of analysis of these projects. It is not a four-day or four-week event, but the forty years plus that we should be concerned with.

LH—There is so much said about Olympic failures, but there have been some successes, too. We could have an entire GDNYU event dedicated to large-scale sporting events in cities around the world—before and after. Maybe that's a way to get good tickets to the next World Cup. But, back to the project at hand, I hope the thinking behind the Cloud Pavilion is realized in one of their future projects.

DAVID KOHN ARCHITECTS is a London-based practice working across the fields of architecture and urbanism. David Kohn has been a diploma tutor at London Metropolitan University since 2003 and previously taught at the University of Bath. He is currently an external examiner at the University of Kingston. Kohn studied architecture at the University of Cambridge and at Columbia University.

DAVID KOHN ARCHITECTS GDNYU ELSEWHERE ENVISONED

DOXIADES+

THOMAS DOXIADIS

LANDSCAPES OF
COHABITATION ON
ANTIPAROS ISLAND,
Greece
The Aegean landscape is
the synthesis of natural
and cultural forms in
a dynamic process of
emergent self-organization.

LANDSCAPES OF COHABITATION | Island Villas Development | Antiparos, Greece

In order to retain the integrity of the ancient Cycladic landscape—currently threatened by a growing tourist economy—Doxiadis+ used the site's existing pezoules (agricultural terraces) and xerolithies (dry stone walls) as this project's skeletal structure. Roads follow either the perpendicular lines of the xerolithies or the parallel lines of the pezoules. New plantings, located close to the residential structures, provide opportunities for a tended garden, while, moving further away from the houses, there are fewer new plantings to allow for natural re-vegetation. The dynamic relationship between the structured environment and natural processes is foregrounded in this project.

Existing and Proposed: Pezoules and Xerolithies

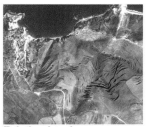

Existing Landscape

The Intervention Areas

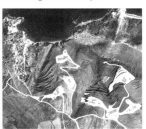

Year 0

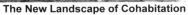

The New Landscape of Cohabitation

Year 6

DOXIADES+
Peder Anker, Louise Harpman, Mitchell Joachim

LH—The Landscapes of Cohabitation engages ecology and the long history of erosion and human incursion in a remote area, Antiparos, Greece. The landscape was scraped for a high-end luxury housing development. When the original project stalled and the new owner came to Doxiadis, he had to answer the question, how can we create a new "dynamic equilibrium" to preserve the dramatic beauty of the area, while acknowledging the tourist economy that funds it? He decided that he had to restore the landscape first. He shows a series of research diagrams, which guided his efforts to reseed and replant the site. He found the types of plants that could survive in this forbidding landscape with driving winds, minimal rainfall, and full sun. He thinks in landscape terms, twenty or thirty years, and was successful in reseeding the slope and undoing much of the damage. The criticism that I would give to a project like this is that the damage and the repair are both part of the same luxury consumption cycle, just with different clients and different architects.

MJ—Where credit is due is probably to the owner of the land, who found a savvy and sensitive office like Doxiadis to allow for this to happen, but the credit for its achievement certainly goes to the developer and then to the scientists who look at the project of ecological restoration. Those are the people that understand botany and soil quality, local climate, and precipitation, and that know how to bring this landscape back to some level of maturity. I think the idea that we are allowing a border for that natural event to restore the landscape is absolutely exceptional, the most exciting thing.

PA—What I think is fascinating here is that you have two professions meeting. There is the sensitive, ecologically-minded architect meeting landscape designers and restoration ecologists, who work on how to restore and design a landscape to make it better. There is, of course, an irony here. Many Greek islands are old ecological disasters. These disasters happened 2,500 years ago, when the islands were deforested. What you see today are islands that have never recovered from these terrible events.

LH—Are you saying that just getting back to groundcover is nothing compared to the full restoration that's needed? If this was an island based on agriculture and pasture-grazing for the last few hundred years, should we really be looking at it before human settlement?

PA—How far will they dig into the history of islands? What is the baseline for the original landscape in a historical site like this? The baseline here is the landscape as it was before development.

LH—Well, if you look at Lesbos, there is evidence of a subtropical forest there. But you'd have to go back about fifteen million years! This island in the Cyclades has a rich archaeological history, with natural features like caves, but more recently, it's been given over to tourism. Doxiadis mentions that finding evidence of a terraced landscape that retained water and reduced erosion informed the current design. They are trying to bring back that agricultural landscape, even if it was one of the more recent historical incursions on the land. I always wonder about the soil in places where there are so few trees. Is it because the soil and the geology cannot support trees?

PA—Some historical records indicate that these lands were once forested, and that the trees were cut down to make boats and to use as firewood. The records are vague, however.

MJ—Landscape architects have outright admitted that in their discipline they do not have a full understanding of the science. The School of Forestry folks at Yale specialize in all different levels of how to restore a landscape that was once agricultural. The idea of succession is extremely important, and we don't hold on to it strongly enough. We can discover new beauty as the system changes and then is reinstated only to change again.

LH—Pollinator populations are key here. Wind matters, too. After the architects and landscape architects leave, things will change.

MJ—We are still learning to find these things beautiful. Doxiadis has actually convinced the client and the community to appreciate a thousand-year system in process.

PA—Doxiadis has an architectural ethic of gentle architecture. It's like Malcolm Wells's projects of designing buildings underground so that one does not harm the landscape.

LH—But there's the money-scape, too. Can we just squint our eyes and ignore that this project is supported by a person making holiday villas for tourists? I think the larger argument is about conservation ecology. Where is the government in all this? Greece is probably not the best example right now, but is this a government job or a private individual's job? I do think we have to ask the question.

MJ—I would say economy is 100% at odds with ecology. There is all this talk about how the two can marry each other and maybe we'll get there. Nobody knows what a stable economy is.

PA—There is no such thing as a stable ecology, either. The idea of a harmony of nature is a myth.

LH—We think of a gentle, harmonious Mother Nature at our peril. But can we use this remote project as a way to talk about ecological restoration more generally? In the next ten years, I predict we will see a real movement toward net-zero buildings in cities, not just as demonstration projects, but as regulations. For example, Philadelphia has just required that any new building in the city center must manage its own storm-water runoff. This is a massive change for how buildings and landscapes are designed, literally starting from the ground up. Rich countries need to lead because we can.

PA—Where does change come from? Does it come from the rich imposing the system? Or does it come from the revolution below? People standing up and fighting? From an efficient Greek government?!

MJ—Change comes from fear.

LH—Are we so stuck in our capitalist mindset that we don't think governments can ever be effective? Not everybody is so skeptical of enlightened government policies. I think America is too disparate, with too many special interests, and too much governed by corporations and private money. Walmart should not gain credibility for promoting "sustainable practices" when they add solar panels to the roofs of their massive refrigeration facilities or boost their truck fleet's efficiency. This is first-order greenwashing—seeking a technological "fix" for what are really human behavioral problems.

MJ—At least Walmart has worked sustainability into its corporate culture. They're going to do it when it makes sense. They could have chosen to simply not recognize these issues. Instead they have made it a point to tell their investors, shareholders, and the public at large that they want to do something different.

DOXIADES+, founded by Thomas Doxiadis and based in Athens, Greece, offers architectural and landscape architectural services. The core team is complemented by a series of specialist collaborators including engineers, agronomists, GIS specialists, and land-use consultants according to the needs of each project. Doxiadis received an M. Arch. and an MLA from Harvard University.

DOXIADES+ GDNYU ELSEWHERE ENVISIONED

GROUNDLAB

**ALFREDO RAMIREZ, EVA CASTRO,
HOLGER KEHNE, EDUARDO RICO**

FLOWING GARDENS
International Horticultural Expo
in China envisions a harmonious
ensemble of water, vegetation,
circulation, and architecture.

FLOWING GARDENS | Xi'an International Horticultural Expo

The International Horticultural Expo in Xi'an, China, initiated the redevelopment of a large area between the airport and the ancient city center of Xi'an, home to the world-famous Terracotta Army, and a major economic center. This proposal includes three main sites—the Guangyun Entrance, which bridges the main road of the site; the Creativity Pavilion, located on the lakeshore; and the Greenhouse, which is reached by boat. The design for the landscape proposes a hybrid of both natural and artificial systems, brought together as a synergy of waterscapes, and uses various sustainable technologies. Rainwater is collected and channeled into the wetland areas, where reed beds clean and store it until it is dispersed throughout the garden and used for irrigation.

GROUNDLAB
Peder Anker, Louise Harpman, Mitchell Joachim

MJ—Groundlab is one of the leaders of landscape urbanism. They were part of making it into a discipline that combines urban design and landscape architecture. Formerly, what we were seeing is that there was a mixed topological mechanism between built or usable program and program that is embedded in the landscape. Yet, there are a lot of crossovers between urban design and landscape architecture. It is absolutely the intention of this team to exploit those crossovers in Xi'an. Their work absolutely recognizes that there should be a distortion of the figure in the ground. Architecture isn't an object plopped into a space, landscape isn't supposed to be separated from the object as far as how it is worked or solved as an active project. In this case, the point is that the two of them are blurred. They're distinguished by materiality and function. Here, materiality means something that is vegetable-based versus something that is stone or glass, but the forms are worked in together. I find this to be a really intriguing project.

LH—I want to foreground the conversation about landscape urbanism. This is not one or two disciplines, but a merging, a third. If one of our goals is to reformat architectural education or rethink the urban environment, then this is a really important development. Training may be discipline-specific, but we cannot make positive proposals if we limit ourselves to our unique disciplines. I think the Architectural Association is leading the way here.

PA—OK, sounds great, but look at the project: is that what's happening? First you get on the highway and drive, and then you go into a giant parking lot and park your car. Then you take your family or loved one and go hand in hand through this meandering garden. But the garden is separated and segmented; the walkways are fenced in, so you end up standing on the walkway looking at the flowers that have all been carefully planted by some hardworking gardeners you do not see. You admire the flowers and agree that they are beautiful, and then after meandering through the garden, you end up at a kind of cultural center and look at scenic views across a lake. This is all cool and a great experience, but tell me, where is the environmental sensitivity? And where can children play?

LH—You can be critical of the place we see now, but you've got to acknowledge that before this project took shape, this was a "non-space" between highways and the lakeside. It was a sandpit next to a polluted lake.

MJ—I think Groundlab has taken a junkspace site that was poisoned and set about remediating it. They have created several different planting zones, testing different plant species that can clean the soil and the embankments of the river. These kind of flowing points were designed to do a series of tests so that they could get to a restored landscape. The paths are networked into a series of zig-zags, so there are no straight lines to go from A to B. The paths really force people to be stuck in the middle of this winding, maze-like garden. I think it allows people to confront nature and think about it.

LH—Plasmastudio and Groundlab won this master-planning project for an international horticultural exposition, like the Olympics of Plants. The original master plan proposal shows ideas about bioremediation, irrigation ponds, reed beds, and constructed wetlands as integral parts of the site development. There was an idea that remediation had to be part of the design, but there was also an idea about cultural landscape, about getting visitors to connect with Guangyun Lake, which was a major port in the Tang dynasty (eighth century AD). But you're right: this is a massive development with paths, and pavilions, and transportation infrastructure. There are a series of active edges that we still see throughout the site and at the lake. This is clearly a destination for the event itself, but remains a cultural center after the expo. Their job was to design a big stitch—to bring the public to an open space or a park space. All of us in healthy cities know that parks are very important.

MJ—It has become an anchor that draws people to the area and creates interest, something spectacular to get people to transverse this ridiculous highway.

PA—The project is beautiful and the meandering garden looks fascinating. All that is good and it should be celebrated, but I am uneasy about this limited role of a park. Here, the park is a destination where you go to do your park thing, take a Sunday stroll, look at some flowers, go see a show. But when you are done, you return to whatever life you've been living. I question whether that is a sustainable way of thinking about the environment and the way we engage with it.

MJ—A lot of people don't think parks should be in the service of playing Frisbee or having a picnic, that parks are not for human recreation, but should be for protecting and restoring or keeping nature in some pristine state. We can have other open spaces where we can enjoy human recreational activity. Many others have stronger stances on what parks should be doing.

LH—I don't think this is a park where you would play Frisbee. It's a formal exhibition space, with big pavilions, not unlike a World's Fair. It has an entrance pavilion, a greenhouse, a "creativity pavilion." And, of course, parking lots. But, as you say, there are at least three layers that keep visitors from actually touching, getting near, or walking on the growing stuff—the path, the curb, and the series of lighting balloons that keep people in their place.

PA—So it has a sort of Marie Antoinette feel: "Nature is to be looked at, otherwise you get dirty."

LH—When Frederick Law Olmsted and Calvert Vaux proposed their design for Central Park, what they called the Greensward Plan, they called it "the lungs of the city." Xi'an is a city that definitely needed a couple of lungs. It is one of the emerging Chinese megalopolises, according to *The Economist*. Short of clearing out a whole part of the city to host this Expo, they put a forlorn site to pretty good use.

MJ—I'm remembering a moment in science fiction where, in the future, nature will become so incredibly valuable and important that it will be locked away by a series of protective barriers, signs, and boundary devices so that people can't get close to it or come in contact with it. If you do, by accident, it means certain death. I think it is in *Star Trek*, but there is an episode where a kid falls into a bunch of shrubs and the community says, "We're so sorry, but you have to report to the disintegration chamber."

PA—From *Star Trek*? Sounds like *Brave New World* to me.

GROUNDLAB, led by Alfredo Ramirez, Eva Castro, Holger Kehne, and Eduardo Rico is a landscape urbanism practice comprised of architects, urban designers, engineers, and landscape architects. Groundlab has offices in both London and Beijing.

GROUNDLAB GDNYU ELSEWHERE ENVISONED

HAUGEN/ZOHAR

MARIT JUSTINE HAUGEN, DAN ZOHAR

CAVE FOR KIDS
Constructed from 1.5 tons of
preindustrial waste, the space
is hollowed out by subtractive
manufacturing technology and
glued up by layering the material
to construct the milled cave.

CAVE FOR KIDS | Breidablikk Kindergarten | Trondheim, Norway

The domain of play brings out experimentation and creativity. It is a form of social interaction that insists upon collective rule-making, mutual dependence, imagination, laughter, and surprise. This structure is a 50-m^3 cave for kids, built on a limited budget using leftover material to form a secretive, spooky space. Constructed with 1.5 tons of preindustrial waste, the space is created by making pressed panels, subtracting certain sections, and layering and gluing the material to construct the milled cave. The primary material is open cell XP foam, collected from various production facilities in the automotive, apparel, and packaging industries. This clean, preindustrial waste material is leftover, collected from foam manufacturers throughout Europe, scrapped into small particles, and then thermally bonded to create panels. This process of reuse and upcycling avoids sending these scrap pieces to a landfill or an incineration facility.

HAUGEN/ZOHAR **GDNYU ELSEWHERE ENVISONED**

LH—The Cave for Kids has relevance and importance for lots of reasons: first, there is the scale, which is the scale of children; second, it is an environment created for play without rules; and third, it occupies public suburban space. But also it is a strategy; it is upcycling a type of plastic that is a waste product from industrial processes. This plastic would normally become plastic water bottles or synthetic timber planks, or go into a landfill. This project gives the plastic a second life to become another type of environment. We are so used to seeing piles of waste as evidence of our excessive levels of consumption, and our despoliation of the environment, but Haugen/Zohar shows us another way to think about waste.

PA—This is not just a proposal, either. This project was built. I think this project conveys links between past and future, culture and memory, between people, their stories and their surroundings. They are concerned with political, social, and environmental urgency confronting contemporary society, and this project focuses on a translation of such urgencies into spatial and material forms of action.

MJ—I think it is fantastic. It relates to a lot of contemporary work that points out how trash is a very important part of our waste stream. In fact, trash can be a nutrient and could be turned into architectural elements that are in service to the public or the needs of a city. This is a premiere example of something like that. If you can show children inside of something that was previously made from waste, it is kind of a symbol of safety, a return of purpose, and confidence that these kinds of methods are workable and safe. It also opens up the discourse on the amount of things that we consume. One questions where all our "things" end up. Being confronted with this is a great way to communicate the amount of waste we produce. In this sense, it is giving it a positive slant or message, not only telling us how much waste we produce, but also that there are ways to repurpose it.

LH—Do you think the value of this project is because of its pedagogical intention? Is this a so-called teachable moment?

MJ—Yes, they make it into a demonstration. The waste becomes the aesthetic, the core visual element. The material itself is something to be celebrated. The images here show just that. I don't think fifty years from now that this is what we will want; the waste will probably be less visible and be something that would be a background issue. But now, we need to accept that we produce far too much waste, and I think the communication and teaching elements are more important than ever.

PA—This project was realized on a very low budget. And that is surely inspiring! You can do something exceptional and beautiful with little money. I'm not sure if I agree that this project is only about education. I see it as creating a sense of wonder. Kids don't come to sit in this cave to learn about recycling, they come here to enjoy climbing and having fun. The structure has a value in itself.

LH—Agreed, but kids don't go to a playscape like this by themselves. They are bringing parents with them or caregivers. So even if the cave is scaled for children to enter, I think there is another level of engagement. The adults that bring the kids can interact with the cave as well. There are multiple constituencies for a project like this, not least the architecture magazines and books that publish it. Yes, the kids are going there to have fun and play, but the teachers or parents that go there have an experience, too. The designers didn't buy something new from a store, or something that you can order from a catalogue. They started at the level of research, well before the design. They found a way to insert themselves into the waste stream in a positive way; they took scraps that would ordinarily be shunted away or taken out of sight and made them into panels that could be reformed and reshaped. This project makes the materials very visible and very active.

MJ—There is an underlying point that I think the children can get to. There is a kind of archaeological strata of waste, layers of some kind: hints of what it used to be are found inside the walls, like fossils. Though kids may not be reading the cave spaces as waste, there is a kind of imaging and remembrance or some kind of connection to these as being whole objects and coming from other sources. I don't think kids can put it together completely, but at the same time a space like this will bring up a series of flashes and questions that will let them think about what made that beautiful play structure that they loved as kids. They can find a part of shoe inside the structure and realize later where that object came from. You do want to start with the children, but it is not a didactic in-your-face lesson. The kids are being exposed to this, and it will seep into them at a psychological level.

LH—There is more and more neurological research that shows the benefits of play—and not just for kids. The Robert Wood Johnson Foundation has been funding a project in the US called Playworks, and they are reporting all kinds of positive effects about how the mind opens up during play. Not always with rules and scripts. I think architecture needs to find ways to more fully engage our environments, and not always in scripted ways.

PA—The firm is young and they do lots of other kinds of projects, but there is a playful element in many of them. The Wooden Hammocks project in Trondheim fits larger kids—even adults—and creates another sense of play. Norwegian Wood is not just a song by the Beatles, of course.

LH—I love that project, too. They are very good about documenting the final project as well as the fabrication processes. Making both design and fabrication part of the story is what I think we all applaud about their work.

PA—But again, they could do more. I want them to be absolutely rigorous about their sourcing of the wood, their commitment to the environment, and the people who will maintain these beautiful play objects. In the photos, it's always a sunny day with smiling children. But what do they look like now? Who takes care of these things? Can the Cave for Kids be maintained, or will it eventually end up as garbage? I hope not.

HAUGEN/ZOHAR ARKITEKTER is an Oslo-based practice established by architect and artist Marit Justine Haugen and architect Dan Zohar. Their works aim to question relationships between architecture, function, and art by integrating the disciplines of landscape architecture and sculpture into their practice. Haugen and Zohar studied architecture at the Norwegian University of Science and Technology and Bezalel Academy of Arts and Design in Jerusalem. They graduated with an M.Arch. in 2001 and 2002.

HHF ARCHITECTS

**TILO HERLACH, SIMON HARTMANN,
SIMON FROMMENWILER**

RUTA DEL PEREGRINO
Client: Secretaria de
Turismo, Gobierno de
Jalisco
Location: State of Jalisco,
Mexico
Completion: 2010

RUTA DEL PEREGRINO | Jalisco, Mexico

Ruta del Peregrino is a path that runs from Ameca to Taipa de Allende in the state of Jalisco, near Guadelajara, Mexico. During Holy Week, approximately two million people make a pilgrimage along this route, which has been active since the seventeenth century. An international team of architects and designers was invited to design a series of shelters and lookout points along the way. The HHF lookout point is designed to be an additional loop in the pilgrims' path. The asymmetric arched openings provide access to a hall covered by the platform above. The inner walls are a shifted repetition of the primary façade in four tangential circles, creating apertures that link to both near and distant views. Between these circles, two staircases define a route up to the platform and back down again.

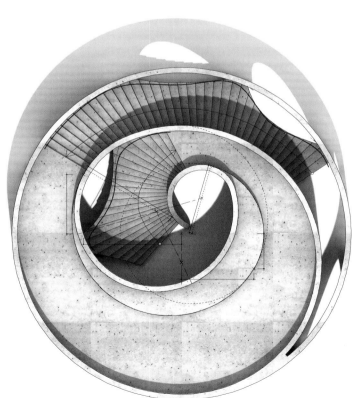

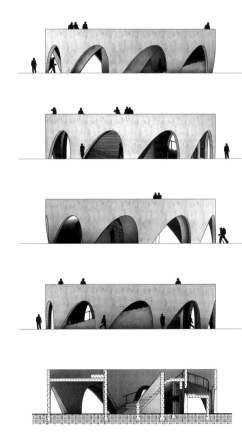

HHF ARCHITECTS
Peder Anker, Louise Harpman, Mitchell Joachim

LH—HHF are Swiss architects with a wide range of beautiful work at small and large scales. The Ruta del Peregrino is a pilgrimage route in the mountains of Jalisco, Mexico. There has been significant degradation to the landscape because of the pilgrimage, and the problem was how to guide the path, how to pace or structure the route, but also how to make some kind of shelter or refuge along the way. Ten architectural firms were commissioned to design pavilions or path markers, which could provide places for people to rest along the route. I think this project isn't necessarily an architecture project, but it is interesting because architects were asked to engage an existing human process that is in direct conflict with a number of natural processes. Landscape can't be trampled to that degree and just "recover" in a year's time.

MJ—What has pilgrimage to do with it?

LH—Well, we know that pilgrimages are important in many Catholic and Islamic countries, and yet the goal for this project, from an architectural point of view, was to somehow protect and enhance the landscape and to create an experience within the experience. I don't think HHF is focused in any way on landscape restoration here as much as trying to enhance the experience—as they say, trying to find a common language in architecture. I think this is an elegant structure, and, for its modest goals, a successful piece of architecture.

MJ—Simon Frommenwiler, the "F" of HHF, asked us why this project would be included in Global Design, especially since they are architects who were flown from Switzerland to build in Mexcio. This certainly brings up the problem of star-chitecture, importing name talent with no boundaries, no borders, and virtually no limits to budget. I think the office was critical of this, and yet they did it.

PA—There are two ways to measure or think about a building's environmental impact. On the one hand, there is the building's footprint, materials, architects traveling around the world on airplanes and overland by cars. From that point of view, this building is a disaster. On the other hand, this building helps people to connect with the environment. Maybe it will alter people's sensitivity so that they will be more aware of environmental issues and appreciate nature? It would be a sad world indeed if the only way to measure environmental success was our ecological footprint.

MJ—Since Stonehenge, we have had structures or monuments that provide a connection to stars or other landforms or the Earth itself, a correlation to nature and all of its mysterious components. I can't really comment about whether this enhances the religious experience or not, or if it meets the constraints of this particular religion. I definitely understand that architects for a very long time have been building elements to view a local landscape in ways that haven't been perceived before. I think this project is coming from that ancient pathway of trying to develop an understanding of the built world.

LH—My question is like yours, I think. Is this project trying to promote a global understanding of, say, humankind's place within the world? Ai Weiwei and Alejandro Aravena were invited to design pavilions, too. I appreciate that HHF are willing to call into question the idea of importing talent to boost a project's marketing appeal and visibility. The flight from Basel, Switzerland, to the western coast of Mexico is not a short hop. It is clearly quite remote. And photos by Iwan Baan don't come at zero cost.

MJ—This brings up questions about what global design is. Here you have an example of a group of architects very far away from their site, yet able to produce something incredible and effective in a place that's deeply remote from where they're located. The fact that they could pull it off is some kind of proof of the thesis that design is now globalized—and has been for quite some time. This is really a case in point. However, HHF as a firm still pays attention and tries to engage the local context, the client's religious needs, and the connection to the environment. But they are exporting their formal concepts and methodology a great distance at the expense of the planet, that is, for the cost of lots of jet fuel.

LH—I suppose it helps that they used local builders and building techniques. The walls are made from poured-in-place concrete, which they say was brought to the site using wheelbarrows. The formwork is all repetitive and reused. I think HHF is getting high formal value out of a humble material. Maybe this becomes a conversation about the vernacular, even though it seems as if that discussion has gone dormant. There is an idea that one could or should work within the vernacular tradition, especially along these remote pilgrimage routes. We saw that discourse emerge decades ago, with critical regionalism. But I see another aesthetic or mindset at work here, one that is about engaging a larger community, whether it is for observant Catholics or "archi-tourists." Does the pavilion promote refuge and prospect, but with a religious or cosmological overlay? Does it call into question a human being's cosmological insignificance?

PA—Perhaps, or at least I would hope so. This project reminds me of the Jantar Mantar architectural constructions used as astronomical and mathematical instruments built in Jaipur, India, in the 1700s. As an observation platform, the Ruta del Peregrino evokes the tension between rationalism and religious longing that I associate with the sublime tradition of European philosophy. It is a beautiful project.

LH—In other words, it is an attempt to locate humans relative to the larger natural celestial-terrestrial environment. I'm always fascinated to look at sixteenth- and seventeenth-century globes that were labeled celestial and terrestrial; they were made and sold as pairs. If you look in antique shops or go to museums, you see this twinning of our relationship to the Earth and the heavens, and the celestial globe is the same size as the terrestrial globe. The globes show a really curious conceit about humans and our need to control both land and sky. Maybe the mapmakers didn't know enough about astronomy to get the distances right, but when you see these kinds of globes right next to each other, something interesting about scale emerges. I think this project has that effect, too. This is a very small pavilion in a vast landscape. I appreciate that humility.

HHF ARCHITECTS was founded by Tilo Herlach, Simon Hartmann, and Simon Frommenwiler. HHF Architects' work ranges from large-scale construction to interior design, master planning, and urban design. The principals of HHF have been visiting professors at the University of Innsbruck. Simon Hartmann is a professor at the HTA in Fribourg, Switzerland. Simon Frommenwiler teaches as a visiting professor at the ENSA in Strasbourg.

J. MAYER H. STUDIO

JÜRGEN MAYER H., ANDRE SANTER, HANS SCHNEIDER

METROPOL PARASOL
These large, mushroom-like structures, built of polyurethane-coated timber, offer more than one possibility: an archaeological site, a farmers' market, and an elevated plaza.

METROPOL PARASOL | Seville, Spain

Metropol Parasol occupies a central plaza in the center of historic Seville. The large, mushroom-like structures, built of polyurethane-coated timber, create a defined zone and a highly visible destination in this emerging part of the city. The Parasol supports an archaeological museum, a farmers' market, and an elevated plaza. The site features numerous bars and restaurants underneath and inside the parasols, as well as a panoramic terrace on the top. Metropol Parasol creates a new landmark for Seville and defines a unique relationship between the historic and the contemporary city.

J. MAYER H. STUDIO **GDNYU ELSEWHERE ENVISONED**

J. MAYER H. STUDIO

Peder Anker, Louise Harpman, Mitchell Joachim

MJ—This project is a relief to the incredibly dense city that is surrounding it. Instead of a relief that would be a void or an open plain, some moment of escape or something that lets the sky in, this project does the opposite. It provides relief by inserting a maximal, monumental, sculptural neoliberal architectural statement with bars and shops and more on top of more. This place is now all about leisure. It is about having a cool drink with friends underneath this massive canopy. It is a ridiculously over-scaled kind of canopy compared to everything around it, but purposely so. It takes quite the opposite approach that everyone has ever thought of when it comes to making a public space in the city. This is going in the exact opposite direction, maybe as an experiment. They don't take away elements, but add more!

PA—Exciting, but sustainable?

MJ—The construction is perhaps the green part. These look like slotted elements built from a computer model that directed the cuts to make elements that could be pieced together and assembled into this seemingly complicated shape and thereby save an awful lot of material. This thing is porous; there is a lot of emptiness inside of that structure for its scale. I see some level of efficiency for a structure of this size. But still, it is an over-scaled umbrella for a place to have a beer.

LH—The Metropol Parasol is a large, very large, urban superstructure in the center of the medieval part of Seville, at the Plaza de la Encarnacion. I see this as an urban regeneration project to promote another type of street life and culture, but not one defined by the existing urban fabric, or the so-called "block and lot" street pattern that we typically see. In other places in Spain there are arcades, covered shopping malls. I see this as a kind of public space that is all about linking the informal networks of streets, alleys, and shop fronts to the new shaded plaza. It is an entertainment destination, to be sure, but it also hosts an archaeological museum and a farmers' market that were designed by other architects. But, for the most part, the big parasol is social. It privileges entertainment and tourism over other public uses, such as a school, a performing arts center, or a library.

PA—For me, this is an example of architects creating amusing sculptures in the city. Yet, Mayer seems to promote his project under a different category. Instead of saying that he is an artist or a sculptor, he says that he is doing something more, like creating a public space. I think he is sailing design under a false flag. I don't see this as being very green. It is beautiful or horrible depending on how you look at it aesthetically. I think in those terms it is actually gorgeous, but in terms of its social success it would be interesting to learn more about who is benefiting from it. I would not be surprised if luxury stores and high-end fashion would move in to the neighborhood, along with five-star hotels and jet set tourists. I wonder how the ladies are doing in their high heel shoes on those roof ramps. My guess is that the city was hoping for a Bilbao effect, right? And I don't see this building as particularly green. Please object, Louise.

LH—This site was used for many years as a surface parking lot. It was viewed as a dead zone between Seville's other urban nodes. During the construction, they found Roman ruins, so there's now an archaeology museum in the basement. It then does two things at the scale of urban design: it becomes an attractor, bringing people to the plaza with an expectation of something new, odd, provocative, and beautiful, where a new type of urbanism is taking shape. And, in the museum, it shows what is old and was previously unseen. But the space also provides what Richard Sennett and Stephen Duncombe might call Theatrum Mundi, a place that it is not completely programmed, where something unexpected could happen, like a performance.

PA—But what about the materials and the extreme construction? How do laminated timber and special UV glue and super-expensive computer-controlled cutting machines promote sustainability?

MJ—The computer can minimize waste from materials. And also prefigure the assembly process, saving time and money.

LH—From a technological point of view, this is pretty fantastic. I applaud the ambition and the intelligence that went into the design and construction. But, if we're looking for more here, maybe we can see this as a rehearsal for a new type of construction system. If they can build something this complicated, they can certainly build things less complicated. Is this a system that could be used for housing, emergency hospitals, schools, refugee camps? I actually think it might be too soon to judge the future of this. I want to offer that this project might be about skill-building and a rehearsal for a future architecture.

MJ—This is an office that prides itself on formal ingenuity. This will not go back to an orthogonal normative architecture; it is not what they do. And I can't see them marshaling all their expertise to make emergency shelters for refugees. On the other hand, there is always skill transfer when people leave offices like this. Those people take their skills with them to build the next platform of architectural innovation. I'm actually very pleased to see this project. I agree that it is definitely an urban attractor. Architecturally, it is an incredible feat and absolutely unique.

J. MAYER H. STUDIO, founded by Jürgen Mayer H. in Berlin, practices at the intersection of architecture, communication, and technology. The studio's work includes urban planning and installation projects. In January 2014, Andre Santer and Hans Schneider joined as partners in the firm. Jürgen Mayer H. has taught at Princeton University, University of the Arts Berlin, Harvard University, Kunsthochschule Berlin, the Architectural Association, Columbia University, and the University of Toronto. He studied at Stuttgart University, The Cooper Union, and Princeton University.

LAVA LABORATORY FOR VISIONARY ARCHITECTURE

CHRIS BOSSE, TOBIAS WALLISSER, ALEXANDER RIECK

MASDAR CITY CENTER
The carbon-neutral city features solar-powered sunflower umbrellas, creating the first perennial outdoor plaza in the Middle East.

GREEN CLIMATE FUND HQ
Curvilinear forms, natural light wells, roof top gardens, and the façade integrate regenerative energy production.

GREEN IS THE NEW BLACK | Masdar City Center

Lava's design for this carbon-neutral city features solar-powered sunflower umbrellas, creating the first perennial outdoor plaza in the Middle East. The umbrellas move with the sun, storing heat during the day and releasing it at night. These organic forms enhance the plaza and forecourt of the adjacent hotel.

GREEN CLIMATE FUND HEADQUARTERS | Bonn, Germany

Proposed as a net-zero energy building, the Green Climate Fund Headquarters in Bonn, Germany, is designed to meet the latest standards in building ecology, realizing Lava's vision for international climate protection. The building includes numerous natural light wells and roof gardens, while the surface of the façade integrates regenerative energy technologies.

LAVA GDNYU ELSEWHERE ENVISONED

LAVA
Peder Anker, Louise Harpman, Mitchell Joachim

LH—I like the fact that we are seeing projects at very different scales from LAVA, the Laboratory for Visionary Architecture. One is at the scale of urban street furniture, the solar umbrella; another is a proposal for a large corporate headquarters. They are also doing building retrofits and façade projects. I like that the office takes on work at so many different scales.

MJ—LAVA is a great example of the "new normal," where an office can work at multiple scales in multiple places with multiple building types and feel comfortable presenting them as such. This group is an authority on these vastly different kinds of projects. A firm that can shift from industrial design to historic preservation to retrofits and also design a new corporate headquarters is now in the general purview of the jack-of-all-trades that we call architects. I find LAVA to be a good example of a multi-scalar practice. It seems to work because they have a continuous theme, which is, "What can we possibly do to make this better for our relationship to the Earth?"

PA—I appreciate that. But to me, it looks like both the Masdar and the Green Climate Fund headquarters in Bonn are separated from the environment they are supposed to protect and engage. Masdar seems to be closed off from any relationship with the desert, and the Bonn building looks like a spaceship stranded on a foreign piece of land. Sorry, I don't see much of a relationship with the Earth going on here.

MJ—Perhaps they're not producing the most sophisticated schemes, but they're definitely sensitive to the existing conditions. The plaza project is working to animate a public space in Masdar, which is the middle of a desert, in the middle of nowhere, and you could easily say we really have no right to build anything there. When LAVA was given the opportunity to question the client and the larger picture they didn't quite do that, but they didn't fully capitulate either. They have produced an element that creates some idea of a better public space that can deal with the totally extreme climate.

LH—One of things I'm really impressed by is that this office thinks about product design, architecture, and landscape simultaneously. We already recognize landscape urbanism, but I don't know that we have a name for this other discipline that is emerging even in our own studios. Industrial design plus architecture plus landscape architecture plus urbanism, what is that?! We could just call it design. But if landscape urbanism has been able to corral new territory for itself, joining landscape architecture and urban design, how can architecture make more space for itself, too? Are we seeing architects going "smaller" by starting to design products, like industrial designers, and also "larger" by integrating their work with landscape architecture? Peder, how do we name this? And is this in any way "new"?

PA—It's called "Bauhaus." What's old is new again. Walter Gropius, the school's founder, designed tea sets, dinner plates, furniture, buildings, urban plans, and landscapes. That school did not operate with the divisions between, say, industrial design, architecture, urban studies, and landscape design that we often find in our current architecture schools. I think LAVA is quite representative of a current trend among designers, namely to move with ease between these different scales or "disciplines" of architecture. It's liberating.

LH—When I look at so many "solutions" to climate problems, I see PV panels mounted on roofs, rain barrels connected to downspouts, external aerobic reactors, or the ubiquitous wind farms. I call those "strap-on" solutions. With these examples, architecture becomes irrelevant if all it takes to be "green" is to add these mitigating elements.

PA—These autonomous technology-driven living machines have been dominating ecological design for so long. This is why I appreciate LAVA's work. They do not strap on technology. Technology drives the building, but it is the language of architecture and design that is at the forefront. The aesthetics and the language of architecture dominate. I like the fact that LAVA has hidden the green technologies. I mean, who wants to look at machinery dealing with our sewage? Yet that is exactly what ecological designers such as Bill McDonough have been doing. Not to mention John Todd's Living Machines.

LH—So how do we look at and evaluate design that is performance and technologically driven, but is not solely judged by those criteria for its success? I want to make sure we're clear about what we're promoting, that design must meet the shared goals of beauty, innovation, and performance, otherwise it fails. Does this have a new name?

PA—I'd still call it Bauhaus, because those were their priorities too: unifying science and design to create culture. But that is a historical name. So let's call it Global Design!

LAVA LABORATORY, a design and research practice founded by Chris Bosse, Tobias Wallisser, and Alexander Rieck, has offices in Sydney, Shanghai, Stuttgart, and Abu Dhabi. Chris Bosse is an Adjunct Professor at the University of Technology, Sydney. Tobias Wallisser is a Professor of Innovative Construction and Spatial Concepts and Vice-President at the State Academy of Fine Arts in Stuttgart. Wallisser received a postgraduate degree from Columbia University. Alexander Rieck works as a senior researcher at Fraunhofer Institute in Stuttgart. He studied architecture in Stuttgart and Phoenix.

MI5 ARQUITECTOS

MANUEL COLLADO ARPIA,
NACHO MARTIN ASUNCION

NEW YOUTH CENTER
Madrid
Future users of the center, as well
as technicians and politicians,
will be able to contribute their
concerns, their fantasies, and
their aesthetics to create a
contemporary "social monument."

NEW YOUTH CENTER | Rivas-Vaciamadrid, Spain

This project was conceived as an opportunity to make the "underground" visible—a manifestation of the vitality of youth groups throughout Madrid's suburbs. The colorful, provocatively shaped project aspires to become a place to support teen communication and activities, by incorporating the needs and aspirations of young people. These program centers are conceived as points of meeting and exchange for Rivas's emerging communities, creating contemporary "social monuments."

TERUEL-ZILLA! | Underground Leisure Lair and Public Space | Teruel, Spain

An influx of theme parks in Dinópolis has created a fantasy landscape against which this new building was conceived. mi5 imagines that this new underground space allows visitors to connect to the archaeology of the place and the origins of the province. This public space and leisure center features a buried depiction of Godzilla, a recognizable cross-cultural pop reference. The structure emerges from the ground and produces a new urban topography. Visitors ramp down into the building to access meeting spaces, entertainment zones, music clubs, and sport halls.

mi5 ARQUITECTOS **GDNYU ELSEWHERE ENVISONED**

NEW YOUTH CENTER
Madrid
The end result of this
process will be a public
structure with a punk
spirit, intensely burdened
with content. These
programmatic centers are
thus conceived as points
of meeting and exchange
for Rivas's emerging
communities.

mi5 ARQUITECTOS **GDNYU ELSEWHERE ENVISONED**

LH—This project in Rivas, a suburb of Madrid, focuses on teenagers as a client group. In libraries, we know that teens want to distance themselves from little kids, but they don't yet connect to the adult world. The idea of this youth center tries to make a space for teens to call their own, to connect to the "underground" aesthetic.

MJ—To some extant, the architects worked assiduously with neighborhood kids to engage them in the pragmatic process. They endeavored to find out, where do they want to go? Where do they congregate? What kinds of spaces felt right to them?

LH—A place like this looks like it erupted from the plaza, that it is radical and not at all a part of normative architectural design. It is designed to be an attractor, with its bright colors and industrial materials, and so I feel like this is part of the social dimension of sustainability. How do we design for inclusion? How do we understand clientele? How do we start to subdivide or fine-tune the social dynamics that occur with different groups of people over time? The strategy to make this space evident from above ground, but also to create a discovery space underneath the ground, really speaks to me about a type of social experiment. This is a space that looks interesting. It's a place to explore.

MJ—It has acute, angular windows and detailing, a truncated star-shaped window pattern system, and is surrounded by glazed orange poles that trace facets of the geometry and in other cases fly off the building. All the colors are obscenely clashing; it is loud and dynamic. It appears like a wicked fun palace for teens, and a fun place for me personally! It's a flamboyant entertainment center, and there is clearly room for theaters and quieter spaces below ground that don't need access to daylight. It has a great punk attitude. I think that is the design intention, to capture that anti-establishment spirit. I can appreciate this building for what it is on its own terms. I don't see any clear links to sustainability. Their mission of catering to groups of low-income people to have access to quality buildings is praiseworthy. But I think that it pushes the term to call the work sustainable. At this point, sustainability is such a broad expression. The challenge is to find a use of it that encompasses specific intentions when it comes to our relationship with the environment.

PA—I feel that young teens do need some sort of access to the natural environment and species other than humans when they go to enjoy their free time and each other. Why is the teen community limited to other teens alone? Why can't they play and make love in the grass? And enjoy other species and animals? Why is this environment stripped of everything natural except the sky and the view?

LH—Do you think this is too reductive, that it's all hardscape? That it has edited out any change, that the building recognizes no seasonal change except for the weather?

PA—From a bird's point of view, this is a terrible place to come. Why does architecture only make structures for humans?

LH—It's a good point. I think dogs and birds and butterflies, not to mention trees, give dimension to cities. In dense urban environments, maybe the zoning needs to change to require this thinking. The twenty-first-century city needs to be a place for people as well as non-human inhabitants.

PA—It is well known that troubled kids are calmed by interactions with animals.

LH—Perhaps, but we have also seen kids torture animals!

PA—All too true. If I had grown up without getting to know animals, I might just have done that as well on my first encounter. . . My point is, why purposely exclude or fail to engage the natural world when building a teen center?

MJ—Yes, even a garden, a swimming pool, a water collector, something beyond the radical punkness of the building that the teens could connect with would be cool, but this was probably not in the mission statement.

PA—So we need a new mission statement then.

LH—mi5 are badass architects. They have a mission statement. It involves science fiction, crashed meteorites, buried creatures, mutant flowers, and space invaders. They are what my teenage self would have loved! They design using comic book style graphics, and really work to connect to youth culture. The project in Teruel, Spain, a partially submerged leisure center, replaces a tired "market hall" in one of the city's central squares. The project, called Teruel-zilla, creates a really engaging set of spaces. The ground plane is warped and folded to create places for viewing, sitting, and strolling on the outside. At the same time, the ground plane presses down to form a ramp to enter the building, which houses a number of entertainment spaces, a climbing wall, sport court, tourist information center, and a bar and restaurant. And it's shiny and red! All the way down!

PA—I think my Norwegian upbringing as a teen hiking in the woods keeps me from appreciating these intense lilac and orange, hard-edged varnished metal surfaces. I will work on it. On the other hand, I like their underground public leisure space in Teruel. Here there seems to be a balance of form and space, of humans and trees, resulting in an inviting place. Besides the trees, how green is it?

MJ—It's an urban park that is built mostly underground. Fire red surfaces and angled lights break up the monotonous big boxy-ness of the project. The mounds of stairs and ramps on the project surface signal to the below grade programs. It's got an invigorating edgy style, yet is done with rigor and parsimony.

PA—I agree. It's a good project. Though, as the saying goes, "The proof of the pudding is in the eating!" The success of architecture for social change cannot be measured by us, but by its users.

mi5 ARQUITECTOS GDNYU ELSEWHERE ENVISONED

mi5 ARQUITECTOS, founded by Manuel Collado Arpia and Nacho Martin Asuncion, is based in London and Madrid. They have taught at various institutions including UAH Madrid, UA Alicante, and UCJC Madrid, the Architectural Association Summer School, and IED Madrid. Currently they are Architectural Association Int. 11 Unit Masters.

MMW ARCHITECTS

MAGNE MAGLER WIGGEN

EQUATOR
Openness, availability, and
low energy consumption
are the key design
elements of the Embassy
at the Equator.

FHILTEX
Fully self-sufficient 60m²
house contains everything
you need for modern life.

EQUATOR

Openness and low energy consumption are the key design elements of the Norwegian Embassy at the Equator. The embassy is designed to be a flexible tool for all Norwegian interests abroad and can be located in any harbor. The floating circular steel construction is connected to land by two docking arms, which pump cold seawater to the top of the structure. A porous exterior skin keeps the cool seawater in constant contact with the façade. When the sun shines on the seawater-soaked façade, the water evaporates, thereby removing heat from the steel construction. This process chills the inside of the embassy, drawing in fresh, cool breezes as a result of the temperature shift.

FHILTEX

This 60m² house is fully self-sufficient—made by upcycling two freight containers—and is fitted with gas and solar panels, as well its own water recycling system. With a roof terrace and three balconies, the house offers 360-degree views and allows for direct sunlight throughout the day. Each component can be dismounted and shipped by boat, train, or car to be reconstructed anywhere in the world. With four foundation points and a hinged staircase, the house can be adapted to any terrain. Fhiltex now stands as an entrance marker on the island of Sukkerbiten in Oslo, an area known for fishing, leisure, and sports.

HOUSE

HOUSE is a self-sufficient dwelling for living on water. HOUSE is conceived as a worldwide home—a new way of living where freedom of movement and sustainability without borders become possible. Infrastructural and geographical independence is the goal of this project: HOUSE can cross the Pacific or sail along the riverways of Europe or navigate the ports of Africa. HOUSE owners can reach almost any destination by shoreline, river, or canal. Generating its own energy and recycling its own water, HOUSE not only participates in the creation of a clean and better world, it also proposes a means of liberation from any national, governmental, or private infrastructure.

HOUSE
Self-sufficient dwelling for use on water. It adapts to its environment to minimize energy consumption and is designed to be a plus-energy home. HOUSE changes colors to absorb and reflect solar energy.

MMW ARCHITECTS **GDNYU ELSEWHERE ENVISONED**

PA—Nomads fascinate MMW. Indeed, they see us all as nomads, constantly traveling in different ways. These three buildings are all traveling buildings. The first one, The Equator, is a suggestion for an embassy for a tropical region that can travel depending on the political situation. If having an embassy in that country is not politically viable, you can just tow the building to a different site or country. It is round and shaped like a beer can, the idea being that when you put a beer can in the water and then back in the sun it will cool. In this case, they spray water on the top of the building, which cools it when the sun evaporates the water in a very efficient way. The second project, Fhiltex, is similar to the zeroHouse project, since it uses modules, in this case shipping containers, one large and one small. You can ship these two containers and reassemble the building anywhere. It has an enclosed bathroom system in the back where, ideally, you recirculate the water. The owner of the Fhiltex can just take it with him or her when traveling from one job to another. That is actually how it has worked. It has been traveling and was once a medical office, a cottage, a showroom in Oslo, and an apartment. The third project is a closed ecosystem concept traveling on the water. Everything is recycled within the boat, and the only thing required is clean water and energy from solar panels. The idea is that you travel in your career from job to job, and the house travels with you. One problem with this conception is that you are detached from society because you travel all the time with your nomadic family. The building is environmentally accountable and tries to achieve a zero footprint, but by doing so it is detached from nature, which it is trying to save.

LH—I'm not sure I agree that Fhiltex is sealed off from the very environment it is trying to preserve. If we actually limit human habitation to a small footprint, and if the energy and space needs for a family of four can be met in this one packet, isn't that another kind of environmental stewardship? If we can have minimal dwellings that solve the basic human needs for shelter, potable water, and domestic waste management, all within a minimal envelope, then that protects open space and minimizes dependence on fossil fuels. That to me is the larger argument. How do we engage the existenz minimum discourse in the twenty-first century? Fhiltex is a great proof of concept. The equatorial embassy project is a bit frivolous, but surely amusing. I love the idea that the law of the sea or low earth orbit would be hashed out in their floating Equator project. Moreover, the houseboat project is enchanting, but maybe that's because I have already drunk the Kool-Aid. I want these kind of sci-fi projects that can get people thinking about other ways of living, with fewer resources. But maybe this is not the house that gets much buy-in. For me, the idea of traveling with the house is actually a problem, and foregrounds the global/local conundrum. I think that this project makes us into perpetual tourists and erodes any chance to learn about local cultures and traditions. If we live in Morocco, for example, we see perforated walls, we come to understand the directionality of winds, and we make use of passive cooling. If those winds pass over a pool of water, then we would get even more cooling. We wouldn't have to "hose down" the outside of the building to promote evaporative cooling like the MMW house.

MJ—I think these are prodigious concepts. They're in the same vein as Norman Bel Geddes or Raymond Loewy, a kind of blurry border between architecture and industrial design or vehicle/transport as in this case boats, making spaces for people to live and work in. I think that there shouldn't be boundaries between those disciplines. I'm certain this view would upset a few industrial designers who believe they're responsible for producing everything from telephones to chairs. Professionals think boat design belongs to the domain of naval architecture or transportation engineering, but that just doesn't seem to be true. This is an architect taking on mobility for dwelling spaces. However, these only work to a point, meaning that I'm sure every single one of these floating projects, no matter which are inhabited, also corresponds to dwellings on the land. It makes it acceptable to have this incredible ability to leave your space, to become a nomad, and transverse the seas as one goes someplace else. I have lived on houseboats, and I know many people that do so. There is a great opportunity to be a part of the collective in an urban setting while still having the capacity to take your home elsewhere. That is a tangible ability for freedom that I think so many of us yearn for. It is much harder and more difficult to live on a boat. As an owner, you understand all of the inputs and outputs; you've got to really rig the system since it becomes a microworld. You could live on a boat with a much smaller footprint than on land. I think confronting the consequence of keeping yourself alive or comfortable on a boat is a really good connection to the limited resources we have.

LH—I think that the boat as an analogy might be right. If zeroHouse and Fhiltex both try to show how daily needs can be solved with minimal external inputs and maximal internal reuse and repurposing, then it is a great story to tell. Twenty-first-century cities should build projects like these to expand affordable housing choices. This could be the beginning of a more robust, more energy-efficient version of the micro-units that we are beginning to see in cities such as San Francisco, Seattle, and New York. If you could opt-in on an annual basis to a net-zero living environment, I think that the results would be utterly transformative. Cities should support the development of this type of experimental housing. Yes, it's social engineering, too. But that's part of the experiment.

PA—But if they're experimental, does that mean they are just on a "trial basis?"

LH—Paul Rudolph, the late architect and former dean of the Yale School of Architecture, built graduate student housing in New Haven that looked a lot like Fhiltex. It was made from modular containers, stacked up, at 90-degree angles to one another, and was called "Oriental Gardens." It was built quickly, occupied for a time, and then demolished—without a trace. Our knowledge of this project is in photographs, technical drawings, and tales. I think we need to make decisions that will create 100-year buildings, not thirty-year buildings.

MMW ARCHITECTS, founded by Magne Magler Wiggen, is located in Oslo, Norway, and works in the areas of architecture, planning, building conservation, stage design, and furniture design. Wiggen received an M.Arch. degree from The Oslo School of Architecture and Design in 1992.

MMW ARCHITECTS GDNYU ELSEWHERE ENVISONED

ORDINARY

MAGNUS LARSSON, ALEX KAISER

CRYSTAL CITY
Buildings made from
harvested materials that
harness processes such as
solidification, sedimentation,
lithification, melting, and
freezing provide the only
unquestionably sustainable
starting point for the creation
of our future built environment.

INVINCIBLE DUNE CITY

In his 1972 novel *Le citta invisibili* (*Invisible Cities*, 1974), Italo Calvino tells the story of the Venetian explorer Marco Polo describing fifty-five cities to the emperor Kublai Khan. It is a tale of tales, stories about storytelling, ideas of cities turned into fanciful theories, and words turned into fabulous cities. For the latest installment of the Dune project, Ordinary uses a Calvinian framework to investigate an urbanism that dares to go beyond biomimicry and toward a harnessing of natural processes in the construction of our future cities—arguments that point toward intelligent and innovative urban concepts seeking to advance discussion about the pivotal role that the city plays in the future of our planet. This urban-scale experiment is an attempt to show a nodal point within a habitable wall network—a solidification of existing sand dunes in the Sahara desert constructed through microbial precipitation. The simultaneous creation of a new material paradigm and a new architectural response to the disastrous natural phenomenon of desertification represents the potential for an invincible, rather than invisible, city of the future.

CRYSTAL CITY

Crystal City investigates how lightweight assemblies dipped in supersaturated solutions can support crystal growth to create structural networks and new construction systems. Ordinary believes that buildings made from harvested materials that harness biological and physical processes such as solidification, sedimentation, lithification, melting, and freezing can provide a new starting point for the creation of new building systems and materials that are truly renewable.

ORDINARY GDNYU ELSEWHERE ENVISONED

INVINCIBLE DUNE CITY
Urban-scale experiment
of solidification of existing
sand dunes in the Sahara
desert constructed through
microbial precipitation.

ORDINARY GDNYU ELSEWHERE ENVISONED

MJ—Dune City is a project that is constantly evolving as the architects understand and gain a level of maturity with the techniques that they have, more or less, invented. The idea is to inject sand with bacteria that allows it to congeal or form a heavier sediment-like substance rather quickly, and then to stage it so that they produce this new substance in an existing desert environment, to stop it from taking over more fertile territory. In earlier iterations of the project, there were images of these beautiful carved dune structures that looked like waves made of rock coming from sand. It didn't seem like it would be possible to inhabit these structures. The average person could probably not connect to those being dwelling spaces. In the current version, they have produced a much more regularized modular housing proposal. It is an idea or concept for how synthetic biology can become a mechanism for creating permanent spaces. This proposal is certainly from the vantage point of people and is a more anthropocentric view of how to work with nature, which privileges human dwelling.

PA—One would think a desert also has its own ecosystem that needs to be respected as much as a forested ecosystem. I am not sure that is happening here.

LH—I connect to this project more now that it's in its second iteration, "Dunescape 2.0." The research came from Larsson's work at the Architectural Association. He looked at sub-Saharan Africa, and connected to mapping that showed the expansion of the desert over the last fifty years. The reason this "desertification" is happening is because humans have cut down the trees and the branches and shrubs that grow there to use for firewood or to create temporary shelters. Larsson is arguing that we as humans need to reverse our negative impacts on the environment. He is not just saying, "let the wind blow," but is advocating for more, not less, human involvement, saying that humans created this problem so we need to be the ones solving it. His bacterial injections are meant to speed up calcification and create a firm edge to the desert. His TED talk and the graphics are all very elegant, but I can't get away from seeing this as a type of biological warfare, and I'm uneasy about this aspect of the project. If the desert were going to make bricks and blocks itself, it would have done so already. This is totally external—a blend of biology and chemistry. I can't help but think of Bernard Rudofsky and his seminal *Architecture without Architects*. Maybe Larsson is looking at this, too, because the formal properties start to look like Morocco and other desert architectures that we have seen. I'm not sure where Larsson and Kaiser locate themselves: are they proposing a biological Maginot Line?

MJ—Are you saying they could do this same kind of project with conventional methods that are already available in climates and cultures that have been building this way for a long time?

LH—I am saying that Rudofsky and others published this research in 1964, but it has been lost. As humans, I think we have these cycles of learning and forgetting. One generation learns something, the next one doesn't, and the one after that thinks it's all new. So these ideas seem "new" to people at the end of each cycle. If you look back at the research, it is there.

PA—Naturally, whenever somebody makes the claim that it is important to understand and teach history, especially the history of architecture, I get excited. Seen historically, what architects really do is just turning the soil. Having said that, I love the project, who doesn't? Yet I am not sure this thing is doable. I don't share your fear that this is biowarfare. When you inject these bacteria, unless you feed them, they will die and will not spread as a wildfire in the desert. The problem is that I have yet to see Larsson and Kaiser and their team build these walls on a large scale. Their proposal seems to be based on very small-scale experiments. Also, here is this Swedish guy coming with a magic silver bullet to Sahara. I can't help but think that that's socio-politically a bit naïve. Environmental IKEA for the world's deserts?

LH—That's not quite fair! I think what is most important is that these ideas become open source. I'm not worried that Larsson is a Swedish guy coming from a British architecture school. Actually I think that is the positive side of this, the fact that ideas circulate and flow and that we can now begin to solve problems in places far away from the accidental place of our birth. That's a positive position to take with Global Design.

MJ—If they were importing some kind of obvious Swedish design that would be egregious. I firmly believe that everything has become globalized, especially ideas, and that we'll see more and more of that. These architects are thinking big. It is wonderful, it stretches our minds and imagination, it questions the possible, it is absolutely necessary to see design as that kind of a tool. What it shows, and where it differs from Rudofsky and *Architecture without Architects*, is that the labor is supposed to be removed. In this case, biological activity interacting with sand will create the space. Humans build the forms or the scaffolding, but all of the rest is done through an organic process that has been accelerated and specifically tuned to the desert conditions. I think this is a project that represents new exploration into how we can use the tools of the Earth for creating architecture and design. It is much different than the steel, glass, and concrete stuff we've had for years.

LH—This definitely links to Rachel Armstrong; it is an idea about accelerating natural processes and guiding them rather than designing them. Maybe this is another type of architecture, a guided architecture, rather than one that is hyper-specific and scripted.

MJ—In architecture we guide other humans to put bricks in place, but this is architects guiding other organisms or creatures to produce forms. If this was a genetically modified material reproduced at this scale, I'd be much more concerned; that would be a different story.

LH—That was my point earlier. There is a relationship to a kind of bio-warfare or terrorism that we need to keep in mind here. We need to think about what we are doing, what we are potentially saving, and how it might create a whole lot of unforeseen effects.

PA—The Crystal City is a more recent experiment from Ordinary. Here they use chemistry to "grow" their architecture. They make literal scaffolding and then dip the elements in a mixture, after which a "matrix" of crystals fills in the structural elements. They are showing this at a small scale, but the demonstration is very clear. This is not only beautiful but radical. They are engaging material science at the laboratory level.

ORDINARY LTD., founded by Magnus Larsson and Alex Kaiser, is a London-based design studio. Ordinary explores strategies for how material research might combine with radically speculative experimentation to push architecture past mere sustainability.

OSA OFFICE FOR SUBVERSIVE ARCHITECTURE

ULRICH BECKEFELD, BRITTA EIERMANN, KARSTEN HUNECK, OLIVER LANGBEIN, ANJA OHLIGER, ANKE STRITTMATTER, BERND TRÜMPLER, SEBASTIAN APPL

KUNSTHÜLLE
Liverpool
Playful, temporary intervention which draws on the industrial hertitage of the buildings and is designed to act as a beacon to draw people to the surrounding area.

THE BLADE FACTORY | Liverpool Biennale for Contemporary Art | Liverpool, England

The Blade Factory is a temporary installation designed for Greenland Street, a major new venue for contemporary art in Liverpool. The rooftop structure is an experimental space for lectures, performances, and events. It merges with the existing factory at the site, incorporating the staircase and rooftop, and extending out over the public façade of the building. The building's translucent skin has two layers: an outer white layer, which protects the space from the weather; and an inner red layer, which adds thermal and noise protection. The building's translucent skin creates a visual link between the arts center and the rest of the city, while also offering views of the River Mersey and Liverpool.

ACCUMULATOR | Public Art Intervention | Leeds, England

This design emphasizes the building's landmark status and its previous use by transforming the former swimming pool into a virtual water collector, thereby opening discussion about resources and sustainability in the face of climate change. Leeds International Swimming Pool, which was constructed from 1965 to 1967, is emblematic of the city during the 1960's, and OSA's design highlights this cultural significance. This much-loved community building was scheduled to be demolished because of a lack of energy efficiency and the need for extensive repairs. This installation became a tribute to the cultural and historical significance of the site, and allowed people a final opportunity to appreciate the site and exchange memories about their experiences.

OSA GDNYU ELSEWHERE ENVISONED

THE ACCUMULATOR
The installation work transforms the former swimming pool into a virtual water collector and raises questions about resources and sustainability based on current discussions on climate change. However, at the same time it symbolizes the emotional charge of an important public space in the city.

OSA **GDNYU ELSEWHERE ENVISONED**

OSA OFFICE FOR SUBVERSIVE ARCHITECTURE

Peder Anker, Louise Harpman, Mitchell Joachim

MJ—The Office of Subversive Architecture (OSA) works in different autonomous cells throughout Europe. It is an architecture firm trying to inject drama or questions into the field of architecture and making it an operation for the public to confront. They work to make architecture relevant. Their projects do this in all kinds of curious and playful ways and investigations.

LH—The Accumulator project forces us to confront dereliction and waste. The building was a swimming pool slated for demolition and was said to have "no value." OSA came in and said that it in fact had a tremendous value—as a public space, a theater space, a space that can be used to engage the community. By creating this light-filled cone inside the space—using fabric and simple rigging—they made the old swimming pool into a theatrical space. They created a space where people could "say good-bye" to a much-loved place. I think they bring incredible value through their collective vision and their installation practice. This installation is an operation that is critical of the "wrecking ball" mentality. They question the logic of "out with the old, in with the new."

MJ—That's true. They use very simple and cheap methods of building to underscore particular issues, and they do it fast. It is successful.

LH—This pool was built in the 1960s, so it was hardly old. The community did go forward with the recommendation of local authorities to demolish the building, but OSA made an event of that loss, like an extended funeral for the building.

PA—It reminds me of Christo's Reichstag project, wrapping the building in order to unwrap it, a way of giving an old building new meaning and celebrating it as something new.

LH—The symbolic aspect of architecture is really important, which this project highlights. Symbolism has meaning and value for a community and even for outsiders like us.

PA—Exactly. The Reichstag was a complicated building with a long, problematic history, so it was wrapped up as new and presented to the public as a present. The unwrapping of it turns it into a new building with new possibilities, closing its history and opening its future. The same thing might happen here. You say good-bye to a building, but it opens the future of the site. But help me, how green is it really?

MJ—It is totally low impact in terms of materials.

LH—Green is process, too. OSA brought a process to engage this community and make them advocates for their own future, I think part of the green mission is to create an engaged citizenry. Architects are agents, agitators, and advocates. Social justice is definitely part of the sustainability discussion. If we support community-based education about the built environment, then I'm all for it.

PA—Remember the neo-avant-garde of the late 1960s? The British Archigram group, or the Austrian Hans Hollein's slogan "Everything is architecture." The same type of playfulness in engaging the public in a discussion of what design is and for whom it is made. OSA is less ideological, of course, though no less subversive.

MJ—Perhaps they represent a renewed appreciation for that period. But they are also getting out and talking to people and making things happen in unexpected ways. They're artists and architects.

PA—Their project inhabiting the roof of the Blade Factory in Liverpool is a case in point. It's a playful, temporary intervention which draws on the industrial heritage of the buildings and is designed to act as a beacon to draw people to the surrounding area. The structure also maximizes the potential of the site and has outstanding views of the Mersey and the city center. To me, it questions the relationship between art and architecture.

LH—I really like that OSA are nimble. They do projects that are sometimes completely small but have a huge impact. Before the London Olympics, for example, they designed and built Point of View, a small wooden staircase that attached to the three-meter high construction enclosure around the Olympic Park. The Olympic Authority was insistent about keeping the public away from the area, with no way to see the amazing transformation taking shape inside. The construction fence was bright blue, and the guards repainted it every day to mask the graffiti from frustrated local residents. OSA designed and painted their platform exactly the same color to "look like" it was supposed to be there. I think it survived almost three days before the authorities knew it was, how do we say, unofficial.

MJ—This is their work. They are stealth and they will show up when they need to. *Blueprint* magazine commissioned OSA for the Point of View project, but they are activists and artists. They have representatives in at least eight cities in Europe. Their work is radical and unexpected.

OSA is a collective of practitioners with similar ideas about architecture and public space. Their consistent aim has been to develop an approach to reinterpret architecture in urban centers. Their projects strive to cross the boundaries between art and architecture, varying from minimal or movable installations to the construction of permanent buildings. They work throughout Europe in cities including London, Berlin, Munich, Frankfurt, Graz, Darmstadt, and Vienna.

OSA GDNYU ELSEWHERE ENVISONED

RAUMLABOR BERLIN

ANDREA HOFMANN, AXEL TIMM, BENJAMIN FOERSTER-BALDENIUS, CHRISTOF MAYER, FLORIAN STIRNEMANN, FRANCESCO APUZZO, FRAUKE GERSTENBERG, JAN LIESEGANG, MARKUS BADER, MATTHIAS RICK

OPEN HOUSE
This vertical village is initiating a process between international and local artists as well as the citizens of the open city, to discuss issues of community against the background of the rapid urbanredevelopments in Anyang, South Korea.

OPEN HOUSE | Anyang, South Korea

Open House is a vertical village and a social sculpture. Raumlabor was asked to design, build, and program the center of the city of Anyang with the purpose of initiating collaboration between international and local artists as well as the citizens of the city. A goal of this project was to facilitate discussion about community issues against the background of rapid urban redevelopments in Anyang, South Korea. Through the creation of Open House, Raumlabor sought to construct a unique form of collective space. The diverse programming of the rooms of Open House combines individual needs and desires with functions for public use: a kiosk, a bar, a business center, a children's home, a recycling workshop, exhibition rooms, and a tea house. A greenhouse is combined with a community farm where vegetables are planted and rabbits are raised. Open House is a new form of collective space for the public activities of its primary users—the local residents. Open House is both temporary and permanent—a self-learning laboratory undergoing continuous renewal and transformation.

RAUMLABOR BERLIN
Peder Anker, Louise Harpman, Mitchell Joachim

LH—I first learned of these guys from their World's Fair project at the old Templehof air field. In that project, The World is Not Fair, Raumlabor curated a set of artist installations and pavilions. To me, it became the anti-Parc de la Villette. They didn't treat the pavilions as all of a piece or part of a formal logic. Raumlabor worked with architects and artists and members of the community to bring a wide range of programming to activate this disused site. The actual World's Fairs were part of a corporate, nation-building agenda. But their work is much more grassroots, curated, and local. They made it a priority to reuse the existing infrastructure or partial buildings. This strategy definitely can be seen in the Open House project, too.

MJ—I think these folks do terrific work. They are definitely in the category of action architects, and there is a gargantuan movement that celebrates this ultra-low-key agnostic form-making. It is as if they refuse to make visual or aesthetic moves or anything with architectural strength. They are the opposite of heavy-handed. It is completely light in touch, gentle to the surroundings, and their whole point is to give the viewer and the visitors a sense of immediacy, place, and recognition that they are not providing answers, but creating questions. I think they are very evocative and provocative in the attitude that they take.

PA—To me there is a Cold-War ring to their "the world is not fair" exhibition and its anti-project mode of reasoning. I do appreciate semi-open spaces for the community to do creative projects. And Raumlabor seems to to engage the community in a non-authoritarian way. Yet, why do we get this "us versus them" rhetoric? What they are doing seems to me very typical for Berlin. Their work is really hyper-local, and it doesn't change the larger regulatory framework at all.

LH—I like that Raumlabor suggests a counter-narrative for architecture. I also like that they think of architecture as a type of performance art. The conception, the scavenging, and the building are all part of the work. In Open House, they even asked local kids to design stencils to decorate the new buildings. The design and construction of the pavilions was equally an effort in community-building, bottom-up as opposed to top-down design. This positions itself as a counter-architecture. I think that it is not an accident that they pick politically charged sites. I wonder, too, about cities like New York and London, where there is a kind of established order in the central business districts that makes those parts of the city feel corporate rather than civic. We need some kind of Raumlabor action in those places, too.

MJ—Raumlabor doesn't yet take on those kind of entrenched interests.

LH—Are you saying that cities need to relax their requirements for orderly sidewalks and peaceful demonstrations?

PA—Absolutely! The sidewalks and plazas and parks should allow for a sense of anarchy, because in those situations you also will have creativity. This is a good attitude to take when thinking about how to use our public or semi-public spaces. You can sharpen and straighten up when you go into your office or into a defined place like a movie theater, but there needs to be more investigation and experimentation into these other kinds of in-between spaces.

MJ—These guys are the wizards of unsolicited proposals and then building projects that nobody necessarily asked for. They are their own client and they do a fabulous job. These are all built by students, volunteers, everybody just kind of jumps in.

LH—With Open House, they recast themselves as Raumlaborkorea and created what they call a "social sculpture," engaging hundreds of people to design and build the community buildings in Anyang, a suburb of Seoul. The Anyang Public Art Project sponsored the efforts, and Raumlabor basically "set up shop" in Anyang to engage local people in discussion, mapping, design, and ultimately construction. Their idea was to make an open master plan that could be upgraded frequently.

PA—Despite it being a community-based project, it is notable that the city took over the financial responsibility for it. I don't know the detailed history for why that happened. Generally, I think we learned from the counterculture of the 1970s that there is a limit to what can be done locally, bottom-up. I believe Raumlabor is an excellent facilitator for the community, but we need to keep in mind that they are also agents with their own agenda.

LH—I think we start to see this emergent agenda in their "summer school" projects like the one at Osthang. Here they set up an experimental educational model that links architects, artists, economists, political scientists, and community members to explore "Future Modes of Living Together." Participants live together, design together, and construct small-scale buildings. The fees are modest (300 euros for three weeks), and students can receive university credit. They are trying to make a place, but also working to teach a process. But your point remains: What is the future of this? Who takes possession, and more to the point, who maintains the structures and the site? It's incredibly wasteful if there's no long-term plan, if nobody really wanted this in the first place.

RAUMLABOR BERLIN is a collective of eight trained architects who have come together in a collaborative work structure. They work at the intersection of architecture, city planning, art, and urban intervention.

SERIE ARCHITECTS

CHRIS LEE, KAPIL GUPTA

BMW OLYMPIC PAVILION
London
This innovative design uses river water to provide a sustainable cooling mechanism for the building. The filtered water is returned to the river via an eye-catching "water curtain" feature.

BMW OLYMPIC PAVILION | London, England

This temporary pavilion is built on an elevated site above the Waterworks River, situated between the Olympic Stadium and the Aquatics Centre. Serie's design uses river water to provide a sustainable cooling mechanism for the BMW building. The filtered water is returned to the river via an eye-catching "water curtain" feature. The top floor houses a number of stand-alone pavilions highlighting BMW's latest vehicle innovations. The lower floor houses a range of interactive exhibits that articulate BMW's vision for sustainable mobility, as well as their support for Team GB and Paralympics GB athletes.

SERIE ARCHITECTS

Peder Anker, Louise Harpman, Mitchell Joachim

LH—The BMW Olympic Pavilion does at least two things—it shows off BMW cars on the top side, but also includes exhibits to show ideas for sustainable mobility. On the architecture side, the building acts as a cooling tower. Part of me really likes the fact that one of the systems we rarely see is made visible. You get this gorgeous curtain of water as an ephemeral façade. I think radical juxtaposition was part of the architectural strategy—highlighting the use of water shows that there is a resource at risk, and that we need to be more aware of this, whether it is water for transportation, industrial processes, agriculture, or potable water. So here's a luxury automaker showing off their new vehicles while spotlighting an at-risk natural resource. I don't know if BMW can have it both ways.

MJ—I wonder if they would recognize the irony? That is, the BMW people trying to create hybrids or something like that. I don't find any of their cars especially green. It seems like the same old sexy, beautiful, decadent BMW. Staring at this image, it looks fantastic, iconic. I think the water creates a shimmering light, an effect of movement on these surfaces that will do nothing but attract the eye. I think there is probably a wonderful sound and fine cooling mist for anybody viewing the cars on top. I think it would have a local effect on the micro-climate in that area. They still have a job to cool the spaces underneath, but I can't see any evidence that the pumping mechanisms, which use a lot of fuel and energy to pump all of this water, thousands of gallons being circulated on the surface, are actually saving any energy.

PA—It is so easy to bring down BMW, and, of course, you are right. On the other hand, isn't it good that we now see sustainability turning into something beautiful and sexy? Isn't it good that cars endorse this agenda, even though it is ironic and filled with problems? Most importantly, we need beautiful sustainable architecture and this might not be down to the numbers the right answer, but it is a step toward trying to answer the question of how to cool a building in a beautiful way and not only an efficient way. I think that is something we should applaud when thinking about sustainability.

LH—I actually think the project is quite subversive: they showcase automotive culture and yet it's the selling of more cars, building more roads, that puts the planet and aquifers at risk. Beauty and subversion.

I find that I want to get out my crystal ball when looking at this project, which was designed and built for the Olympics. I want to know its afterlife, to ask, when the cars are gone, could this be a science museum? A library that floats and visits underserved communities? Could it have solar panels on the roof? Could it be more of a demonstration project for sustainable technologies? If that is the case, then I want BMW to be the leaders. I love the idea that it could be BMW taking the lead—and that is the issue for the architects, to hold their feet to the fire, to say "do more" and don't only use this project to celebrate your hybrid vehicles.

MJ—I think BMW should keep investing in public transportation, which is the best thing that they could do for the environment. I absolutely agree that sustainable design, whatever that means, needs, if not begs, to look fabulous. There is no doubt this has an incredible shimmering quality that does that job.

PA—They point us a in a new direction; so many green projects are all about technologies and how to implement them. Serie reminds us that green global design also has to be beautiful, marvelous, and aesthetic. Yet I fear that BMW is not serious and that this pavilion is just an attempt to greenwash their brand.

LH—Perhaps, but I do think that the architecture and design community still needs to partner with industry. If you have a good idea as a student, or as a young designer, we need to create more ways to partner with industry. Where is the X Prize for architects? I look at the work coming out of the Audi Urban Future initiative. They seem to be really trying to make a place for architects and planners to think about future cities.

MJ—Audi is scared, they are in fear that more people are moving into cities and cars are less and less relevant. They absolutely know that and have seen the trend. That is why they are dumping money into these Audi Urban Future projects, so they can get some stylish propositions about what should happen architecturally and urban design-wise when it comes to cars in cities. How can we design cars to fit cities better? They want to design a vehicle that makes sense for urban dwelling.

PA—Among environmentally concerned students and activists, there is this sense of not wanting to work with the car industry, for a whole set of good reasons: pollution, oil production, and so on. There is the push for everybody to use bikes or their feet instead. And that's good. Yet we need to engage with the car industry in order to change things in the future.

MJ—I think these guys are just trying to turn the wheel on the Titanic. If we are up to 400 parts per million of carbon in the atmosphere, the shift should have happened years ago and if it is going to happen today these are one of the major agencies that need to turn that steering wheel to prevent us hitting the iceberg. They're producing an awful lot of carbon. There are just so many cars, new cars, and so much energy to make cars. We have been convinced that we need cars, so the automotive industry people just have to be at the table. And unlike other companies, the automotive companies are very keen on working with the environment. They have children too!

SERIE ARCHITECTS, founded by Chris Lee in London and Kapil Gupta in Mumbai, India, Serie is an international architectural firm with offices in the UK, India, and China. Chris Lee is an Associate Professor in Practice of Urban Design at Harvard University's Graduate School of Design. He received his D.Phil. in Architecture and Urbanism from the Berlage Institute and TU Delft.

STIG L. ANDERSSON

THE CITY DUNE | Copenhagen, Denmark

On the harbor front of Copenhagen, which is widely criticized for its low-quality office buildings and few public spaces, SLA created a revitalized public plaza for Swedish Bank SEB. This urban space called City Dune engages the buildings with the surrounding area, the harbor, and the rest of Copenhagen. City Dune is made of white concrete, borrowing its folding forms from the sand dunes of Northern Denmark and the snow dunes of the Scandinavian winter. The folding technique has several benefits, including a surface with high albedo-effect, creating a cooler microclimate during the warm periods of the year by reflecting as much of the incoming heat radiation as possible. The cooling effects are further enhanced by water atomizers, utilizing rainwater and emitting moist air spread by the wind, thus creating an experience of being in the middle of a lush environment. The City Dune promotes the sustainable use of concrete, and also gives much-needed recreational value to a part of Copenhagen long neglected by city planners.

SLA GDNYU ELSEWHERE ENVISONED

SLA

Peder Anker, Louise Harpman, Mitchell Joachim

LH—The charge seems to have been to humanize this bland office-park landscape, which had a dead central plaza. One of the problems with these undifferentiated large public plazas is that there is always this wind-blown placelessness to these kinds of spaces. I think City Dune is trying to knit the various buildings together by creating a consistent, active "surface," which they call "folded." Within the surface, they try to create microclimates and distinct zones. We are seeing places where they have introduced cooling mists, and places with trees and plants. But the proposal is shown to us like twenty years too early. When you imagine the tree canopy that would develop and become another kind of subspace within what they call "the folded landscape," it actually might be quite lovely.

PA—First of all, there is this old fascination in the modern architectural tradition with concrete. Ever since Lubetkin's penguin pools we have seen this, but despite their claims, it is not a sustainable material, at least not now. There is a lot of research going on and a few start-ups, but at the moment concrete is not ideal, and thus choosing this as a green building material is not supported. The second problem, I think, is that this a project about cooling in a country that has very few summer days. Yes, there are some beautiful summer days that require cooling in Denmark, but most of the year it is rainy, wet, and cold. With three semi-warm summer months, and nine months of winter, why focusing on cooling?

LH—You fault them on their premise?

PA—They're building a project that looks like it fits in a plaza in Miami. In Scandinavia, you need places to protect you from wind and rain when you have to be outside. I'm not sure they have really taken environmental issues into account, as well as the Scandinavian climate. Having said that, the project is stunning.

MJ—They're importing some idea of a Scandinavia in their use of light woods. They're also proposing some kind of ecological patch in the city. Their concrete forms represents stones, or sand, or some glacial shift that you would find in lightly wooded areas. All of this is very beautifully designed, but also very artificial and missing some big marks. A cooling mist in Denmark? I'm not quite sure that it makes sense. It definitely challenges my observations of what Denmark is normally like, and to do all of this for a month or two in the summer is not enough. I wonder what this place looks like in the cold, driving rain or the snow? I'd like to see the seasonal shift.

PA—Though there is some snow in the hard months of winter, Copenhagen is generally cold, windy, and gray. Those are the climate conditions this project should be confronting.

MJ—Maybe they are working with a new idea about sheltering where the folded plates create buttresses against the wind. There are places to rest and benches to sit on.

LH—City Dune offers those options, but will people be sitting here? I see that pedestrians and skaters and cyclists might really enjoy this environment, but more so when the trees and plantings have taken hold. The idea of the dune is just an urban fantasy. I don't think language helps here.

MJ—Is the dune the right metaphor?

PA—All right, enough criticism. Let's also hail the designers, as well as the SEB bank who paid the bill for creating a sort of public park in the city. It may not protect you against cold winds or warm you in the winter, but it does create some interesting and beautiful meandering paths on which you can enjoy a stroll with a date or take a break during lunch hour. I believe these in-between mini-parks in cities are crucial to make urban life more pleasurable. Also, look at the liberated glass façades of the surrounding office buildings.

These buildings are not that unique, perhaps, but let's not forget the original intention behind modernist glass buildings, namely providing sun, light, and views for their inhabitants. It was important back then when they were first invented, and it's equally important today.

LH—For a huge retrofit, the project definitely merits acclaim. Doing these kinds of projects after the buildings are in place is really very difficult. And parks and plazas definitely sponsor a type of urban regeneration that can't be totally predicted. If you look at the new Brooklyn Bridge Park in New York or even Park Güell in Barcelona, you see what might happen to the surrounding area if the space is more fully programmed.

MJ—Or even the Tiergarten in Berlin. Or the High Line in New York. The City Dune needs many more active uses, and probably better buildings, to make it into that discussion.

SLA, located in Copenhagen, Denmark, is an architecture studio that also works in the areas of urban space, city planning, and landscape. Stig L. Andersson is the Founder and Creative Director of SLA. Andersson received an MA in Architecture from the School of Architecture at the Royal Danish Academy of Fine Arts.

STUDIO WEAVE

JE AHN, MARIA SMITH

PALEYS UPON PILERS
Locally sourced wood
structure designed as a
pavilion for the London
Olympic Games.

PALEYS UPON PILERS | London, England

Paleys Upon Pilers marks the location of historic London Wall and the entry at Aldgate, which existed from Roman times until 1781. Aldgate's distinguished literary resident, Geoffrey Chaucer, lived above this historic eastern gateway into the City of London. The design was inspired by two dream poems written by Chaucer while he was a resident in the rooms above the gate from 1374 to 1386. "The House of Fame" and "The Parliament of Fowls" both describe fantastic scenes of dream-like temples—precarious, precious structures of impossible materials and scale. The site remains in a strategic position in London today, standing at the beginning of a major reconstruction site which leads to the Olympic Park.

STUDIO WEAVE GDNYU ELSEWHERE ENVISONED

STUDIO WEAVE
Peder Anker, Louise Harpman, Mitchell Joachim

LH—How do we transform a space into a place? To create one, Paleys Upon Pilers creates a marker and a gathering space along a common path. They are playful in their work, bringing history and metaphor into their design process. I like that the structure "riffs" on the church steeple, which signals a very purpose-driven architecture, a space for worship, versus this, which is outside in daylight, not fully enclosed, and not at all precious. I see their work as a way to activate another type of public that is ecumenical as opposed to ecclesiastical. The structure looks handmade, like a big birdhouse. There is friendliness to this project. I think that the juxtaposition between the transparency of the timber structure and the opacity, authority, and dour character of the brick and limestone steeple couldn't be more evident. This speaks to and for another type of public.

MJ—This is classic Kevin Lynch. In Lynch's view, urbanity can be visualized as "a picture especially in the mind," a demonstrative mixture between impartial urban perspective and subjective individual reflections. This is a reciprocal procedure between the viewer and the perceived effects of the urban environment imagined. The viewer, with boundless flexibility and in their own idiom, picks, classifies, and provides with meaning what he/she visualizes. Consequently, the explicit image can be wholly different from the diverse viewpoint of spectators, just like there are a million Shakespearean villages in a million people's minds. How we image a city is different for us all. Yet the multitudes of distinguishing moments help the denizens capture the city as a whole.

PA—You need markers or structures that stand out. In the city of Bergen, Norway, the city put up a big blue stone in the middle of town and it became a marker. It is a tool for getting familiar with a place—and this building could do that, too. There is a remembrance of things past in Paleys Upon Pilers that I appreciate as a historian, though the progressive side of me wonders who's benefiting. Why not put a glass roof or something on the structure so that the homeless could shelter under it?

MJ—The crisscrossing of these wood members is reminiscent of E. Fay Jones. It is a rousing simple, sculptural, geometric fantasy. These are triangles within triangles; you cannot escape the patternization of the system. It is built from these reduced elements of wood that are manufactured for rapid assembly. The angular opposing, structural systems against one another in this lattice are very legible. They make the strongest configuration within this public folly that really emphasizes the space. It is unquestionably a marker, and it is an attraction to people into the area. I don't see this as being permanent on any level and I don't think it was intended to be. I consider it as a well-crafted temporary structure that could end up in many other places. I admire the care in the assembly and the way the designers reveal the layers of the studs becoming lattices, triangles, and diamonds.

LH—I first came to hear about Studio Weave through their project the Longest Bench. In that project, which they built in West Sussex on the southern coast of England, they used reclaimed wood, worked with local schoolchildren and other members of the community, and created a sinuous, delightful, beautiful marker for the seashore. They tick three of my boxes for green architecture with that single project. It also helps that they conceived of the project as open-ended, so that more could be built in successive years. . .

PA—. . . making sure the Longest Bench will stay the longest! Clever. You know, Studio Weave brings something to the green Global Design table which I find truly refreshing, and that is color and humor. Their "Ecology of Color" cabin in Dartford, Kent, is like the primitive hut on steroids. A totally wonderful intervention in the world of green design, which all too often is weighed down by the seriousness of the subject matter, namely our common survival. My personal favorite of theirs is the "Lullaby Factory" of musical instruments placed on a building, not to mention their humongous "Hear Hears" alpenhorn-like objects out in the fields. It's out of this world.

MJ—"Common survival"? Yes, that is the way sustainability is often described. It is a tired movement meant to regulate our need to simply live and breathe for the next generation. What about terms such as evolution, exuberance, innovation, prosperity, radicalization? Sustainability as both a term and a movement is really a conventional set of survivalist routines. It doesn't evoke brilliance or invention. I find its aspirations to be limited as it castigates us toward energy responsibility. Studio Weave reminds me of the time our culture was celebrated with wit, charm, and great fanfare. Their projects supersede the platitudes of "energy responsibility" and get us to someplace more fantastical. These artisanal follies and colorful insertions remind me of Halloween. A festival of vibrant masks, music and tricks that spill over into the public realm, if only momentarily. The late John Hejduk would have much in common with this group. He was a true poet-architect, unafraid to weave splendor into the quotidian. I can see how Studio Weave embraces elemental forms and playfulness.

STUDIO WEAVE, directed by Je Ahn and Maria Smith, is a London-based architecture practice.

TOPOTEK 1

MARTIN REIN-CANO, LORENZ DEXLER

HEERENSCHÜRLI
Zurich
The new facilities will be turned
into an independently present
ensemble of a compact, high-
frequency sports world.

SUPERKILEN | Copenhagen, Denmark
Superkilen is a heterogeneous site-collage in a densely populated area in central Copenhagen. The environment for this diverse and multicultural neighborhood is revitalized through a framework of open spaces. Propelling the site beyond its current role as a mere place of transit, this project transforms the area into an ambassador for global urban culture.

SPORT FACILITIES, HEERENSCHÜRLI | Zurich, Switzerland
This sports complex, one of the largest in Zurich, is situated among a nature reserve, a highway crossing, housing, and large-scale industrial buildings. The complex includes a sports field situated between three new buildings—an ice rink, a workshop, and a locker-room building. The complex also includes twelve soccer fields and Switzerland's first standard baseball field. The sport fields are enclosed by eight-meter-high fences made of transparent wire mesh, allowing for interaction between athletes and onlookers.

TOPOTEK 1 GDNYU ELSEWHERE ENVISONED

SUPERKILEN
Over the course of many months, conversing with residents and local associations, the community has been mobilized to develop an international catalogue of urban design elements.

TOPOTEK 1
Peder Anker, Louise Harpman, Mitchell Joachim

MJ—Superkilen is a super exciting landscape project that incorporates a lot of found objects, like swings, strange flagpoles, benches, and other odd items that have become street furniture. It is a cabinet of curiosities and filled with artifacts that have been found far and near. Each item has been brought to this site, presented and represented, embedded in the landscape of brilliant color. Everywhere is this blood-red pigmentation that really takes note and displays these objects rather well. It's like a menagerie of found relics collected together in a wonderful assembly to create this open space. Talking about the green city, and reusing/upcycling, this is a fantastic case. They took ordinary or utilitarian objects and made them into something profound. The ordinary becomes the climax, or at least that is the arc of how they present these curious items. It does not mean that all the objects are treated the same; some objects will still probably be perceived as mundane. Overall it is a congenial space to visit these diminutive items fastened into the landscape and serving as whimsical articles for the public to ingest.

LH—I find their design process so compelling. This park is along a transit corridor, so it is a space that could also be conceived of as a right-of-way or a non-space, and yet, the architecture and landscape architecture teams worked together to develop this zooming and quirky park. Most of the residents in this part of Copenhagen are recent immigrants. The designers brought together community and local associations and asked people to think about what they remember, or recall, from their home countries. They asked them to identify the markers that could only be found back in their previous towns or cities. That is how the collage was made. In the park, the designers created three different zones: the red square, the green park, and the black market. I think the "cabinet of curiosities" is a good metaphor—there's novelty and interest round every bend. I think what the park is not is also important to talk about. It is an active space, a place for kids and adults, and it is not overly scripted. It doesn't say, "Here is the quiet zone for the grandmas and here is the skateboard zone." It is all a really interesting mash-up of urbanisms. I think the degree to which it is a combination of architects, landscape architects, and civil engineering is exactly the kind of hybrid teaming that makes it so vital. This project has gotten a lot of notice because of the design, but also because of the program and its high-profile designers.

PA—What is the difference between this and PoMo architecture, where you take some sort of historical object from the Greeks and ironically put it into a modern setting? Or you take an iconic object situated in a physical and historical context and rip it out and place it in another? Take, for example, this star, which to me, looks like it is taken out of some Eastern Bloc former communist country and replaced in Denmark, a liberal democracy. It's playful and clever, but a play on what?

MJ—A postmodernist would not take the actual star, but would redraw it and rebuild it, making a reference to that star. It would be stylized into the system, whereas these are original objects and have a provenance that is discreet. They are presented to the public in order to reach a new level of engagement. The elements do, however, have a postmodernist aesthetic. I love that the park includes this assemblage or pastiche of different objects. It is exclusive rare antique paraphernalia put out into the open for civic display.

LH—One could make an argument that a new part of a city does not need to be as buttoned up as a historic area. I definitely think that we could have a bit more urban irreverence in our old-growth cities, too! There is something about Topotek's design and the community-engagement strategy that has a playfulness and an informality. We should see more of this, not less.

MJ—There were many difficulties in producing the WWII veterans memorial in Washington, DC. It was in many ways a struggle to find appropriate representation. The thought was that there would be 400 marble stars representing American lives lost. The problem was that the "star symbol" is not necessarily owned by any particular nation. It could be a star for the Soviets, China, and all kinds of other military forces. These symbols have meanings that are distorted, if not lost, when they move between cultures and contexts.

PA—I think you see it that way, Mitch, because you live in a city built by immigrants. Believe me, Copenhagen is not like Brooklyn. In Copenhagen there is a tiny minority of immigrants coming in from all kinds of different cultures and backgrounds, and they feel that they are coming to a foreign place. They feel lost in a world of Danes. The Danes then install objects from a culture the immigrants associate with so they can feel more at home and maybe less foreign. Right? I am not sure if it is an invitation to social inclusion, but more a type of distortion. It is an act of generosity to put up a huge donut sign so that that immigrants with a love for donuts can feel more at home, though I doubt they will. After all, it's the donut context they miss the most. Yet it is comfortable for the Danes to point to the donut at Superkilen and say, '"Hey hey, aren't we tolerant and inclusive?" I think that is the underlying agenda. Instead, the Danish government and local councils should address the tougher question of why immigrants tend to be poor and are segmented in one area of the city. This is not a criticism of Topotek, whose work I admire. It is a criticism of the larger issues surrounding poor immigrant communities in wealthy host countries.

LH—Well, then let's look at their work in Zurich; that's certainly another test case.

MJ—The Topotek 1 project in Zurich seems to fit a tight budget into an even tighter design program. They are again using ultra-bright color to rethink and activate quotidian places. All of the typical lighting, fencing, bleachers, and other sports elements are coated in acid-green enamel. They strike a signature look and create continuity in a program that has a limited scope, as it's mostly playing fields. The corrugated shed component is the most striking. It is a great swooping wave of lime/caustic green surface that is smattering acid colored chairs in two directions. I feel as if I will be electrocuted gazing at it too long.

PA—Their sports complex in Zurich is located between a nature reserve and a highway interchange. I think they have built a beautiful buffer to the cars and a way to welcome people to the nature reserve. The same is true for the open space built on the top of train tracks going through a residential community in Munich, creating a huge boost for its residents.

TOPOTEK 1 is directed by founder Martin Rein-Cano and Lorenz Dexler. The Berlin-based studio works in the field of landscape architecture and takes an interdisciplinary approach. Rein-Cano studied art history at Frankfurt University and landscape architecture at the Technical Universities of Hannover and Karlsruhe. Dexler studied landscape architecture at Hannover Technical University.

ACKNOWLEDGMENTS

This book grew out of exhibitions for Global Design New York University (GDNYU) organized at the Jerry H. Labowitz Theatre and Galleries at NYU's Gallatin School of Individualized Study and at the Building Centre in London, in collaboration with NYU London. Our first round of thanks goes to all the designers who generously provided us with images and models, in addition to sharing their thoughts with us in the symposia associated with our exhibitions.

Arranging exhibitions is no small task, and our next round of applause therefore goes to our curatorial assistants, Elisabeth Dearden, Adrian De Silva, Jacqueline Hall, Eva Jaeger, James Schwartz, Laura Seach, and Jana Walters, along with our exhibit assistants, Dylan Butman, Clay Doggett, Emma Goode, Coralie Harmache, Everett Hollander, Devin Keyes, Ben Lang, Jason Lindy, Greg Mulholland, Belinda Rodriguez, Melody Song, Jonathan Stone, Katherine Sullivan, Daniel Swartz, Ally Trevorrow, and Ethan Zisson. Special thanks go to Melanie Fessel for her installation expertise and Terreform ONE for their support.

We are also grateful to the many people who have helped us turn the exhibitions into a book. In particular we would like to thank Hashim Sarkis for his essay and Jonathan Bell and Ellie Stathaki for their introduction and curatorial advice. We have benefited tremendously from the work of our managing editor, Caroline Klein, our design editor, Melanie Fessel, and from the editorial work of Carly Krakow and David Maruzzella. The first-rate work of our digital assistant, Jake Madoff, is evident at www.gdnyu.com, twitter.com/gdnyu, facebook.com/gdnyu, and nyudesign.blogspot.com.

We are also grateful to the NYU Office of the Provost, Global Research Initiatives Program, NYU Office of Sustainability, Gallatin Community Learning Initiative, Department of Environmental Studies at NYU, The London Design Festival, NLA, Bloomsbury Festival, and Nancy Levinson with the Design Observer, who was our media partner for the New York show and symposium. Special thanks also to the staff of the Gallatin School of Individualized Study at NYU, who with their work in so many ways made the exhibitions and our book possible.

Finally, neither the exhibitions nor the book would have been realized without the highest level of support from Susanne Wofford, Dean of the Gallatin School of Individualized Study, who has been our prime benefactor. Without her ongoing commitment, neither the exhibitions nor the book would have happened.

Thank you all for your support.

PEDER ANKER

Peder Anker is an Associate Professor at the Gallatin School of Individualized Study and the Chair of the Environmental Studies Department at New York University. His works include *Imperial Ecology: Environmental Order in the British Empire, 1895–1945* (Harvard University Press, 2001) and *From Bauhaus to Eco-House: A History of Ecological Design* (Louisiana State University Press, 2010). Anker received his PhD in the History of Science from Harvard University.

LOUISE HARPMAN

Louise Harpman is an Associate Professor of Practice in the areas of Architectural Design, Urban Design, and Sustainability at New York University's Gallatin School of Individualized Study and the Wagner Graduate School of Public Service. She is a founding partner of Specht Harpman, a multidisciplinary architecture, urban design, and design research firm in NYC. Specht Harpman was recognized by *Wallpaper** magazine as one of the "top 50 up and coming architectural practices from around the world." The firm has received multiple Honor Awards from the American Institute of Architects and was recognized in the "Emerging Voices" series at the Architectural League of New York. Specht Harpman's solar-powered house, zeroHouse, has won a number of design awards and has been published in over forty-five international books and magazines. Harpman previously taught architecture at the Yale School of Architecture, the University of Pennsylvania, and the University of Texas at Austin, where she was the Associate Dean for Undergraduate Programs. She is the coeditor of *Perspecta 30: Settlement Patterns* (MIT Press, 1999). She is a graduate of Harvard University, Cambridge University, and the Yale School of Architecture, where she earned her M.Arch. degree.

MITCHELL JOACHIM

Mitchell Joachim is a cofounder of Terreform ONE. He is an Associate Professor of Practice at New York University's Gallatin School of Individualized Study. He was formerly an architect at Gehry Partners and at Pei Cobb Freed. He is a TED Senior Fellow and has been awarded fellowships with Moshe Safdie and the Martin Society for Sustainability, MIT. He was chosen by *Wired* magazine for "The Smart List: 15 People the Next President Should Listen To." *Rolling Stone* magazine honored him in "The 100 People Who Are Changing America." He and his design firm, Terreform ONE, have won many awards, including an AIA New York Urban Design Merit Award, Victor Papanek Social Design Award, Zumtobel Group Award for Sustainability, History Channel Infiniti Award for City of the Future, Architizer A+ Award, and Time Magazine Best Invention, with MIT Smart Cities Car. *Dwell* magazine featured him as "The NOW 99" in 2012. He is the coauthor of *Super Cells: Building with Biology* (TED Books, 2014). He earned a PhD at Massachusetts Institute of Technology, an MAUD at Harvard University, and an M.Arch. from Columbia University.

ACKNOWLEDGEMENTS GDNYU ELSEWHERE ENVISONED

CREDITS

SCAPE: ZEREGA AVENUE STATION: Smith Miller & Hawkinson Architects and LANGAN Engineering. BLUE WALL ENVIRONMENTAL CENTER: Studio Gang Architects. **BIG:** W57: Principal: Bjarke Ingels. Design Team: Beat Schenk, Soren Grunert, Thomas Christoffersen, Celine Jeanne, Daniel Sundlin, Allesandro Ronfini, Aleksander Tokarz, Allessio Valmori, Alvaro Garcia Mendive, Felicia Guldberg, Gabrielle Nadeau, Ho Kyung Lee, Julian Liang, Julianne Gola, Lucian Racovitan, Marcela Martinez, Dominyko Mineikyte, Elvor Davidsen Maria Nikolova, Minjae Kim, Mutesh Dixit, Nicklas Rasch, Riccardo Mariano, Stanley Lung, Steffan Heath, Thilani Rajarthna, Xu Li. AMAGER RESOURCE CENTER: Principals: Bjarke Ingels, David Zahle. Project Leader: Claus Hermansen. Project Architect: Nanna Gyldholm Møller. Team Members: Brian Yang, Nanna Gyldholm Møller, Jakob Ohm Laursen, Lise Jessen, Espen Vik, Narisara Ladawal Schröder, Mads Enggaard Stidsen, Jesper Boye Andersen, Ryohei Koike, Anders Hjortnæs, Henrick Poulsen, Annette Jensen, Jeppe Ecklon, Kamilla Heskje, Frank Fdida, Alberto Cumerlato, Gonzalo Castro, Chris Zhongtian Yuan, Aleksander Wadas, Liang Wang, Alexander Ejsing, Chris Falla, Mathias Bank, Katarzyna Siedlecka, Jelena Vucic, Alina Tamosiunaite, Armor Gutierrez, Maciej Zawadzki, Jakob Lange, Andreas Klok Pedersen, Daniel Selensky, Gül Ertekin, Xing Xiong, Sunming Lee, Long Zuo, Ji-young Yoon, Blake Smith, Buster Christensen, Simon Masson, Brygida Zawadzka, Zoltan David Kalaszi. **LATERAL OFFICE:** NEXT NORTH: Image Credits: Iceberg Riggings (Lateral Office/InfraNet Lab), Arctic Food Network (Lateral Office/InfraNet Lab), Active Layer. **SIDL:** AIR TRACKS, BEIJING: Research Associates: Minna Niova, Robert Viola, Cressica Brazier. **RICHARD SOMMER:** Daniel Adams of Landing Studio. **RUR ARCHITECTURE:** O-14: Principals: Jesse Reiser, Nanako Umemoto. Design Team: Mitsuhisa Matsunaga, Kutan Ayata, Jason Scroggin, Cooper Mack, Michael Overby, Roland Snooks. Interns and Assistants: Tina Tung, Raha Talebi, Yan Wai Chu. Structural Engineer: Ysrael A. Seinuk, PC, New York. Architect of Record: Erga Progress, Dubai. Window Wall Consultant: R. A. Heintges & Associates. KAOHSIUNG PORT TERMINAL: Principals: Jesse Reiser, Nanako Umemoto. Design Team: Neil Cook, Michael Overby, Kris Hedges, Eleftheria Xanthouli, Juan DeMarco, Massimiliano Orzi. Interns and Assistants: Toshiki Hirano, Sonya Chao, Imaeda Ryosuke. Structural Engineering: Ysrael A. Seinuk, PC, New York, NY (Schematic Design) Supertek, Taiwan (Detailed Design) MEP, Sustainability, Port Planning and Logistics ARUP, Hong Kong. Façade Consultant: Meinhardt, Hong Kong. Lighting Consultant: Izumi Okayasu Lighting Design Office, Japan. Local Architect: Fei and Cheng and Associates, Taipei, Taiwan. SHENZHEN INTERNATIONAL AIRPORT – TERMINAL 3: Principals: Jesse Reiser, Nanako Umemoto. Project Architect: Mitsuhisa Matsunaga. Design Team: Mitsuhisa Matsunaga, Kutan Ayata, Michael Overby, Roland Snooks, Neil Cook, Michael Loverich. Assistants: Steven Lauritano, Juan De Marco, Lindsey Cohen, Luis Costa, Yan Wai Chu, Roselyn Shieh, Max Kuo, Robin Liu, Devin Jernigan, Robert Soendergaard. Structural Engineer: ARUP New York. Technical Development Team: Mitsuhisa Matsunaga, Kutan Ayata, Michael Overby, Juan De Marco, Neil Cook, Michael Loverich, Lindsey Cohen, Jonathan Solomon, Luis Costa, Devin Jernigan. Structural Engineer: ARUP New York, ARUP Hong Kong / Shenzhen. Architect of Record: AEDAS New York, AEDAS Hong Kong. Façade Consultant: FRONT, Inc., New York. **AXEL KILIAN:** ATHLETE CAR: Axel Kilian, Patrik Kunzler, Oeter Schmitt, Mitchell Joachim, Enrique L. Garcia. **WHOWHATWHENAIR:** ACUTATED TOWER: Support for the project was provided by Professor Yung Ho Chan, Professor John Ochsendorf, Chris Dewart, and many volunteers. The competition-wining proposal was built at MIT for $7,000, with pneumatic actuators provided by FESTO. Design/Build Team: Philippe Block, Axel Kilian, Peter Schmitt, John Snavely. **RACHEL ARMSTRONG:** THE FUTURE VENICE PROJECT: Neil Spiller, Director of AVATAR, Martin Hanczyc, and Christian Kerrigan. **PNEUMASTUDIO:** SPIRABILIS: Cathryn Dwyre, Chris Perry, Justin Snider, Dave Mulder. **ARCHITECTURE RESEARCH OFFICE:** NEW URBAN GROUND (RISING CURRENTS ZONE: 0): Designed with dlandstudio landscape architecture. **NEA STUDIO:** LATITUDE LIGHTS: Interns: Sofie Vertongen, Ninni Rautianien. Electrical Engineer: Michael Edwards. **SPECHT HARPMAN:** Scott Specht and Louise Harpman; Amy Lopez-Cepero, Devin Keyes, Brett Wolfe, Frank Farkash; Bear Ventures, DuPont Corporation. **RUY KLEIN:** KNOT GARDEN: Andrew Lucia, Andrew Ruggles, Matthew Lake, Megan Born, Aaron Jezzi. Assistants: Brandon Gerke, Jessica Hogue, Robert May,

Jean-Baptiste Rufineau, David Schweim, Lisa Schwert, Lara Thrasher, Ashley Wendela. Consultants: Bora Temelkuran. Product Design: Katrin Mueller. Fabrication Consultant: Ken Tracy and Associated Fabrication. Structural Engineer: Mathew Clark and ARUP. PANGAEA: Eric Ellingsen, Chris Junkin, Jeffrey Chen, Hoon Kim. **INTERBORO PARTNERS:** THE ARSENAL OF EXCLUSION & INCLUSION: Tobias Armborst, Daniel D'Oca, Georgeen Theodore, Rebecca Beyer Winik, Lesser Gonzalez Alvarez. **TERREFORM ONE/PLANETARY ONE:** RAPID RE(F)USE: Mitchell Joachim, Maria Aiolova, Melanie Fessel, Emily Johnson, Ian Slover, Philip Weller, Zachary Aders, Webb Allen, Niloufar Karimzadegan. BIO CITY MAP OF 11 BILLION: WORLD POPULATION IN 2110: Mitchell Joachim, Nurhan Gokturk, Melanie Fessel, Maria Aiolova, Oliver Medvedik. Research Fellows; Chloe Byrne, Adrian De Silva, Daniel Dewit, Renee Fayzimatova, Alena Field, Nicholas Gervasi, Julien Gonzalez, Lucas Hamren, Patty Kaishian, Ahmad Khan, Laasyapriya Malladi, Karan Maniar, Ricardo Martin Coloma, Puja Patel, Merve Poyraz, Mina Rafiee, Mahsoo Salimi, Manjula Singh, Diego Wu Law. SUPER DOCKING: Brooklyn Navy Yard, NY: Mitchell Joachim, Maria Aiolova, Nurhan Gokturk, David Maestres, Jason Vigneri Beane. Carlos Barrios, Alex Felson, Walter Meyer, Melanie Fessel, Zafirah Bacchus, Ivy Chan, Courtney Chin, Adrian De Silva, Julianne Geary, Francisco Gill, Shima Ghafouri, Jacqueline Hall, Kelly Kim, Florian Lorenz, Bart Mangold, Dustin Mattiza, Chema Perez, Alsira Raxhimi, Daniel Russoniello, Melody Song, Allison Shockley, Katherine Sullivan. **R&SIE(N):** TBWND: François Roche, Stephanie Lavaux, Kiuchi Toshikatsu, Sandra Meireis, Ulrike Marie Steen, Hamish Rhodes, Sina Momtaz. Light Engineer: Benoit Lalloz. Glass Craftsmen: Stephane Rivoal, Pedro Veloso. OLZWEG: François Roche, Stephanie Lavaux, Jean Navarro, Pierre Huyghe. Artist: Mathieu Lehanneur. Furniture Designer: Stephan Henric. Robotic Designer: Nicholas Green. Façade Engineer: Ami Barak. Museum Expert: Sibat. Basic Engineer: Julien Blervaque. Script Programmers: Alexander Römer, Agnes Vidal, Daniel Fernández Florez, Gaëtan Robillard. I'MLOSTINPARIS: François Roche, Stéphanie Lavaux, Jean Navarro. Structural Development and Construction of the Green Prototype: Christian Hubert De Lisle & Cie. Glass Beakers: Produced by Pedro Veloso (including the consulting of Vanessa Mitrani). Ferns: Dryopteris filix-mas. **WORKAC:** PLUG-OUT TOWER: Principals: Amale Andraos & Dan Wood. Design Team: Anne Menke, Anna Kenoff. **AUM STUDIO:** SUTURE: Programming Design: G. Showman. LODI LIBRARY: Rendering and Imaging: E. Blassetti, T. Branquinho. Research Assistant: J. Locke. ENANTIOMORPHAO: Design Team (NY): D. Pigram, E. Blasetti, R. Snooks. Site Research (Los Angeles): D. Vasini, E. Espasandin. Landscape and Engineering (Lisbon, Portugal): C. Sisti, V. Leitao. **BLOOM: THE GAME:** Principal Designers: Alisa Andrasek and Jose Sanchez. Plastic Manufacturing: Atomplast. Steel Manufacturing: JMR Section Benders. Thanks to all the staff from The Bartlett, UCL. **ABERRANT ARCHITECTURE:** TINY TRAVELLING THEATRE: Image Credits: Jim Stephenson, Simon Kennedy, Mark Cocksedge. **ACME:** UN MEMORIAL: Kelvin Chu, Daewon Kwak, Friedrich Ludewig, Isabel de la Mora, Monica Preziuso, Teresa Yeh. **ATMOS:** THE MOBILE ORCHARD: Alex Haw, Jeg Dudley, Natalie Chelliah, Xiaolin Gu, Maite Parisot, Juan Carlos Bueno, Adamantia (Mando) Keki, Miriam Fernandez. Structural Engineering: Blue Engineering (James Nevin). Lighting Design: Arup Lighting (Arfon Davies, Dwayene Shillingford). Lighting all sponsored by: LED Linear / Wibre / Architectural FX (Stuart Knox). Plywood sponsored by: DHH Timber. Microsite Web Design: Eightfold (Sinead Mac Manus). Fabrication: Nicholas Alexander (Jak Drinnan, Nicholas Runeckles, Anna Baker). Festival Tree Sponsor: Bloomberg. Real orchard trees donated by: YouGarden (Peter McDermott) & The Worshipful Company of Fruiterers. Hosts: Broadgate Estates, Devonshire Square Management, Land Securities, 30 St Mary Axe Management Company Ltd. Logistics: Tellings Transport. Special Thanks: Sinead Mac Manus, Professor John Price (WCoF), Ed Gillespie, Olivia Sibony, Corporation of London. WORLDSCAPE: Concept & Design: Alex Haw, Pablo Milara, Friedrich Vitzthum. Development: Alex Haw, Pablo Milara, Friedrich Vitzthum, Dom Rago-Verdi, Xiaolin Gu, Melissa Reynaud, Ana Maria Diaz, Ana Sidorova, Nick O'Neill, Dan Mahoney, Chris Green, Jeg Dudley, Rowan Taylor. Construction: above + Anibal Puron, Martin, Sinead Mac Manus, Stefan Simanowitz, Marcus Keohane, Jonathan Taylor, Leo, William Hardie, Andrew Atkins, Anke Weber. Fabrication: The Cutting Room (very special thanks to Mark Durey). Plywood: DHH Timber. Special Thanks: Thomas Ugo Ermacora (Lime Wharf), Alison Davenport (Stratford Old Town Hall), Sinead Mac Manus. **AWP:** PAVILIONS AND FOLLIES OF THE "PARC DES BORDS DE SEINE": Consulting Assistance: HHF, EVP (structure), Ginger (engineering/QS). Image Credits: AWP, HHF, SBDA. **CREUS E CARRASCO ARQUITECTOS:** HARBOR REMODELING: Work Directors: Juan Creus, Covadonga Carrasco. Collaborators: Francisco Rosell, Felipe Riola, Roi Feijoo, Belén Salgado, Alexandre Antunes, Bárbara Mesquita, Laura Coladas.

Photographs: CREUSeCARRASCO arquitectos, Xoan Piñón. **CUAC ARQUITECTURA:** ABOVE CORDOBA: Authors: Javier Castellano Pulido, Tomás García Píriz. Collaborators: Antonio Monterroso Checa (archaeology) Miguel Hernandez Valencia (structures), Samuel Dominguez Amarillo (installations), Miguel Gomez Losada (artist), Raffaella Grossi (architect), Alvaro Castellano Pulido, Biamca Bamares Rodriguez, Alba Marcos Ramirez, Antonio Perez Blanco (students), Carmen Orega (architect) Andrea Ninni (engineer), Fernando Alvarez Cienfuegos (CUACS graphic), Javier Callejas (CUACS photography). TETRABRIK PAVILION: Architects: Tomás García Píriz, Javier Castellano Pulido, with help from Sugarplatform (Julien Fajardo, Christophe Beaveuz). Production: BABYDOG S.L. Professors: Rafael Sánchez Sánchez, Elisa Valero Ramos,Miguel Martinez Monedero, Proyectos I. Etsag Arquitectura Granada. Promoters: Area de Medioambiente, Diputacion de Granada, Junta de Andalucia. Photography: Pavilion: Javier Callejas Sevilla. Process: Julian Fajardo. **DAVID KOHN:** CLOUD PAVILION: Landscape: David Buck Landscape Architects. Play Strategy: Davies White Landscape Architects. Structures: Alan Baxter & Associates. Environment: Max Fordham LLP. Costs: Jackson Coles. Graphics: Sara de Bondt Studio. **DOXIADIS+:** LANDSCAPES OF COHABITATION: Island Villas Development, Antiparos Greece: Landscape Architects: Doxiadis+ (Thomas Doxiadis, Terpsy Kremaly). Photographers: Clive Nichols, Cathy Cunliffe, Thomas Doxiadis. **GROUNDLAB:** FLOWING GARDENS: Plasmastudio with LAUR studio, ARUP and BAID. Project Team: Eva Castro, Holger Kehne, José Alfredo Ramírez, Eduardo Rico, Hossein Kachabi, Jorge Ayala, Mehran Garlegui, and Evan Greeberg with Nadia Kloster, Steve De Micoli, Elisa Kim, Filipo Nassetti, Federico Ruberto, Rui Liu, Kezhou Chen, and Clara Oloriz. **HAUGEN/ZOHAR:** CAVE FOR KIDS: Marit Justine Haugen, Espen Bærheim, Dan Zohar. Image Credit: Grethe Fredrikse. **HHF ARCHITECTS:** RUTA DEL PEREGRINO: Alexa den Hartog, Janna Jessen. Image Credit: Iwan Baan. Curatorial Team: Tatiana Bilbao and Derek Dellekamp. Master Plan and Project Coordination: Rozana Montiel and Derek Dellekamp. **J. MAYER. H:** METROPOL PARASOL: Management Consultant: Dirk Blomeyer. Realization: Arup GmbH. Technical Support for Plants Competition: Coqui-Malachowska-Coqui with Thomas Waldau. Timber Model: Finnforest Merk, Bremen. Photography: Fernando Alda. **LAVA:** MASDAR CITY CENTER: Kann Finch Group, Arup SL Rasch, Transsolar, EDAW. GREEN CLIMATE FUND HEADQUARTERS: Fraunhofer IAO, Fraunhofer Allianz Bau, Fraunhofer IGB. **MI5 ARQUITECTOS:** NEW YOUTH CENTER IN RIVAS-VACIAMADRID: Architects: Manuel Collado Arpia, Nacho Martín Asunción. Collaborators: Eider Holgado, Richar y Diego Barajas. Engineering: Juan Travesí. Image Credit: Miguel de Guzmán. TERUEL-ZILLA: Collaborators: PKMN. Architectural Technologists: María del Carmen Nombela, Ana Macipe. Structure Engineering: Mecanismo Diseño y Cálculo de Estructuras S.L. Systems Engineering: Solventa Ingenieros Consultores S.L. Geotechnics: Geodeser S.A. Topography: Julia del Toro. Image Credit: Miguel de Guzmán, Javier de Paz. **MMW ARCHITECTS:** EQUATOR: Visualization: Kjetil Johansen. Partner: Magne Magler Wiggen. FHILTEX: Image Credit: Nils Petter Dale, Eirik Forde. Architects: Sindre Ostereng, Vibeke Thoresen Dahle, Maiken Seglem, Lon Sjoli. Visualization: Kjetil Johansen. Partner: Magne Magler Wiggen. Project Manager: Rebekka Bondesen. Lawyer: Tore Magler Wiggen. Other Team Members: Jo Epsen Bjerk, Trine Hauge. HOUSE: Lead Architect: Hallstein Guthu. Project Team: Martin Adolfsson, Inger Andresen (SINTEF), Trond Andresen (SINTEF), Håvard Arnhoff, Dino Beslic, Espen Bjerk (Elbil Norge), Rebekka Bondesen, Martin Braathen (Projekt 0047), David Brassfield, Jostein Edvardsen, Lars Ellingsen Bæren, Harald Egeberg, Ines Fritz, Åsmund Gamlesæter, Gabriel Schanche Gilje, Gunnar Gjerde, Stig Grani (Festo), Helle Sara Gundersen, Fred Guthu, Torgrim Guthu, Kristina Jullum Hagen, Jørgen Hals (SINTEF), Bjørn Staff Halvorsen, Terje Gorm Hansen (Helly Hansen Spesialprodukter), Tuva Hansen, Tina Hasaas, Paul Heisholt, Käthe Hermstad (SINTEF), Richard Horden (TU München), Margrethe Jakola, Jon Arne Jørgensen, Ottar Jørgensen (ALUNOR), Peder Jørgensen (composer), Carl Hall-Karlstrøm, Tommy Kleiven (SINTEF), Bernard Kristensen, Kristian, Hanne Jacobsen Lillevold, Thomas Mikarlsen, Björn Munch, Ole Nielsen, Robert Nilssen (NTNU), Torkel Njå, Jorun Schanche Olsen (NTNU), D.I.Michael "Palli" Palfinger, Alexandra von Petersdorff (TU München), Reiulf Ramstad, Sami Rintala, Jo Rognaldsen, Øystein Rø (Projekt 0047), Espen Røyseland (Projekt 0047), Anne Sandnes, Klaus Schubert (Brødrene Bøckmann), Fredrikke Finne Seip, Bjørn Spjutøy, Hans Erik Standal (Electrolux), Sverre Steen (NTNU), Jørn Stene (SINTEF), Perann Sylvia Stokke, Ivar Sørlie (Festo), Lars Tallhaug (Kjeller Vindteknikk AS), John Olav Tande (SINTEF), Charles Wara, Magne Magler Wiggen, Erik Young (PKL), Sindre Østereng. **ORDINARY STUDIO:** CRYSTAL CITY: Curator: Chris Hatherill (agency super/collider). Sponsor: Selfridges Festival of Imagination. DUNE CITY: Consultants: Bio-Soil Improvements, Scott Howard, Earthen

Hand. Collaborator: BLDG Blog. Images: Magnus Larsson. **OSA:** ACCUMULATOR: KHBT Karsten Huneck, Bernd Trümpler. Collaborators: Darren Paine, Structural Engineering; Greg Scarth, Music Composition. Photographer: Phillip Day. KUNSTHÜLLE: KHBT Karsten Huneck, Bernd Trümpler. Photographer: Johannes Marburg. **RAUMLABOR BERLIN:** OPEN HOUSE: Matthias Rick with Florian Stirnemann. **SERIE ARCHITECTS:** BMW OLYMPIC PAVILION: Chris Lee, Bolam Lee, Martin Jameson, Patrick Usbourne, Simon Whittle, Fei Wu, Kapil Gupta, Santosh Thorat. Physical Model: Huida Xia, Lola Lozano. Executive Architect: Franken Architekten. Structural Engineering: AKT II. Mechanical Engineering: Atelier Ten. Water Feature Specialist: Fountains Direct. Interiors: Mutabor. Project Managers: KSV Krüger Schuberth Vandreike. Images: Edmund Sumner; Clive Barker (aerial). **SLA:** THE CITY DUNE: Stig L. Andersson, Malene Krüger, Ulla Hornslyd, Rikke Geertsen, Alexandra Vindfeld Hansen. Collaborators: Lundgaard & Tranberg Architects, Rambøll. **STUDIO WEAVE:** PALEYS UPON PILERS: Studio Weave worked with Structural Engineers, Structure Workshop; Pattern and Print Designer, Linda Florence; Development Managers, M3 Consulting; and Planning Consultants, DP9. The project is made from British Timber grown by the Forestry Commission Wales and supplied by BSW Timber, and is fabricated and installed by AB3 Workshops with streetworks by Conways and concrete donated by Laing O'Rourke. The project was funded by 4C Hotel Group. **TOPOTEK 1:** SPORT FACILITIES | HEERENSCHÜRLI: Architecture: Dürig Architekten AG. Cooperation: Tiefbau: Büro Moser. SUPERKILEN: BIG Partner In Charge: Bjarke Ingels. BIG Project Leader: Nanna Gyldholm Møller, Mikkel Marcker Stubgaard. Big Design Team: Ondrej Tichy, Jonas Lehmann, Rune Hansen, Jan Borgstrøm, Lacin Karaoz, Jonas Barre, Nicklas Antoni Rasch, Gabrielle Nadeau, Jennifer Dahm Petersen, Richard Howis, Fan Zhang, Andreas Castberg, Armen Menendian, Jens Majdal Kaarsholm, Jan Magasanik. Topotek 1 Partner In Charge: Martin Rein-Cano, Lorenz Dexler. Topotek 1 Project Leader: Ole Hartmann, Anna Lundquist. Topotek 1 Design Team: Toni Offenberger, Katia Steckemetz , Cristian Bohne, Karoline Liedtke. Superflex Design Team: Jakob Fenger, Rasmus Nielsen, Bjørnstjerne Christiansen. Collaboration: Lemming Eriksson, Help PR & Communication. Photography: Hanns Joosten, Torben Eskerod.

Front cover and main title p.2/3, p.9: source by NASA
p.6/7: Wikimedia GPL/GNU 2014

Prestel Verlag, Munich
A member of Verlagsgruppe Random House GmbH

Prestel Verlag
Neumarkter Strasse 28
81673 Munich
Tel. +49 (0)89 4136-0
Fax +49 (0)89 4136-2335

www.prestel.de

Prestel Publishing Ltd.
14-17 Wells Street
London W1T 3PD
Tel. +44 (0)20 7323-5004
Fax +44 (0)20 7323-0271

Prestel Publishing
900 Broadway, Suite 603
New York, NY 10003
Tel. +1 (212) 995-2720
Fax +1 (212) 995-2733

www.prestel.com

Library of Congress Control Number is available; British Library Cataloguing-in-Publication Data: a
catalogue record for this book is available from the British Library; Deutsche Nationalbibliothek holds a
record of this publication in the Deutsche Nationalbibliografie; detailed bibliographical data can be found
under: http://www.dnb.de

Editorial management: Caroline Klein
Project management, Prestel: Anja Besserer
Copyediting: Rita Forbes, Germering
Layout design: Melanie Fessel, Terreform ONE
Production: Andrea Cobré
Origination: digital print solutions Milan
Printing and binding: APPL aprinta druck GmbH & Co. KG, Wemding
Printed in Germany

ISBN 978-3-7913-5358-6

Verlagsgruppe Random House FSC® N001967
The FSC®-certified paper Hello Fat matt
was supplied by Deutsche Papier